SBAC
SMARTER BALANCED
GRADE 7 MATH

By Wendy Huang Lu

About the Author

Wendy Huang Lu received her bachelors in Business Administration from Texas A&M University (whoop!) and majored in Management Information Systems. After 6 years of working in the private sector, she decided to turn the passion to teach from a hobby to a full time career. She is currently a middle school math teacher in Los Altos School District. Previously, she taught middle school math at Lanier Middle School, an International Baccalaureate World School, in Houston, Texas where she taught remedial, on-level, and accelerated math.

While she was born in Taipei, Taiwan, she lived most of her life in Dallas, Texas with short stints in College Station, Houston, Cologne (Germany), and Cambridge, MA. She and her husband have been living in the San Francisco Bay Area for 5 years now. She enjoys doting on her Goldendoodle Mochi Doodle Lu and good eats in the Bay Area.

Acknowledgments

To my husband Dennis, without your constant support and encouragement, this book would have never materialized. To my daughter Kaylee Pei-Chan, we can't wait to see where life takes you. To my Goldendoodle Mochi, may there always be a beach for you to romp on. To my family—mom, dad, sister Jane, and brother Cary—for always keeping it real. I would not be the teacher I am if not for my students and my mentors, Dr. Jackie Sack, Ann Crowley, Michael Bordelon, and Stephanie Tyson, who believed in me and helped me nurture my development as a teacher. Thank you to all the other dedicated teachers I have met who inspire me to become a better version of myself every day.

The Smarter Balanced screenshots, in Chapter 1, pages 6–7, Chapter 2, page 33, Chapter 4, pages 47–49, Chapter 5, pages 85–89, Chapter 5, pages 112–114, and Chapter 6, page 170, are reprinted with permission courtesy of The Regents of the University of California. The publishing of this information does not represent an endorsement of products offered or solicited by Barron's Educational Series, Inc.

All inquiries should be addressed to:
Barron's Educational Series, Inc.
250 Wireless Boulevard
Hauppauge, NY 11788
www.barronseduc.com

ISBN: 978-1-4380-1093-9
Library of Congress Control Number: 2017942582

Date of Manufacture: December 2017
Manufactured by: B11R11

Printed in the United States of America
9 8 7 6 5 4 3 2 1

**10%
POST-CONSUMER
WASTE**
Paper contains a minimum
of 10% post-consumer
waste (PCW). Paper used
in this book was derived
from certified, sustainable
forestlands.

Contents

Introduction

Welcome to Barron's SBAC Grade 7 Math study guide.

This book is the only book that offers a comprehensive, affordable, flexible manual for all student levels. It is a great aid for teachers when they design their lessons, is informational for parents, and most importantly . . . is to the point.

Having worked with remedial, on-level, accelerated, and advanced students from fifth through ninth grade, I have not seen it all but I have seen a lot. This book will help students build a solid seventh grade foundation for all levels of work but still be rigorous and challenging.

Overview

The **Smarter Balanced Assessment** is given at the end of the year in both English and Math to grades 3–8. It is used to measure student achievement and growth. In Grade 7, the focus is on: (1) developing understanding of and applying proportional relationships; (2) developing understanding of operations with rational numbers and working with expressions and linear equations; (3) solving problems involving scale drawings and informal geometric constructions, and working with two- and three-dimensional shapes to solve problems involving area, surface area, and volume; and (4) drawing inferences about populations based on samples. The overarching goal is that at the end of grade 8, students "can demonstrate progress toward college and career readiness in mathematics."

The recent SBAC test, compared to the previous assessment, is less about the calculations and more about different ways to solve the problems and then using the applications of math in a real-world context.

SBAC Blueprint

The seventh grade SBAC math is divided into two parts: a **Computer-Adaptive** summative and a **Performance Task**. See the table below for how the exam is broken up for grades 6–8.

Claim/Score Reporting Category	Content Category	Stimuli		Items		Total Items by Claim
		CAT	PT	CAT	PT	
1. Concepts and Procedures	Priority Cluster	0	0	12-15	0	16-20
	Supporting Cluster	0		4-5		
2. Problem Solving	Problem Solving	0				
3. Modeling and Data Analysis	Modeling and Data Analysis	0	1	6	2-4	8-10
4. Communicating Reasoning	Communicating Reasoning	0		8	0-2	8-10

Blueprint Table Mathematics Grades 6–8 — Estimated Total Testing Time: 3 Hours

Task Types

The main types of questions you will encounter:

1. **Multiple-Choice, Single Response Tasks** These are straightforward and require you to click on the right answer.

2. **Multiple-Choice, Multiple Response Tasks** These are a bit trickier. These questions may contain more than one correct answer. The key here is to show all your work from the original problem AND work out the solutions if possible.

3. **Open Response Tasks** There are two types of open response answers. (1) On the summative test, these questions are likely short text where once you arrive at your solution, you will need to type in your solution. (2) On the performance test, you will be asked to explain how you arrived at your solution and explain your reasoning. When explaining how you arrived at the solution, make sure to not only include the calculations you made but why you made them in terms of the problem.

For more information about the Smarter Balanced
Assessment Consortium, go to *www.smarterbalanced.org*.

Test-Taking Strategies

The best way to use this book and be ready for the seventh grade SBAC math test is to show all work and look for patterns to extend your understanding of the math concepts. All the problems in this workbook are open response. To best prepare for this test, it is crucial that you show all your work, even the steps you can easily do in your head.

This book cannot replace the instruction a classroom teacher can provide, but I wrote it anticipating all the careless mistakes I have seen from thousands of students. For example, in the Distributive Property section, the most common mistake is forgetting to distribute the negative term. To help with this, think about the distributive property in terms of the area of a rectangle and draw an area model.

There are also a lot of nuances of a concept that are addressed in the classroom that I tried to include in this book. The hardest part to put on paper, that we address in the classroom, is to reason abstractly and quantitatively, which I tried to include. For example, in the Scale Factor section, instead of going straight into the calculations, we need to first think of the scale and if it is a reduction or enlargement of the original, etc.

Showing your work means showing the calculations as well as articulating in sentences what the numbers mean during the process of solving the problem and the final solution. Organizing your thoughts as you solve the problem is really important. The assessment not only values your solutions but different ways to get to the answers and other equivalent answers.

Practice, Practice, Practice

This book contains examples and practice problems at the end of each lesson for reinforcement. I advise students to use these as a diagnostic tool before completing the full-length practice test in Chapter 7. The practice test will mirror the types of questions and tasks students will encounter on the actual SBAC. At the conclusion of the practice test, students will find the answers explained for both the practice questions throughout the lessons as well as the answers for the practice test. Good luck!

Rational Numbers

Real numbers are numbers that represent a quantity on the number line. These numbers can be rational or irrational. Rational numbers are numbers that can be expressed as the ratio of two integers. Irrational numbers are numbers that cannot be expressed as a ratio of two integers.

Example of Rational Numbers	Nonexample of Rational Numbers (also known as Irrational Numbers)
$-\frac{2}{3}$, $\frac{3}{2}$, $0.2 = \frac{2}{10}$, $6 = \frac{6}{1}$, $\sqrt{9} = 3 = \frac{3}{1}$, $0.2 = \frac{2}{10}$, $2\frac{1}{2} = \frac{5}{2}$, $0.21 = \frac{21}{100}$, $-1.4 = -1\frac{4}{10} = -1\frac{2}{5} = -\frac{7}{5}$, $\frac{1}{3}$, $\frac{2}{3}$, $20\% = \frac{1}{5}$, $120\% = 1.2 = 1\frac{2}{10} = \frac{12}{10} = \frac{6}{5}$, $\sqrt{100} = \frac{10}{1}$, $\sqrt[3]{8} = \frac{2}{1}$	$\sqrt{2}$, $\sqrt{3}$, $-\sqrt{5}$, $-\sqrt{10}$, π (pi)

Types of Rational Numbers

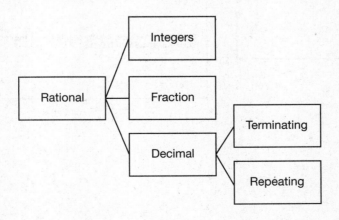

5

Standards

7.NS.A.1 Apply and extend previous understandings of addition and subtraction to add and subtract rational numbers; represent addition and subtraction on a horizontal or vertical number line diagram.

7.NS.A.2 Apply and extend previous understandings of multiplication and division and of fractions to multiply and divide rational numbers.

7.NS.A.3 Solve real-world and mathematical problems involving the four operations with rational numbers.

Sample Questions from the SBAC

The following are examples of question types that you will see on the SBAC Grade 7 Math test. We will cover them in this chapter. Notice in the first image below the **Equation Response Editorial Tool**. It is a tool that will be provided to help you enter your answers that are numbers, expressions, or equations. Questions with this tool will appear throughout the SBAC test.

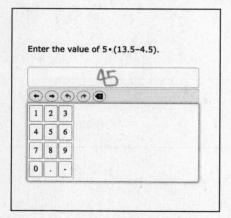

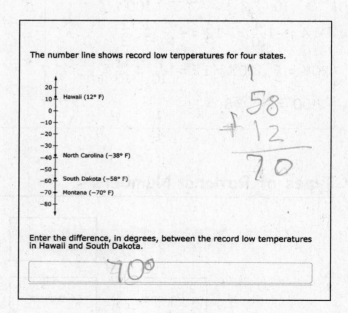

Enter the decimal equivalent of $\frac{11}{8}$.

1.405

1	2	3
4	5	6
7	8	9
0	.	-

$$\begin{array}{r} 125 \\ 8\overline{)1000} \\ \underline{-8\downarrow} \\ 020 \\ \underline{-16} \\ 040 \end{array}$$

×125
11

125
+1250
1405

1405

***Remember** the equation response editorial tool in the image above is NOT a calculator. You will need to work out your own calculations on scrap paper, then use the tool to input your responses.

Select **all** values equivalent to $-\frac{10}{7}$.

☐ $\frac{-10}{-7}$

☐ $-3\frac{1}{7}$

☐ $1\frac{3}{7}$

☐ $-\frac{-10}{-7}$

☐ $-1\frac{3}{7}$

Maria claims that any fraction located between $\frac{1}{5}$ and $\frac{1}{7}$ on a number line must have a denominator of 6.

Enter a fraction that shows Maria's claim is incorrect.

1	2	3	+	-	*	÷
4	5	6	<	≤	=	≥	>
7	8	9	$\frac{a}{b}$	$\square^\square$	( )	||	π
0	.	-

Lesson 1.1: Integer Operations

1.1A: Adding and Subtracting Positive and Negative Integers

An integer is a number that can be written without a fraction or decimal component. They are also referred to as whole numbers.

Examples	Nonexamples
−55, −1, 0, 1, 55, 100	−2.3, $2\frac{6}{7}$, 120%, 5.7

Here is the general rule for adding positive and negative numbers.

Situation	Solution	Think	Example
Positive + Positive	Positive	Start off with positive numbers. Add more positive numbers. End up with a positive solution.	9 + 3 = 12 12 + 16 = 28 50 + 30 = 80
Larger Negative + Smaller Positive	Negative	Since you have more negative units than positive, the answer will be negative. Then find the difference between the two.	−9 + 3 = −6 12 + (−16) = −4 −50 + 30 = −20
Smaller Negative + Larger Positive	Positive	Since you have more positive units than negative, the answer will be positive. Then find the difference between the two.	9 + (−3) = 6 −12 + 16 = 4 50 + (−30) = 20
Negative + Negative	Negative	Start off with negative numbers. Add more negative numbers. End up with a negative solution.	−9 + (−3) = −12 −12 + (−16) = −28 −50 + (−30) = −80

General rules for subtracting negative numbers: Always convert to a positive expression first.

Situation	Convert to Positive Expression	Example	Think
$a - b$	$a + (-b)$	$3 - 5 = 3 + (-5)$ $5 - 3 = 5 + (-3)$	Subtracting a positive is the same as adding a negative.
$-a - b$	$-a + (-b)$	$-3 - 5 = -3 + (-5)$ $-13 - 19 = -13 + (-19)$	Subtracting a positive is the same as adding a negative.
$-a - (-b)$	$-a + b$	$-3 - (-5) = -3 + 5$ $-5 - (-3) = -5 + 3$	Subtracting a negative is the same thing as adding.
$a - (-b)$	$a + b$	$3 - (-5) = 3 + 5$ $13 - (-19) = 13 + 19$	Subtracting a negative is the same thing as adding.

Example 1 Add $-8 + 3$.

Solution

METHOD 1 Think

Think of the signs first. Do you have more positive or negative units? *Negative*.

Then think about the units. How many more negative units do you have? *5.*

The answer is **−5**.

METHOD 2 Number line

Start at −8 on the number line. Add 3 by moving 3 units to the right. You are now at −5 units.

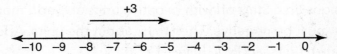

Example 2 Dhruv pulled his pull-back toy car 3 inches and it traveled for 15 inches. If Dhruv started at 0 inches, what is the net distance his toy car went?

Solution

METHOD 1 Think

Convert to a numerical statement:

Pull back 3 inches = −3

Car traveled for 15 inches = +15

The numerical statement is −3 + 15

Think about the signs first. Do you have more positive or negative units? *Positive.*

Then think about the units. How many more positive units do you have? *12.*

The answer is **+12**.

METHOD 2 Number line

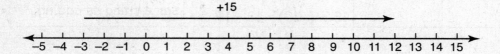

Start at −3 on the number line. To add 15 units, move to the right on the number line. From −3 to 0, the distance is 3. Since the total distance is +15, you have to move to the right 12 more units. The answer is **+12**.

Example 3 −4 − 11

Solution

Rewrite the expression as a positive expression. One way to think about it is to add the opposite: −4 + (−11)

METHOD 1 Think

Think about the signs first. Start off with negative units and add more negative units. The answer must be negative. Then think about the units. Add 4 negative units and 11 negative units, and you have −15.

METHOD 2 Number line

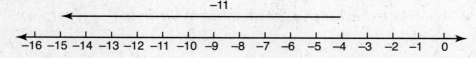

Start at −4 on the number line. Add −11 by moving 11 units to the left. You are now at −15.

Example 4   Bryceton lost two bets with his friend and lost $10 and $20 on both bets. Write an expression and draw a number line to represent how much he lost in all.

Solution

Write the expression −10 + (−20)

METHOD 1   Think

Think about the signs first. Start off with negative units and add more negative units. The answer must be negative. Then think about the units. You have 10 negative units and 20 negative units and you have 30 negative units total.

METHOD 2   Number line

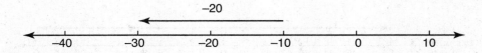

Start at −10 on the number line. Add −20 by moving 20 units to the left. You are now at −30 units.

Example 5   −11 − (−23)

Rewrite the expression as an addition of the opposite: −11 + 23

METHOD 1   Think

Think of the signs first. Since there are more positive units than negative units, the answer will be positive. The difference between 23 and 11 is 12. The answer is **12**.

Another way to think about it is the difference between −11 and −23 are the number of units in between. There are 12 units in between. Therefore, the difference between −11 and −23 is the same as −11 + 23.

METHOD 2   Number line

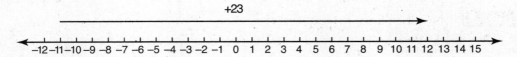

Start at −11 on the number line. Add +23 by moving 23 units to the right. The distance between −11 and 0 is 11. How many units do you have left to move after you move the 11? 12. Move 12 more units to the right. You are now at +12.

Example 6   Peyton went scuba diving. She submerged 5 feet below sea level, took a quick break, and then submerged another 12 feet. Rewrite the numerical expression using addition instead of subtraction.

Solution

Write it like a numerical expression: $0 - 5 - 12$

Rewrite as an addition of the opposite: $0 + (-5) + (-12)$

METHOD 1   Think

Negative units added to more negative units results in a negative answer. *5 plus 12 is 17*. The answer is **−17**.

METHOD 2   Number line

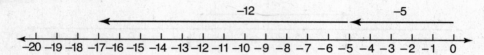

Start at 0 and move 5 units to the left. Add −12 by moving 12 units to the left. You are now at −17 units.

Example 7 $-3 + 12 - (-5) - 7$

Solution

Write the numerical expression using addition instead of subtraction.
$-3 + 12 + 5 + -7$

METHOD 1   Think

Rewrite and group the units: $12 + 5 + -3 + -7$

Are there more positive units or negative units? The answer is **positive units**.

How many more positive units are there? **7.**

METHOD 2   Number line

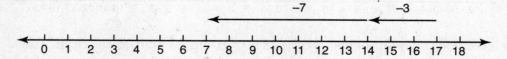

Start at 17 on the number line. Add −3 by moving 3 units to the left. Add −7 by moving 7 more units to the left. You are now at +7 units.

Example 8 Areli is in an elevator. She started at the fifth floor, went up 18 floors, down 9 floors, down 7 floors, and up 2 floors. Rewrite the numerical expression using addition instead of subtraction. Then regroup the positive integers together and negative integers together.

Solution

Translate the word problem into a numerical statement.

Keywords are: *Start at 5th floor, up 18, down 9, down 7*, and *up 2*

This translates to: 5 + 18 + (−9) + (−7) + 2

Rewrite and group the positive and negative units: 5 + 18 + 2 + (−9) + (−7)

Simplify: 25 + (−9) + (−7)

METHOD 1   Think

Think of the signs first. Do you have more positive or negative units? *Positive.* How many more positive units do you have? *9.* The answer is **+9**.

METHOD 2   Number line

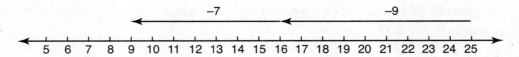

Start at 25 on the number line. Add −9 by moving 9 units to the left. Add −7 by moving 7 more units to the left. You are now at +9 units.

PRACTICE

Directions: Find each sum or difference. Use a number line to show your work.

1. −18 + 6 = −12
2. −23 + 36 = 13
3. −19 + −28 −47
4. −102 + −234 336
5. −19 − (−25) 6

6. −123 − (−432) 309
7. −7 − (−9) − 10 −8
8. 8 − (−11) − 19 0
9. −19 − (25) + 14 − 82
10. −12 − 18 − (−25)

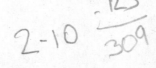

11. A submarine is situated at 345 feet below sea level. If it ascends 168 feet, what is its new position?

12. A submarine is situated at 789 feet below sea level. It then descends 231 feet. What is its new position?

13. The highest recorded temperature in New York was 108°F. The lowest recorded temperature was −15°F. What is the difference in the temperatures?

14. Even though it is currently −4°F in Central Park, New York, the weatherman predicts it will be 12 degrees warmer tomorrow. How much warmer does the weatherman think it will be?

15. A golfer scores the following for a three-day tournament: −4, −5, and −1. What is the golfer's total score?

16. A football team gained 23 yards, lost 16, gained 3, and then lost 7 more. What is the overall change in field position?

17. Beatrice's pet fish started off at 15 inches below the surface of the water of the fish tank. It ascended 3 inches up to retrieve some treats. How many inches below the surface is it now?

18. The sum or difference of two integers with different signs is 5. What are some possible solutions?

19. Use the following numbers 2 and −3 and create a math story. Create a number line and expression to represent the situation. Solve.

20. Your solution is 0. Create a word problem and include the addition and subtraction of two positive integers and two negative integers.

(Answers are on pages 205–206.)

1.1B: Multiplying and Dividing Positive and Negative Integers

General rules for multiplying and dividing positive and negative numbers:

Situation	Fun way to remember these rules. Good = positive Bad = negative (Please do not take this shortcut literally!)	Examples
Positive x ÷ Positive = Positive	Good things happening to good people = good	$3 \times 5 = 15$ $15 \div 3 = 5$
Positive x ÷ Negative = Negative	Good things happening to bad people = bad	$3(-5) = -15$ $15 \div (-3) = -5$ $\frac{15}{-3} = -5$
Negative x ÷ Positive = Negative	Bad things happening to good people = bad	$-3(5) = -15$ $-15 \div 3 = -5$ $\frac{15}{-3} = -5$
Negative x ÷ Negative = Positive	Bad things happening to bad people = good	$-3(-5) = 15$ $-15 \div (-3) = 5$ $\frac{-15}{-3} = 5$

Example 1

A. $-2(12) = -24$

B. $2(-12) = -24$

C. $-2(-12) = 24$

D. $2(12) = 24$

E. $-24 \div 2 = -12$

F. $\frac{24}{-2} = -12$

G. $24 \div 2 = 12$

H. $\frac{-24}{-2} = 12$

Example 2   Aryan is playing a video game and loses four points each time he misses the basket. He has lost 12 points. How many baskets did he miss?

$$-12 \div -4$$

Solution

METHOD 1 Think

Think about the signs first. A negative divided by a negative = a positive. Then think about the numbers: −12 ÷ −4 = 3. When you divide, your answer is **3**.

METHOD 2 Number line

How many times does −4 go into −12?

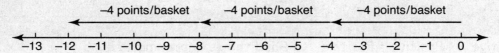

Example 3 In Michigan, the temperature has been dropping two degrees every hour. It has been three hours. How many degrees has it dropped?

Write the numerical expression to represent the situation: −2(3)

Solution

METHOD 1 Think

Think about the signs first. Negative times positive = negative. Then think about the numbers: −2 × 3 = −6. When you multiply, your answer is **−6**.

METHOD 2 Number line

Move to the left two units to represent the first hour. Move −4 units to represent the next 2 hours.

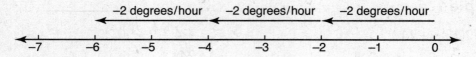

 PRACTICE

Directions: Find each product or quotient.

1. (−3)(−5) $= 15$
2. (−3)(5) $= -15$
3. 15 ÷ (−3) $= -5$
4. (11)(−11) $= -121$
5. 28 ÷ −4 $= -7$

6. (−15)(−15) $= 225$
7. −100 ÷ (−5) $= 20$
8. (−1)(−1)(−1) $= -1$
9. (−1)(−1)(−1)(−1) $= 1$
10. (−2)(−3)(−5)(−6)(−1) $= -180$

11. Jade received a one-point deduction for every problem that she did not show her work. She did not show her work for six problems. What was her total deduction? −6

12. Tammy is paying it forward by paying for the next seven people's drinks at Starbucks. If each drink costs $3, how much less does she have in her wallet? −21

13. Jeshua withdraws $115 every month to pay for his cell phone bill. How much will his cell phone bill cost him after one year? −1380

14. Eric is mountain climbing and descends 98 feet in 4 hours. How many feet does he descend per hour? −24.5

15. Tasmin went scuba diving and descended 2 feet every 5 minutes. How many feet did she descend after one hour? 24 feet

16. At the Holiday Craft Fair, Zoe decided to reduce her knitted scarves by $1 every hour left for a quicker sale. If she started off at $13 a scarf, how much will her scarves cost after 4 hours? $9

17. Describe a situation to fit the expression −48 ÷ 6.

18. If −8 is the product of two integers, what are four possible products?

19. What are three possible products of −12 if it is a product of three integers?

20. What are three possible products of −24 if it is a product of four integers?

(Answers are on pages 207–208.)

Lesson 1.2 Fraction Operations

The same rules apply when adding, subtracting, multiplying, and dividing fractions.

Example 1 Solve: $-\dfrac{1}{3} - \dfrac{4}{5}$

Solution

Change to common denominators: $-\dfrac{5}{15} - \dfrac{12}{15}$

Change to an addition expression: $-\dfrac{5}{15} + \left(-\dfrac{12}{15}\right)$

METHOD 1 Think

Think about the signs first. You start out with negative units, then add more negative units. So the answer must be negative.

Then think about the units: $-\dfrac{5}{15} + \left(-\dfrac{12}{15}\right) = \dfrac{-17}{15} = -1\dfrac{2}{15}$

METHOD 2 Number line

Start at $-\dfrac{5}{15}$. Add $-\dfrac{12}{15}$ by moving $\dfrac{12}{15}$ units to the left. You are now at $\dfrac{-17}{15}$.

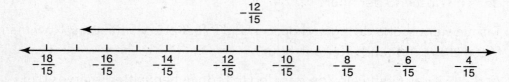

Example 2 $-\dfrac{2}{7} - \left(-\dfrac{3}{14}\right)$

Solution

Change to common denominators: $-\dfrac{4}{14} - \left(-\dfrac{3}{14}\right)$

Change to an addition expression: $-\dfrac{4}{14} + \dfrac{3}{14}$

METHOD 1 Think

Think about the signs first. Do you have more positive or negative units? *Negative.*

Then think about the units. The difference between $\dfrac{4}{14}$ and $\dfrac{3}{14}$ is $\dfrac{1}{14}$. The answer is $-\dfrac{1}{14}$.

METHOD 2 Number line

Start at $-\dfrac{4}{14}$. Add $+\dfrac{3}{14}$ by moving 3 units to the right. You are now at $-\dfrac{1}{14}$.

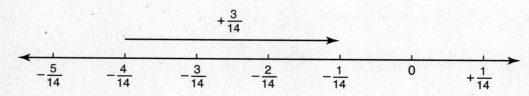

Example 3 $-\dfrac{1}{2}\left(-\dfrac{4}{13}\right)\left(-\dfrac{6}{18}\right)$

Solution

Cross cancel by factoring out 2: $-\dfrac{1}{\cancel{2}}\left(-\dfrac{\overset{2}{\cancel{4}}}{13}\right)\left(-\dfrac{6}{18}\right)$

$\quad\quad\quad\quad\quad\quad\quad\quad\quad\quad\;\;1$

Cross cancel by factoring out 2 again: $-\dfrac{1}{1}\left(-\dfrac{\overset{1}{\cancel{2}}}{13}\right)\left(-\dfrac{6}{\underset{9}{\cancel{18}}}\right)$

Cross cancel by factoring out 3: $-\dfrac{1}{1}\left(-\dfrac{1}{13}\right)\left(-\dfrac{\overset{2}{\cancel{6}}}{\underset{3}{\cancel{9}}}\right)$

Multiply and simplify: $-\dfrac{1}{1}\left(-\dfrac{1}{13}\right)\left(-\dfrac{2}{3}\right)=-\dfrac{2}{39}$

Example 4 $-\dfrac{18}{5}\div-\dfrac{3}{25}$

Solution

Multiply by the reciprocal of the second fraction: $-\dfrac{18}{5}\left(-\dfrac{25}{3}\right)$

Cross cancel by factoring out 3 and 5: $-\dfrac{\overset{6}{\cancel{18}}}{\underset{1}{\cancel{5}}}\left(-\dfrac{\overset{5}{\cancel{25}}}{\underset{1}{\cancel{3}}}\right)$

Multiply the simplified fractions: $-\dfrac{6}{1}\left(-\dfrac{5}{1}\right)=30$

Example 5   Mochi eats three half cups of his kibble twice a day. How much less kibble will he have after one week?

Solution

Translate three half cups of kibble twice a day to a numerical expression: $-\dfrac{3}{2}(2)$.

This is the amount of kibble he eats each day. Since there are seven days in a week, multiply this amount by 7: $-\dfrac{3}{2}\left(\dfrac{2}{1}\right)\left(\dfrac{7}{1}\right)$

Cross cancel by factoring out the 2: $-\dfrac{3}{\underset{1}{\cancel{2}}}\left(\dfrac{\overset{1}{\cancel{2}}}{1}\right)\left(\dfrac{7}{1}\right)$

Multiply: $-\dfrac{3}{1}\left(\dfrac{1}{1}\right)\left(\dfrac{7}{1}\right)=-21$

Mochi consumes **21 cups** of kibble each week.

Example 6   Jasmin owes her neighbor $\frac{1}{3}$ cups of sugar. Her mom gave her three cups of sugar. After she reimburses her neighbor, how much sugar does Jasmin have left?

Solution

Translate the word problem into a numerical expression: $-\frac{1}{3} + 3$

Change the fraction to common denominators in order to add: $-\frac{1}{3} + \frac{9}{3}$

Solve: $\frac{8}{3} = 2\frac{2}{3}$

Jasmin has **$2\frac{2}{3}$ cups** of sugar left after she pays her neighbor back.

✎ PRACTICE

Directions: Evaluate each expression.

1. $-\frac{3}{5} \div -\frac{6}{15}$

2. $-\frac{4}{5} - \left(-\frac{8}{15}\right)$

3. $-\frac{3}{5}\left(-\frac{10}{13}\right)$

4. $-\frac{3}{5} - \frac{3}{4}$

5. $-\frac{9}{26} - \left(-\frac{2}{13}\right)$

6. $3\frac{11}{20} + \left(-\frac{11}{2}\right)$

7. $-\frac{7}{5} - \left(-\frac{5}{6}\right)$

8. $-\frac{3}{5} - \frac{6}{15}$

9. $-\frac{4}{5} \div \left(-\frac{8}{15}\right)$

10. $-\frac{3}{5} + \left(-\frac{10}{13}\right)$

11. $-\frac{3}{5} \div \frac{3}{4}$

12. $-\frac{9}{26} - \frac{2}{13}$

13. $\frac{6}{26} \div \left(-\frac{12}{2}\right)$

14. $-\frac{4}{6} + \frac{8}{5}$

15. $-\frac{1}{2}\left(-\frac{1}{2}\right)\left(-\frac{1}{2}\right)$

16. $-\frac{1}{2}\left(-\frac{1}{2}\right)\left(-\frac{1}{2}\right)\left(-\frac{1}{2}\right)$

17. $-\frac{12}{28}\left(-\frac{6}{12}\right)\left(-\frac{5}{10}\right)\left(\frac{3}{4}\right)$

18. $-\frac{1}{2} - \frac{1}{2} - \frac{1}{2}$

19. Find the area of a rectangle with a length of $4\frac{5}{6}$ units and width of $3\frac{3}{5}$ units.

20. Tina needs $2\frac{1}{4}$ cups of sugar to make one batch of cookies. How many batches of cookies can she make with $12\frac{1}{2}$ cups of sugar? How much sugar will she have left?

21. Stefani had a bag of red rope candy. She gave one-half of it to her sister. She gave three-fourths of whatever she had left to her friends. How much did she give away? How much does she have left?

22. Create a scenario for $-\frac{1}{2} + \left(-\frac{4}{5}\right)$.

23. Create a scenario for 12 times $\frac{3}{8}$.

(Answers are on pages 208–210.)

Lesson 1.3 Decimal Operations

The same rules apply when adding, subtracting, multiplying, and dividing decimals.

Example 1   Add −8.47 and 3.52

Solution

METHOD 1   Think

Think about the signs first. Do you have more positive or negative units? *Negative.*
Then think about the units. How many more negative units do you have? *4.95.*
The answer is **−4.95**.

METHOD 2   Number line

Start at −8.47 on the number line. Add +3.52 units by moving 3.52 units to the right.
You are now at −4.95.

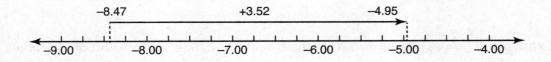

Example 2   Johnny owes his mother $29.50. He washed the dishes and did the laundry and earned $5.50. Write an expression and draw a number line to represent how much more he owes his mother.

Solution

Translate the word problem into a numerical statement: −29.50 + 5.50

METHOD 1   Think

Think of the signs first. Do you have more positive or negative units? *Negative.* Then think about the units. How many more negative units do you have? *24.* The answer is **−24**.

METHOD 2   Number line

Start at −29.50. To add +5.5, move 5.5 units to the right. You are now at −24.

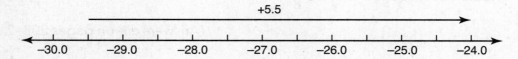

Johnny owes his mother **$24 more**.

Example 3   Add −2.45 and −12.85

Solution

METHOD 1   Think

Think about the signs first. Start off with negative units and add more negative units. The answer must be negative. Then think about the units. Add 2.45 negative units to 12.85 negative units and you have 15.3 negative units.

METHOD 2   Number line

Start at −2.45. Add −12.85 by moving 12.85 units to the left. You are now at **−15.3**.

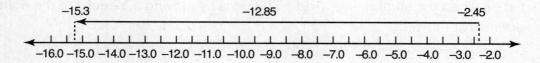

Example 4   Ayaka brought $20 to the Sweet Shop. She spent $3.50 on gummies and $4.25 on a cup of tea. Draw a number line to represent how much she spent and how much she has left.

Solution

Translate the word problem into a numerical statement: 20 − 3.5 − 4.25

You can subtract like you normally do for this! Here is another way:

Rewrite as an addition expression: 20 + (−3.5) + (−4.25)

METHOD 1 Think

Think about the signs first. Do you have more positive or negative units? *Positive.* Then think about the units. You are taking 7.75 total away from 20. The answer is **12.25**.

METHOD 2 Number line

Start at 20. Add −3.5 by moving 3.5 units to the left. You are now at 16.5. Then add −4.25 by moving 4.25 units to the left. You are now at 12.25.

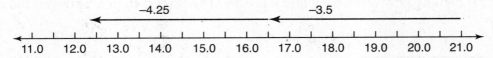

Example 5 Evaluate: −5.21 − (−5.72)

Solution

Convert to a positive expression: −5.21 + 5.72

METHOD 1 Think

Think about the signs first. Do you have more negative or positive units? *Positive.* Then think about the units. How many more positive units do you have? *0.51.* The answer is **0.51**.

METHOD 2 Number line

Start at −5.21. Add +5.72 by moving 5.72 units to the right. The distance between −5.21 and 0 is 5.21. How many units do you have left to move after you have moved 5.21 units? 0.51 more units. Your answer is **0.51**.

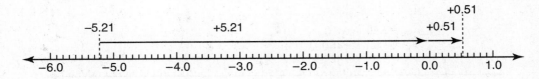

Example 6 The highest elevation in the world is Mount Everest at 8.85 km. The lowest point in the world is the Dead Sea at 0.42 km below sea level. What is the distance between the two?

Solution

METHOD 1

Translate the word problem into a numerical statement: $8.85 - (-0.42)$

Convert to an addition expression: $8.85 + 0.42$

Simplify and your answer is **9.27**.

METHOD 2

Locate 8.85 and −0.42 on the number line. The distance between −0.42 and 0 is 0.42. The distance between 8.85 and 0 is 8.85. The total distance between the two is 9.27.

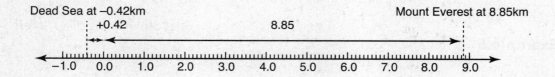

Example 7 $-3.45 - (-2.31)$

Solution

Change to an addition expression: $-3.45 + 2.31$

METHOD 1 Think

Think about the signs first: Do you have more positive or negative units? *Negative.* Then think about the units: How many more negative units do you have? *1.14.* Your answer is **−1.14**.

METHOD 2 Number line

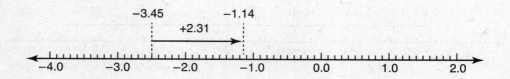

 **PRACTICE**

Directions: Evaluate the expressions.

1. −4.5 + 2.7
2. −4.5 − 2.7
3. −4.5 − (−2.7)
4. −18.23 − 17.8
5. −18.23 − (−17.8)
6. −18.23 + 17.8
7. −6.3 − 9.1 − (−2.8)

8. 0.21 ÷ −0.3
9. (−0.11)(0.3)
10. −0.2 ÷ −0.3
11. 0.3 ÷ −0.2
12. (−0.1)(−0.1)(−0.1)(−0.1)
13. (−0.2)(−0.2)(−0.2)(−0.2)(−0.2)

14. Kevin forgot his wallet and owes the candy store $3.58 for gumdrops and another $8.14 for chocolate brownies. How much does he owe the candy store all together?

15. Stock prices for Apple fell $0.88 after news broke that Steve Jobs died. It fell another $1.32 the day after. How much did it fall in two days?

16. The highest elevation in the U.S. is Mount McKinley in Alaska at 6.194 km. The lowest elevation is Death Valley at 0.282 km below sea level. What is the difference in kilometers between the two?

17. Does Tyson have enough to purchase three books from the bookstore at $5.95, $11.95, and $7.95 if he only has $25?

18. The largest snail in the world is the African giant snail. It measures 39.3 cm from snout to tail. If the average length of a garden snail is about 3 cm, how many more times longer is the African giant snail?

19. William is playing a video game and gets 1.25 points for each apple he picks. He loses 1.45 points if he does not use the apples and lets them rot. How many points does he have if he started from 0, picked up 12 apples, and only used 3 of them?

20. Oliva went scuba diving and descended at a rate of 12.5 feet every two minutes. If she started right at the surface, how far has she descended after 10 minutes?

21. Jake went mountain climbing and descended at a rate of 0.75 meters every 10 minutes. How far has he descended after an hour?

22. Create your own word problem for the following expression: −2.1 − (4.5)

23. Create your own word problem for the following expression: −2.3(4)

(Answers are on pages 210–212.)

Lesson 1.4 Fractions, Decimals, and Percents

Rational numbers can be written as terminating or repeating decimals. **Terminating decimals** are decimals that end or do not go on forever. If you take the fraction equivalent of the decimal, find the quotient of the numerator and denominator, the remainder will be 0. A **repeating decimal**, also known as a recurring decimal, is a decimal that has a digit, or block of digits, that repeats over and over again without ever ending.

A **vinculum** is a horizontal line used in mathematical notation for a specific purpose. It is most commonly used today to indicate the repetend of a **repeating decimal**. For example, $0.\overline{3}$ means the 3 repeats until infinity. If multiple digits repeat until infinity, then a vinculum is drawn over all the digits that repeat. For example, $0.\overline{123}$ looks like 0.123123123…etc.

Example 1 Which of the following are equivalent to $-\frac{1}{5}$? Explain your reasoning.

A. -0.2

B. $\frac{-1}{5}$

C. $\frac{1}{-5}$

D. $\frac{-1}{-5}$

E. -20%

Solution

A. -0.2 is equivalent because you can convert $-\frac{1}{5}$ into a decimal using long division and get -0.2.

		−	0.	2
+	5	−	1.	0
		−		0
			1	0
		−	1	0
				0

B. $\frac{-1}{5}$ is equivalent because a negative divided by a positive is negative. The answer is $-\frac{1}{5}$.

C. $\frac{1}{-5}$ is equivalent because a positive divided by a negative is negative.

The answer is $-\frac{1}{5}$.

D. $\frac{-1}{-5}$ is not equivalent because a negative divided by a negative is positive.

The answer is $+\frac{1}{5}$.

E. −20% is equivalent because $-20\% = -\frac{20}{100} = -\frac{1}{5}$.

Example 2 Use long division to write the rational number $\frac{3}{8}$ as a terminating decimal.

Solution

		0.	3	7	5
8	3.	0	0	0	
−	0				
	3	0			
−	2	4			
		6	0		
	−	5	6		
		4	0		
		−	4	0	
			0		

Example 3 Use long division to write the rational number $\frac{1}{9}$ as a repeating decimal.

Solution

		0.	1	1	1
9	1.	0	0	0	
−	0				
	1	0			
−		9			
		1	0		
	−		9		
			1	0	
		−		9	
				1	

Since the 1 repeats, the answer is written as **$0.\overline{1}$**.

Example 4 What is the difference between $\frac{0}{12}$ and $\frac{12}{0}$?

Solution

12 goes into 0, zero times. Therefore, $\frac{0}{12} = 0$.

It is impossible for 0 to go into 12, therefore, $\frac{12}{0}$ = **no solution**.

 PRACTICE

Directions: Use long division to write each rational number as a decimal. Determine if the decimal is terminating or repeating.

1. $-\frac{23}{20}$ 4. $-1\frac{1}{8}$ 7. $\frac{4}{33}$

2. $8\frac{3}{5}$ 5. $\frac{2}{9}$ 8. $-\frac{9}{11}$

3. $\frac{9}{200}$ 6. $-\frac{56}{99}$ 9. $\frac{3}{125}$

10. Which of the following are equivalent to $-\frac{2}{3}$? Select **all** that apply.

☐ A. $\frac{-2}{-3}$

☐ B. 0.6

☐ C. $0.\overline{6}$

☐ D. $-\frac{-2}{-3}$

☐ E. $-66\frac{2}{3}\%$

11. Select the following that are equivalent to $\frac{1}{8}$. Explain your reasoning below.

☐ A. 0.125

☐ B. $\frac{-1}{-8}$

☐ C. 12.5%

☐ D. $-\frac{1}{-8}$

☐ E. $\frac{2}{16}$

12. Which of the following are equivalent to 7.5? Explain your reasoning below.

    ☐ A. 750%

    ☐ B. 7500%

    ☐ C. $7\frac{1}{2}$

    ☐ D. $\frac{15}{2}$

    ☐ E. $\frac{-15}{-2}$

For the following, write five more rational numbers that are equivalent and include the percent and decimal equivalent.

13. $\frac{7}{8}$

14. $-\frac{3}{2}$

15. $-\frac{3}{4}$

(Answers are on pages 212–214.)

Lesson 1.5 Order of Operations

Apply the order of operations: parentheses, exponents, multiplication, division, addition, or subtraction for every problem.

Example 1 $-1 \div (-1)(-1) - 1 - (-1)$

Solution

Since you see multiplication and division, perform the operation on the left.

$-1 \div (-1)(-1) - 1 - (-1)$

$1(-1) - 1 - (-1)$

$-1 - 1 - (-1)$

Change to an addition expression. $-1 + (-1) + 1$

Another method is to simplify $-1 + 1 = 0$, because the commutative property of addition allows you to add numbers in any order. Then you are left with -1.

$-2 + 1 = -1$

Example 2 $-0.1 \div (-0.01)\frac{1}{10} + 0.1 - 1.1$

Solution

Since you see multiplication and division, perform the operation on the left.

$$-0.1 \div (-0.01)$$

$$\frac{1}{10} + 0.1 - 1.1$$

$$10\left(\frac{1}{10}\right) + 0.1 - 1.1$$

$$\mathbf{1 + 0.1 - 1.1}$$

Another method is to rewrite as an addition expression: $1.1 + (-1.1)$. Since 1.1 and -1.1 are zero pairs, the answer is **0**.

Example 3   Dennis is checking out from the pet store. He receives a refund for three Frisbees at $2.25 each and purchases five dog treats at $0.65 each and two bags of dental treats at $7.45 each. How much does he end up paying?

Solution

Translate the word problem into a numerical expression.

$3(-2.25) + 5(0.65) + 2(7.45)$

Multiply. $-6.75 + 3.25 + 14.9$

Add. 11.40

The total cost is **$11.40** for Dennis's purchase at the pet store.

 PRACTICE

Directions: Evaluate each expression.

1. $-2 - 2 \div 2 \times 2 + 2 - 2 \div 2$

2. $10 \div -10(-10) - 10 + 10 \div (-10)(-10)$

3. $0.25 \div -0.5(0.5) \div (-5)$

4. $-0.1 \div 0.1(0.1) - 0.1$

5. $-0.8 - (-0.04) \div 2(20\%) + 1.6 \div \frac{2}{5}$

6. $-10(-10) \div 10(10) \div 10$

7. $1 \div -1 - (-1)(-1)$

8. $\frac{1}{10} \div 0.1(10\%) - \frac{1}{10}$

9. $20\% \div \frac{3}{25}(0.4) - \frac{10}{20}$

10. $-\frac{7}{20} - 45\% - (-0.95)$

11.   What is halfway between $3\frac{1}{2}$ and $7\frac{1}{3}$?

12.   What is one-quarter of the distance between $\frac{2}{5}$ and $\frac{9}{10}$?

(Answers are on pages 214–216.)

## CHAPTER 2

Algebraic Expressions

An expression is a mathematical phrase. There are two common types of expressions: numerical and algebraic. A **numerical expression** contains numbers and operations. An **algebraic expression** is an expression built up from integer constants and variables and the algebraic operations.

Below is an algebraic expression. There are three terms that are unlike: $\frac{1}{2}xy$, $3y^2$, and -10. There are no like terms. There are two operators: $+$ and $-$.

$$\frac{1}{2}xy + 3y^2 - 10$$

Variables

Coefficients

Constant

Please see these helpful terms.

Keyword	Definition	Example
Constant	The term in an algebraic expression that never changes. The number by itself, without the variable.	$3x - 2y - 1$ $-4x$ (no constant)
Variable	Unknown value represented by a letter in an algebraic expression or equation you are trying to solve.	$3x - 2y - 1$ $-4x$
Coefficient	A number used to multiply the variable.	$3x - 2y - 1$ $-4x$
Terms	Part of the expression separated by addition or subtraction.	$3x - 2y - 1 => 3$ terms $-4x => 1$ term

Keyword	Definition	Example
Like Terms	Terms whose variable and exponents are the same.	$-x$ and $-7x$ $9xy$ and $-6xy$ -9 and $+1$ $5x^2$ and $-2x^2$
Unlike Terms	Two or more terms that are not alike. They do not have the same variables or powers.	$3x - 2y - 1$ (all unlike terms)
Algebraic Operation	Also known as the operator, this symbol tells you what to do. Traditional operation of arithmetic: addition, subtraction, multiplication, raising to an integer power, and taking roots.	$3x - 2y - 1$ (both subtraction signs)

Standards

7.EE.A.1 Apply properties of operations as strategies to add, subtract, factor, and expand linear expressions with rational coefficients.

7.EE.A.2 Understand that rewriting an expression in different forms in a problem context can shed light on the problem and how the quantities in it are related. For example, $a + 0.05a = 1.05a$ means that "increase by 5%" is the same as "multiply by 1.05."

7.EE.B.3 Solve real-life and mathematical problems posed with positive and negative rational numbers in any form (whole numbers, fractions, and decimals), using tools strategically. Apply properties of operations to calculate with numbers in any form; convert between forms as appropriate; and assess the reasonableness of answers using mental computation and estimation strategies.

Sample Questions from the SBAC

The following are examples of question types that you will see on the SBAC Grade 7 Math test. We will cover them in this chapter.

Select the expression equivalent to $(4x + 3) + (-2x + 4)$.

Ⓐ $-2x + 12$

Ⓑ $-8x + 12$

Ⓒ $6x + 7$

Ⓓ $2x + 7$

Select **all** expressions that are equivalent to $-3.75 + 2(-4x + 6.1) - 3.25x$.

☐ $7x - 2x + 8.1$

☐ $8.45 - 8x - 3.25x$

☐ $-1.75 - 7.25x + 6.1$

☐ $-11.25x + 12.2 - 3.75$

Lisa wrote the expression $(3 + 6x) - 2(x + 1) + 5$. She simplified the expression using the following steps:

Step 1: $3(1 + x) - 2(x + 1) + 5$

Step 2: $3(x + 1) - 2(x + 1) + 5$

Step 3: $(x + 1) + 5$

Step 4: $x + 6$

Lisa says that $(3 + 6x) - 2(x + 1) + 5 = x + 6$. Lisa's statement is incorrect.

In which step did Lisa first make a mistake, and what is a correct expression for that step?

Ⓐ Step 1; $3(1 + 3x) - 2(x + 1) + 5$

Ⓑ Step 1; $3(1 + 2x) - 2(x + 1) + 5$

Ⓒ Step 3; $5(x + 1) + 5$

Ⓓ Step 3; $6(x + 1) + 5$

Lesson 2.1 Factoring and Expanding Algebraic Terms

Factoring is the process of deciding what to multiply together to get an expression. It is splitting an expression into a multiplication of simpler expressions. Expanding the algebraic expression means to get rid of the parentheses or brackets.

Example 1 Expand $3(4 - a)$

METHOD 1   Distribute numerically.

$3(4) + 3(-a)$ Distribute +3.

$12 + (-3a)$ Simplify.

$12 - 3a$

METHOD 2   Use an area model.

The area of a rectangle equals length times width. Think about the area of the entire rectangle, your width is three units and your length is $(4 - a)$ units. The total area of the rectangle is the area of the left one plus the area of the right one. See the diagram below.

	4	−a
3	$3(4) = 12$	$3(-a) = -3a$

Area of left rectangle + Area of right rectangle = $12 + (-3a) = 12 - 3a$

Example 2 Factor $24x - 8y$

METHOD 1   Factor the expression.

The greatest common factor (GCF) between $24x$ and $-8y$ is 8.

Divide each term by the GCF into both terms: $\dfrac{24x}{8} = 3x$ and $\dfrac{-8y}{8} = -y$

The answer is **8(3x − y)**.

METHOD 2   Use an area model.

	3x	−y
8	$8(3x) = 24x$	$8(-y) = -8y$

Example 3 Are the following expressions equivalent? $-2a + 10$ and $-2(a + 5)$

Set them horizontally side by side. $-2a + 10$ and $-2(a + 5)$

Distribute where you can. $-2a + 10$ and $-2(a) + (-2)(5)$

If there are terms that are exactly the same, subtract them from both sides.
$-2a + 10$ and $-2a - 10$

See what is left. $10 \neq -10$

The expressions are not equivalent.

Example 4 Expand the following expression: $-(6b - 7)$

METHOD 1 Distribute numerically.

$-(6b - 7)$ Distribute -1 to both terms inside the parentheses.

$-1(6b) + (-1)(-7)$ Show the distribution numerically.

$-6b + 7$ Simplify.

METHOD 2 Use an area model.

	$6b$	-7
-1	$-1(6b) = -6b$	$-1(-7) = 7$

Example 5 $-a - 6b$

METHOD 1 Factor numerically.

The GCF between $-a$ and $-6b$ is -1.

Divide each term by the GCF into both terms: $\frac{-a}{-1} = a$ and $\frac{-6b}{-1} = 6b$

The answer is **$-1(a + 6b)$**

METHOD 2 Use an area model.

	a	$6b$
-1	$(-1)a = -a$	$-1(6b) = -6b$

Example 6 $-\frac{1}{5}(-20y - 35x)$

METHOD 1   Distribute numerically.

$-\frac{1}{5}\left(-\frac{20y}{1}\right)+\left(-\frac{1}{5}\right)\left(-\frac{35x}{1}\right)$ Distribute $-\frac{1}{5}$ to both terms inside the parentheses.

$4y + 7x$ Simplify.

METHOD 2   Use an area model.

	$-20y$	$-35x$
$-\frac{1}{5}$	$-\frac{1}{5}\left(-\frac{20}{1}y\right)=+4y$	$-\frac{1}{5}\left(-\frac{35}{1}x\right)=+7x$

Example 7 $-0.2(-3x + 8y)$

METHOD 1   Distribute numerically.

$-0.2(-3x) + (-0.2)(8y)$ Distribute -0.2 to both terms inside the parentheses.

$0.6x - 1.6y$ Simplify.

METHOD 2   Use an area model.

	$-3x$	$8y$
-0.2	$-0.2(-3x) = 0.6x$	$-0.2(8y) = -1.6y$

PRACTICE

1. Factor the following expressions using both methods.

   A. $81a + 9$

   B. $81 - 9a$

   C. $-81a - 9$

   D. $-81a + 9$

   E. $-24x + 12y - 6$

   F. $3a - 12b + 18$

   G. $-x - 2y$

   H. $-10x + 20y$

   I. $-3x - 3y$

   J. $-5a - 10b$

2. Expand the following expressions.

   A. $2(3a + 4)$

   B. $-2(3a + 4)$

   C. $2(3a - 4)$

   D. $-2(3a - 4)$

   E. $-2(-3a - 4)$

   F. $-(4a + 13)$

   G. $-(4a - 13)$

   H. $-(-4a - 13)$

   I. $-(-a - b)$

   J. $-(-2 + c)$

   K. $\frac{1}{2}(-4x - 10y)$

   L. $\frac{3}{4}(-16x + 12y)$

   M. $-\frac{1}{3}(12x - 18y)$

   N. $-\frac{2}{3}(-7x - 4y)$

   O. $-\frac{1}{4}(-10x + 22y)$

   P. $-0.5(6y + 3x)$

   Q. $-0.5(-6y - 3x)$

   R. $0.3x(10 - x)$

   S. $1.2(12x + 1.2y)$

   T. $-(-0.7x - 0.7y)$

3. Which of the following expressions are equivalent? Select **all** that apply.

   ☐ **A.** $-6(x + 3)$ and $3(-2x + 6)$

   ☐ **B.** $-6(x + 3)$ and $6(x - 3)$

   ☐ **C.** $\frac{1}{3}(-9x - 15)$ and $-\frac{1}{3}(9x + 15)$

   ☐ **D.** $\frac{2}{3}\left(\frac{6}{4}y - 1\right)$ and $-\frac{2}{3}\left(-\frac{6}{4}x - 1\right)$

   ☐ **E.** $0.1(82x + 95y)$ and $-0.01(-820x - 950y)$

   ☐ **F.** $-10(2.9x - 9.2y)$ and $10(-2.9x - 9.2y)$

   (Answers are on pages 216–221.)

Lesson 2.2 Adding and Subtracting Algebraic Terms

Simplifying an algebraic expression means to write it in the most compact or efficient manner without changing the value of the expression. This can be done by combining like terms.

Example 1   Write an equivalent expression for $-5(x - 4) + 3$.

$-5(x) + (-5)(-4) + 3$ Distribute the -5.

$-5x + 20 + 3$ Simplify.

$-5x + 23$ Combine like terms.

Example 2 $\frac{3}{4}x - \frac{1}{2}y + \frac{2}{3}x - \frac{1}{6}y$

$\frac{3}{4}x + \frac{2}{3}x - \frac{1}{2}y - \frac{1}{6}y$ Group the like terms.

$\frac{9}{12}x + \frac{8}{12}x - \frac{6}{12}y - \frac{2}{12}y$ Change to equivalent fractions with common denominators.

$\frac{9}{12}x + \frac{8}{12}x + \left(-\frac{6}{12}y\right) + \left(-\frac{2}{12}y\right)$ Change to an addition expression.

$\frac{17}{12}x + \left(-\frac{8}{12}y\right)$ Combine like terms.

$\frac{17}{12}x - \frac{2}{3}y$ Simplify.

Example 3 $3.4x - 2.3y - 1.6x - 0.6y$

$3.4x - 1.6x - 2.3y - 0.6y$ Group like terms.

$1.8x + (-2.9y)$ Combine like terms.

$1.8x - 2.9y$ Simplify.

PRACTICE

Directions: Simplify the expressions. Expand if necessary.

1. $-(-3x + 5) - 6x$

2. $-3(-5x + 3) + 15x$

3. $-(x - 4) + 8x - 10$

4. $-3x - 7(-2 + 3x) - 8$

5. $-3(x + 5y) - 9x$

6. $-x(4 - y) - 12x - 3xy$

7. $-9(9x - 5) - 3(7 - x)$

8. $3(-4y - 2x) - 2(17x - 6y)$

9. $-(11x - 9) - 2x(3 - 6y) - 2(x + 8)$

10. $-\dfrac{1}{2}x - \dfrac{3}{5}y + \dfrac{7}{10}x - \dfrac{9}{10}y$

11. $-\dfrac{1}{4}x + \dfrac{5}{6}y - \dfrac{11}{12}x + \dfrac{2}{3}y$

12. $-\dfrac{2}{5}x + \dfrac{1}{4}y + \dfrac{19}{20}x - \dfrac{9}{10}y$

13. $\dfrac{1}{5}x - \dfrac{2}{3}y - \left(\dfrac{11}{15}y - \dfrac{7}{15}x\right)$

14. $-\dfrac{3}{8}x - \dfrac{4}{3}y + \dfrac{2}{3}\left(\dfrac{5}{16}x - \dfrac{3}{4}y\right)$

15. $4.5x - 0.8y + 1.2x - 3.3y$

16. $-0.6x - 0.2y - 0.4y - 0.5x$

17. $2 + 2.3x + 2.4 - 6.3x$

18. $-7.3x - 8.1y + 3.7x + 5.9y$

19. $0.1(-3x + 4y) - 10x$

20. $-0.1(-3x - 4y) - 9x - .6y$

(Answers are on pages 221–222.)

Lesson 2.3 Writing Algebraic Expressions

The key to word problems is treating them like another language. It is also helpful to translate the words first and then simplify if necessary. Here are some helpful keywords to help with the translation.

Addition	Subtraction	Multiplication	Division
Plus	Minus	Multiple of	Quotient
Increased by	Decreased by	Times of	Divided by
More than	Less than	Product	Ratio of
Added to	Take away		Per
More than	Fewer than		
Sum	Difference between		

Example 1   Write the algebraic expression for each verbal phrase.

Problem #	Verbal Phrase	Algebraic Expression
A	Two less than x	$x - 2$
B	x less than 2	$2 - x$
C	The quotient of m and 3	$\frac{m}{3}$ or $m \div 3$
D	The quotient of 3 and m	$\frac{3}{m}$ or $3 \div m$
E	y subtracted from x	$x - y$
F	x subtracted from y	$y - x$

Example 2 Write at least two verbal statements for each numerical statement.

Problem #	Algebraic Expression	Verbal Statement
A	$(3a)^2$	The quantity of three times a, squared.
		The quantity of three times a, to the second power.
B	$3a^2$	Three times a squared.
		The product of three and a squared.
C	$\dfrac{2x-7}{3y}$	The quantity of seven less than $2x$ divided by the product of three and y.
		The quotient of $2x$ reduced by seven and three times y.
D	$\dfrac{2x}{3y}-7$	The quotient of $2x$ and $3y$ decreased by seven.
		Seven subtracted from $2x$ divided by $3y$.
E	$2x-\dfrac{7}{3y}$	The quotient of seven and $3y$ subtracted from the product of 2 and x.
		The quotient of seven and $3y$ less than two times x.

Example 3 The length of a rectangle is three times its width. What is the area of the rectangle? Use w for width.

Let w equal the rectangle's width.   Define the variable using "let" statements.

Width $= w$

Length $= 3w$

Area of rectangle $=$ length(width)   Start with the formula.

$\qquad\qquad\quad = 3w(w)$ Plug in the expressions.

$\qquad\qquad\quad = 3w^2$ Solve.

Example 4 The neighborhood gym charges $50 for the signup fee and $25 per month. How much will the gym charge Gaby to go for m months?
Use a table to show your work.

STEP 1 Set up the table.

# of Months	Total Cost
m	

STEP 2 Plug in or substitute the numbers. If Gaby only used the gym for two months, how much would she pay?

# of Months	Total Cost
2	50 + 25(2)
3	50 + 25(3)
4	50 + 25(4)
m	

STEP 3 Look for the pattern and use m for months instead of a number. Simplify the expression.

# of Months	Total Cost
2	50 + 25(2)
3	50 + 25(3)
4	50 + 25(4)
m	50 + 25(m) = 50 + 25m

STEP 4 Answer the question using a sentence.

Gaby would be charged $(50 + 25$m$) for using the gym after m months.

Example 5   Yankee the Goldendoodle has not been eating her meals. She gets 680 grams of kibble every day. On Monday, she ate 78%, on Tuesday, she ate $\frac{7}{8}$, and on Wednesday, she ate 0.8 of her kibble. Which day did Yankee have the best appetite?

Solution

Monday: $680(78\%) = 680(0.78) = 530.4$

Tuesday: $680\left(\frac{7}{8}\right) = 680(0.875) = 595$

Wednesday: $680(0.8) = 544$

Yankee had the **best appetite on Tuesday** since she ate most of her kibble that day.

Example 6   Farmed salmon costs $13.99 per pound. Wild salmon costs $23.97 per pound. Chloe is splitting the cost with her neighbor. She will pay for 70% of the salmon and her neighbor will pay 30%. They chose salmon that weighs 2.4 pounds. How much more does Chloe pay for wild salmon vs. farmed salmon?

Solution

Round the farmed salmon to **$14 per pound** and wild salmon to **$24 per pound**.

The cost of 70% of an 2.4-pound farmed salmon = $70\%(2.4)(14) = 0.7(33.6) = 23.52$

The cost of 70% of an 2.4-pound wild salmon = $70\%(2.4)(24) = 0.7(57.6) = 40.32$

The difference between the costs is $40.32 - 23.52 = 16.8$.

Chloe pays **$16.80 more** for her 70% of the 2.4-pound wild salmon.

PRACTICE

1. Write the numerical expression for the following verbal expressions. Then simplify if possible.

   A. Two-thirds x increased by 9.

   B. The sum of one-sixth x and 7.

   C. Three fewer than the product of x and y.

   D. The quotient of one and six x reduced by 7.

   E. Twenty percent of the sum of one-half x and 10.

   F. The difference between y squared and x cubed.

   G. Double the sum of x and y.

   H. The product of negative x and negative x.

   I. The product of negative 1 and x squared.

   J. The product of negative 1 and double the amount of x.

   K. The product of $6x$ and 7 divided by 2.

   L. The sum of one-third x, two-thirds x, and three-fourths y.

   M. One-half subtracted from the product of $9x$ and $7y$.

   N. Four-fifths of the sum of $8x$ and 2 less than 10.

   O. The quotient of 6 and x reduced by y.

2. Write at least **two** verbal statements for the following numerical statements:

   A. $3a - 7b$

   B. $7b - 3a$

   C. $\dfrac{3a}{7b}$

   D. $\dfrac{7b}{3a}$

   E. $(3a)(7b)$

   F. $5a^2$

   G. $(5a)^3$

   H. $\dfrac{x+2}{6y}$

   I. $(x-9)^2$

   J. $x^2 - 9^2$

   K. $x^2 + y^2$

   L. $\dfrac{1}{4}xy^2$

   M. $9x^2y^3$

   N. $8a + \dfrac{2}{b}$

   O. $\dfrac{3x-1}{y+2}$

3. The length of a rectangle is eight less than three times its width. What is the area of the rectangle?

4. The width of a rectangle is one-fifth of its length. What is the perimeter of the rectangle?

5. The length of a rectangle is 350% of its width. What is the area of the rectangle?

6. The area of a rectangle is 20 times the length. If the width is half of the length, what is the length?

7. What is the area of a square if each side measured $7x$ units?

8. Mark wrote the expression $-(2x + 9) - (-7 - 5x)$. He simplified the expression using the following steps:

   STEP 1 $-2x - 9 + 7 - 5x$

   STEP 2 $-2x - 5x - 9 + 7$

   STEP 3 $-7x - 2$

   Which step(s) did Mark make mistakes with and what is the correct expression for that/those step(s)?

9. Stefani wrote the expression $-10x - 20xy$. She factored the expression by dividing both terms by the GCF into both terms. Here are her steps:

   STEP 1 $\dfrac{-10x}{10x} - \dfrac{20xy}{10x}$

   STEP 2 $-1 - 2y$

   STEP 3 The factored expression is $10x(-1 - 2y)$

   Which step(s) did Stefani make mistakes with and what is the correct expression for that/those step(s)?

10. Ellen wrote the expression $-3(x - 1) - (6 - x)$. She simplified the expression using the following steps:

    STEP 1 $-3x + 3 - 6 - x$

    STEP 2 $-3x - x + 3 - 6$

    STEP 3 $-4x - 3$

    Which step(s) did Ellen make mistakes with and what is the correct expression for that/those step(s)?

    (Answers are on pages 223–225.)

Algebraic Equations and Inequalities

The purpose of algebraic equations and inequalities is to represent relationships between quantities algebraically using numbers, letters, and symbols.

Standards

7.EE.B.4 Use variables to represent quantities in a real-world or mathematical problem, and construct simple equations and inequalities to solve problems by reasoning about the quantities.

Sample Questions from the SBAC

The following are examples of question types you will see on the SBAC Grade 7 Math test. We will cover them in this chapter.

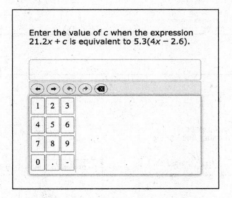

Enter the value of c when the expression $21.2x + c$ is equivalent to $5.3(4x - 2.6)$.

Jenny has $25 and she earns $10 for each lawn that she mows. Jenny wants to buy a concert ticket that costs $65.

Enter the minimum number of lawns Jenny needs to mow to be able to buy the concert ticket.

David goes into a candy store with $5.00. He buys 9 peppermints for $0.15 each, and some sour candies. Each sour candy costs $0.25.

Enter the maximum number of sour candies David can buy.

←	→	↶	↷	⌫

1	2	3
4	5	6
7	8	9
0	.	-

Marcus has a pool that can hold a maximum of 4500 gallons of water. The pool already contains 1500 gallons of water. Marcus begins to add more water at a rate of 30 gallons per minute.

Enter an inequality that shows the number of minutes, m, Marcus can continue to add water to the pool without exceeding the maximum number of gallons.

←	→	↶	↷	⌫

1	2	3	m
4	5	6	+	-	*	÷
7	8	9	<	≤	=	≥	>
0	.	-	$\frac{a}{b}$	$\square^{\square}$	( )	| |	π

Values for variables a, b, and c are graphed on the number line shown.

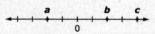

Use the graph to evaluate the expressions in the table. Select one column for each row in the table to indicate whether the expression is less than 0, equal to 0, or greater than 0.

Expression	< 0	= 0	> 0
$a - b$			
$a + b$			
$b - c$			
$c - a$			
$a + c$			

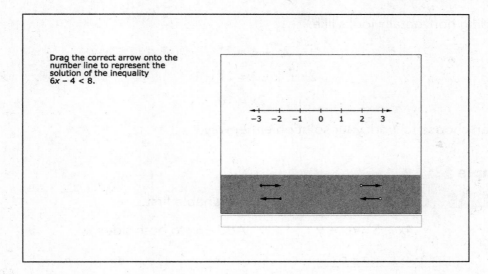

Drag the correct arrow onto the number line to represent the solution of the inequality $6x - 4 < 8$.

Lesson 3.1 Solving Algebraic Equations

An **equation** is a statement where the values of two mathematical expressions are equal as indicated by the = symbol. It is also the process of equating one thing to another. Solving the equation consists of determining which values of the variable make the equality true. Components of an algebraic equation are the same as that of an algebraic expression except for the equal sign.

To solve for the unknown of an equation, you want to isolate your unknown, also known as your variable, and move everything to the opposite side.

$$0.5x - 6 = 14$$

Variable — x

Coefficient — 0.5

Constant — 6, 14

There are two ways to show your work when adding terms to both sides of the equation. You can add either vertically or horizontally. For example,

Adding vertically or writing like terms in columns:

$$2x + 1 = 11$$
$$+ \qquad -1 \quad -1$$
$$2x = 10$$

Adding horizontally looks like:

$$2x + 1 = 11$$
$$2x + 1 - 1 = 11 - 1$$
$$2x = 10$$

You can choose to work your solution either way.

Example 1

METHOD 1 Consolidate the term with the variable first.

$$4x - 5 = 6x + 9 \qquad \text{Add } -6x \text{ to both sides.}$$

$$\underline{+\ -6x \qquad = -6x}$$

$$-2x - 5 = 9$$

$$\underline{+ \qquad +5 \quad +5} \qquad \text{Add } +5 \text{ to both sides.}$$

$$\frac{-2x}{-2} = \frac{14}{-2} \qquad \text{Divide by } -2 \text{ to both sides.}$$

$$x = -7$$

METHOD 2 Consolidate and combine the constants first.

$$4x - 5 = 6x + 9$$

$$4x - 5 + 5 = 6x + 9 + 5 \qquad \text{Add } +5 \text{ to both sides.}$$

$$4x = 6x + 14$$

$$4x - 6x = 6x - 6x + 14 \qquad \text{Add } -6x \text{ to both sides.}$$

$$4x - 6x = 14$$

$$-2x = 14$$

$$\frac{-2x}{-2} = \frac{14}{-2} \qquad \text{Divide by } -2.$$

$$x = -7$$

Check your answer by plugging the solution back into the original equation. You know you have the right answer when both sides are equivalent to each other.

$$4(-7) - 5 = 6(-7) + 9$$

$$-28 - 5 = -42 + 9$$

$$-28 + (-5) = -42 + 9$$

$$-33 = -33$$

Example 2

METHOD 1 Consolidate or combine the constants first.

$$-\frac{2}{3}x + 8 = 7$$

$$+\underline{\qquad -8 \quad -8 \qquad}$$ Add −8 to both sides.

$$-\frac{2}{3}x = -1$$

$$-\frac{3}{2}\left(-\frac{2}{3}x\right) = -\frac{3}{2}(-1)$$ Multiply both sides by the reciprocal of $-\frac{2}{3}$ by putting parentheses around both sides first.

$$x = \frac{3}{2}$$

METHOD 2 This method is less direct and longer than method 1 but it shows that it does not matter which one you do first, you will get the same answer.

$$-\frac{2}{3}x + 8 + \frac{2}{3}x = 7 + \frac{2}{3}x$$ Add $+\frac{2}{3}x$ to both sides of the equation.

$$8 = 7 + \frac{2}{3}x$$ Simplify by combining the zero pairs.

$$8 - 7 = 7 + \frac{2}{3}x - 7$$ Add −7 to both sides of the equation.

$$1 = \frac{2}{3}x$$

$$\frac{3}{2}(1) = \frac{3}{2}\left(\frac{2}{3}x\right)$$ Multiply by the reciprocal of $\frac{2}{3}$.

$$\frac{3}{2} = x$$

Check your answer:

$$-\frac{2}{3}\left(\frac{3}{2}\right) + 8 = 7$$

$$-1 + 8 = 7$$

$$7 = 7$$

Example 3 $-\dfrac{5}{6}x - \dfrac{3}{2} = \dfrac{4}{3}x - \dfrac{5}{12}$

METHOD 1 Combine the algebraic terms first.

$$-\dfrac{5}{6}x - \dfrac{3}{2} = \dfrac{4}{3}x - \dfrac{5}{12}$$ Convert all the fractions to common denominators.

$$\dfrac{+\quad +\dfrac{5}{6}x \qquad\quad +\dfrac{5}{6}x}{\qquad\qquad -\dfrac{3}{2} = \dfrac{13}{6}x - \dfrac{5}{12}}$$ Add $\dfrac{5}{6}x$ to both sides.

Combine $\dfrac{4}{3}x + \dfrac{5}{6}x = \dfrac{8}{6}x + \dfrac{5}{6}x = \dfrac{13}{6}x$

$$\dfrac{+\quad +\dfrac{5}{12} \qquad\quad +\dfrac{5}{12}}{\qquad\quad -\dfrac{13}{12} = \dfrac{13}{6}\,x}$$ Add $\dfrac{5}{12}$ to both sides.

$$\dfrac{6}{13}\left(-\dfrac{13}{12}\right) = \dfrac{6}{13}\left(\dfrac{13}{6}x\right)$$ Multiply by the reciprocal of $\dfrac{13}{6}$.

$$-\dfrac{6}{12} = x$$ Simplify.

$$-\dfrac{1}{2} = x$$

METHOD 2 Combine the constants first.

$$-\dfrac{5}{6}x - \dfrac{3}{2} + \dfrac{3}{2} = \dfrac{4}{3}x - \dfrac{5}{12} + \dfrac{3}{2}$$ Add $\dfrac{3}{2}$ to both sides.

$$-\dfrac{5}{6}x = \dfrac{4}{3}x - \dfrac{5}{12} + \dfrac{18}{12}$$ In order to combine the fractions, convert both to equivalent fractions with common denominators.

$$-\dfrac{5}{6}x = \dfrac{4}{3}x + \dfrac{13}{12}$$ Simplify $-\dfrac{5}{12} + \dfrac{18}{12} = \dfrac{13}{12}$

$$-\dfrac{5}{6}x - \dfrac{4}{3}x = \dfrac{4}{3}x + \dfrac{13}{12} - \dfrac{4}{3}x$$ Add $-\dfrac{4}{3}x$ to both sides.

$$-\dfrac{5}{6}x - \dfrac{8}{6}x = \dfrac{13}{12}$$ Change to equivalent fractions with common denominators in order to combine the like terms.

$$-\dfrac{13}{6}x = \dfrac{13}{12}$$

$$-\dfrac{6}{13}\left(-\dfrac{13}{6}x\right) = -\dfrac{6}{13}\left(\dfrac{13}{12}\right)$$

$$x = -\dfrac{6}{12}$$

$$x = -\dfrac{1}{2}$$

METHOD 3 Multiply by the LCM of 2, 3, 6, and 12.

$$\frac{12}{1}\left(-\frac{5}{6}x - \frac{3}{2}\right) = \frac{12}{1}\left(\frac{4}{3}x - \frac{5}{12}\right)$$

$$\frac{12}{1}\left(-\frac{5}{6}x\right) + \frac{12}{1}\left(-\frac{3}{2}\right) = \frac{12}{1}\left(\frac{4}{3}x\right) + \frac{12}{1}\left(-\frac{5}{12}\right)$$

Distribute 12 to both terms inside the parentheses.

$$-10x - 18 = 16x - 5$$ Multiply the fractions and simplify.

$$-10x - 18 + 10x = 16x - 5 + 10x$$ Add +10x to both sides.

$$-18 + 5 = 26x - 5 + 5$$ Add +5 to both sides.

$$-13 = 26x$$

$$-\frac{13}{26} = \frac{26x}{26}$$

Divide by 26 on both sides to isolate the variable.

$$-\frac{1}{2} = x$$

Example 4 $\dfrac{3}{4}\left(-\dfrac{1}{2}x + 5\right) = 9$

METHOD 1 Distribute

$$\frac{3}{4}\left(-\frac{1}{2}x + 5\right) = 9$$

$$\frac{3}{4}\left(-\frac{1}{2}x\right) + \frac{3}{4}\left(\frac{5}{1}\right) = 9$$

$$-\frac{3}{8}x + \frac{15}{4} = 9$$

$$\underline{+ \qquad -\frac{15}{4} \quad -\frac{15}{4}}$$

$$-\frac{3}{8}x = \frac{21}{4}$$

$$-\frac{8}{3}\left(-\frac{3}{8}x\right) = -\frac{8}{3}\left(\frac{21}{4}\right)$$ Multiply by the inverse of $-\dfrac{3}{8}$.

$$x = -14$$

> Perform the fraction operation on the side:
> $$\frac{9}{1} - \frac{15}{4} = \frac{36}{4} - \frac{15}{4} = \frac{21}{4}$$

METHOD 2 Divide by $\frac{3}{4}$ or multiply by the reciprocal of $\frac{3}{4}$.

$$\frac{4}{3}\left(\frac{3}{4}\right)\left(-\frac{1}{2}x+5\right) = \left(\frac{9}{1}\right)\left(\frac{4}{3}\right)$$

$$-\frac{1}{2}x + 5 = 12 \qquad\qquad \text{Add } -5 \text{ to both sides.}$$

$$\underline{+ \qquad -5 \ -5}$$

$$-\frac{1}{2}x = 7 \qquad\qquad \text{Multiply by the reciprocal of } -\frac{1}{2}.$$

$$-\frac{2}{1}\left(-\frac{1}{2}x\right) = -\frac{2}{1}\left(\frac{7}{1}\right)$$

$$x = -14$$

Check your answer:

$$\frac{3}{4}\left(-\frac{1}{2}\left(-\frac{14}{1}\right)+5\right) = 9 \qquad\qquad \text{Plug } -14 \text{ in for } x.$$

$$\frac{3}{4}(7 + 5) = 9$$

$$\frac{3}{4}(12) = 9$$

$$9 = 9$$

Example 5 $\quad 0.1(7x + 5) = 46$

METHOD 1 Distribute 0.1

$$0.1(7x) + (0.1)(5) = 46$$

$$0.7x + 0.5 = 46 \qquad\qquad \text{Add } -0.5 \text{ to both sides.}$$

$$\underline{+ \quad -0.5 \ \ -0.5}$$

$$0.7x = 45.5$$

$$\frac{0.7x}{0.7} = \frac{45.5}{0.7} \qquad\qquad \text{Divide by the coefficient of } 0.7x \text{ to both sides.}$$

$$x = 65$$

METHOD 2   Divide by 0.1

$$\frac{0.1(7x+5)}{0.1} = \frac{46}{0.1}$$

Think of how the area of the rectangle is length times width. Divide by 0.1 on both sides.

$$(7x + 5) = 460$$

Add −5 to both sides.

$$+ \quad -5 \quad -5$$
_____

$$7x = 455$$

$$\frac{7x}{7} = \frac{455}{7}$$

Divide by the coefficient of 7x.

$$x = 65$$

Check your answer:

$$0.1(7 \cdot 65 + 5) = 46$$

Plug in or substitute 65 for x.

$$0.1(455 + 5) = 46$$

$$0.1(460) = 46$$

$$46 = 46$$

Example 6 $0.3x + 14 = -0.7x - 2.4$

METHOD 1   Combine like terms by adding −14 on both sides.

$$0.3x + 14 = -0.7x - 2.4$$

$$+ \quad -14 \quad -14$$
_____

Add the inverse of +14.

$$0.3x = -0.7x - 16.4$$

$$+ \quad +0.7x \quad +0.7x$$
_____

Add the inverse of −0.7x.

$$x = -16.4$$

METHOD 2   Combine like terms by adding −0.3x on both sides.

$$0.3x + 14 = -0.7x - 2.4$$

$$0.3x + 14 - 0.3x = -0.7x - 2.4 - 0.3x \qquad \text{Add the inverse of } +0.3x.$$

$$14 = -x - 2.4$$

$$14 + 2.4 = -x - 2.4 + 2.4 \qquad \text{Add } +2.4 \text{ to both sides.}$$

$$16.4 = -x$$

$$16.4(-1) = -x(-1) \qquad \text{Multiply by } -1 \text{ or divide by } -1 \text{ to get a positive } x.$$

$$-16.4 = x$$

Check your answer:

$$0.3(-16.4) + 14 = -0.7(-16.4) - 2.4$$

$$-4.92 + 14 = 11.48 - 2.4$$

$$9.08 = 9.08$$

Example 7 $\dfrac{4}{3}x - \dfrac{5}{6} = \dfrac{1}{9}x - \dfrac{7}{18}$

METHOD 1   Use fraction operations to solve for x.

$$\frac{4}{3}x - \frac{5}{6} + \frac{5}{6} = \frac{1}{9}x - \frac{7}{18} + \frac{5}{6} \qquad \text{Add } \frac{5}{6} \text{ to both sides.}$$

$$\frac{4}{3}x = \frac{1}{9}x + \frac{8}{18}$$

$$-\frac{7}{18} + \frac{5}{6} = -\frac{7}{18} + \frac{15}{18} = \frac{8}{18} \qquad \text{Combine like terms.}$$

$$\frac{4}{3}x - \frac{1}{9}x = \frac{1}{9}x + \frac{8}{18} - \frac{1}{9}x \qquad \text{Add } -\frac{1}{9}x \text{ to both sides.}$$

$$\frac{11}{9}x = \frac{8}{18}$$

$$\frac{9}{11}\left(\frac{11}{9}x\right) = \left(\frac{8}{18}\right)\left(\frac{9}{11}\right)$$

$$x = \frac{4}{11}$$

METHOD 2   Multiply by the LCM of 3, 6, 9, and 18 to solve for x.

How do you find the **L**east **C**ommon **M**ultiple (LCM) of 3, 6, 9, and 18? Write out the multiplication table for each number and find the multiple they have in common:

3: 3, 6, 9, 12, 15, <u>18</u>, 21

6: 6, 12, <u>18</u>, 24

9: 9, <u>18</u>, 27

18: <u>18</u>, 36

$$18\left(\frac{4}{3}x - \frac{5}{6}\right) = 18\left(\frac{1}{9}x - \frac{7}{18}\right)$$

$$\frac{18}{1}\left(\frac{4}{3}x\right) + \frac{18}{1}\left(-\frac{5}{6}\right) = \frac{18}{1}\left(\frac{1}{9}x\right) + \frac{18}{1}\left(-\frac{7}{18}\right) \qquad \text{Distribute.}$$

$$24x - 15 = 2x - 7$$

$$24x - 15 + 15 = 2x - 7 + 15 \qquad \text{Add the inverse of } -15.$$

$$24x = 2x + 8$$

$$24x - 2x = 2x + 8 - 2x \qquad \text{Add the inverse of } +2x.$$

$$22x = 8$$

$$\frac{22x}{22} = \frac{8}{22} \qquad \text{Divide by the coefficient of } 22x.$$

$$x = \frac{8}{22} = \frac{4}{11}$$

✎ PRACTICE

Directions: Solve the algebraic equations.

1. $3x - 12 = 7x + 21$

2. $-5x - 13 = -x - 11$

3. $-0.5x - 0.13 = -0.1x - 0.11$

4. $-\dfrac{3}{4}x + 12 = 28$

5. $-17 + 2x = -6x - 33$

6. $-2x - 12 + 5x = -9x + 21 - 2x$

7. $\dfrac{3}{5}\left(\dfrac{1}{4}x + 1\right) = 4$

8. $\dfrac{-x - 4}{7} = 2$

9. $-5 - \dfrac{2}{3}x = -9$

10. $-\dfrac{2}{9}\left(-\dfrac{1}{6}x - 18\right) = -27$

11. $-\dfrac{7}{8}x + 14 = \dfrac{1}{2}x - 2$

12. $-\dfrac{2}{5}x - \dfrac{1}{6} = -\dfrac{1}{2}x - 2$

13. $0.4(-0.2x - 3) = 0.5$

14. $-14 = \dfrac{-90 - 5x}{10}$

15. $-(-x - 1) + 6 = -2(-3x + 4) - 8x$

16. $\dfrac{-6x + 24}{-12} = -9$

17. $-3(0.5x - 4) - 2(-4x - 1) = 1$

18. $\dfrac{1}{2}\left(-\dfrac{1}{2}x + \dfrac{1}{2}\right) = \dfrac{1}{2}$

19. $-0.8(2.3x - 0.1) = -0.4(2 - 6x)$

20. $\dfrac{1}{2}\left(-\dfrac{2}{3}x + \dfrac{3}{2}\right) = \dfrac{1}{3}\left(\dfrac{5}{2}x - \dfrac{7}{12}\right)$

(Answers are on pages 225–234.)

Lesson 3.2 Real-World Problems: Algebraic Equations

When working with word problems, translate the words into symbols and numbers first. Remember to check your answers by plugging the value of the unknown back into the original equation to see if it works. Equations are either equal to each other, or not equal to each other. Here are helpful keywords to look for:

=	≠
is/are equal to	is not equal to
costs	is not the same as
has/had	is different
was/were	differs from
will be	
gives	
yields	

Example 1 Write an equation for each sentence. Then solve the equation.

#	Sentence	Equation and Solution	Check
A	9 less than the product of 7 and x is 75.	$7x - 9 = 75$ $7x - 9 + 9 = 75 + 9$ $7x = 84$ $\dfrac{7x}{7} = \dfrac{84}{7}$ $x = 12$	$7(12) - 9 = 75$ $84 - 9 = 75$ $75 = 75$
B	Three subtracted from the product of $2x$ divided by negative 5 equals −48.	$-\dfrac{2x}{5} - 3 = -48$ $-\dfrac{2x}{5} - 3 + 3 = -48 + 3$ $-\dfrac{2x}{5} = -45$ $-\dfrac{5}{2}\left(-\dfrac{2x}{5}\right) = (-45)\left(-\dfrac{5}{2}\right)$ $x = 112.5$	$-\dfrac{2(112.5)}{5} - 3 = -48$ $-\dfrac{225}{5} - 3 = -48$ $-45 - 3 = -48$ $-48 = -48$

#	Sentence	Equation and Solution	Check
C	x more than the quotient of $16x$ and 2 equals negative 81.	$x + \dfrac{16x}{2} = -81$ $x + 8x = -81$ $9x = -81$ $\dfrac{9x}{9} = -\dfrac{81}{9}$ $x = -9$	$-9 + \dfrac{16(-9)}{2} = -81$ $-9 + \dfrac{-144}{2} = -81$ $-9 + (-72) = -81$ $-81 = -81$
D	The quotient of the sum of $3x$ and 4, and negative 7 equals 13.	$\dfrac{3x + 4}{-7} = 13$ $-\dfrac{7}{1}\left(\dfrac{3x + 4}{-7}\right) = (13)(-7)$ $3x + 4 = -91$ $3x + 4 - 4 = -91 - 4$ $3x = -95$ $\dfrac{3x}{3} = -\dfrac{95}{3}$ $x \approx -31.67$	$\dfrac{3(-31.67) + 4}{-7} = 13$ $\dfrac{-95.01 + 4}{-7} = 13$ $\dfrac{-91.01}{-7} = 13$ $13.0014 \approx 13$ Since we plugged in an approximate number for x, the solution will not be exact.
E	17 more than the product of -6 and x equals the sum of 55 and the product of -2 and x.	$-6x + 17 = -2x + 55$ $-6x + 17 + 6x = -2x + 55 + 6x$ $17 = 4x + 55$ $17 - 55 = 4x + 55 - 55$ $-38 = 4x$ $-\dfrac{38}{4} = \dfrac{4x}{4}$ $-9.5 = x$	$-6(-9.5) + 17 = -2(-9.5) + 55$ $57 + 17 = 19 + 55$ $74 = 74$

Example 2 The sum of 3 consecutive numbers is 213. Write an equation to represent this situation and find all 3 numbers.

Solution

Think of three consecutive numbers:

$$4, 5, 6$$

$$7, 8, 9$$

$$10, 11, 12$$

$$121, 122, 123$$

Come up with expressions that work for all of them:

$4 = x$	$7 = x$	$10 = x$	$121 = x$
$5 = x + 1$	$8 = x + 1$	$11 = x + 1$	$122 = x + 1$
$6 = x + 2$	$9 = x + 2$	$12 = x + 2$	$123 = x + 2$

Define the variable: Let x = the value of the smallest number.

Write your equation in words first. Then use the expressions and set the sum equal to 213.

Small number + middle number + large number = 213

$$x + x + 1 + x + 2 = 213$$

$$3x + 3 = 213 \qquad \text{Combine like terms.}$$

$$3x + 3 - 3 = 213 - 3 \qquad \text{Add } -3 \text{ to both sides.}$$

$$3x = 210$$

$$\frac{3x}{3} = \frac{210}{3} \qquad \text{Divide by the coefficient of } 3x.$$

$$x = 70$$

Once you plug in or substitute the value of x for your expression, find the other values.

$$\text{Small number} = x = 70$$

$$\text{Middle number} = x + 1 = 70 + 1 = 71$$

$$\text{Large number} = x + 2 = 70 + 2 = 72$$

Example 3 Mrs. McFarland's dog Pino refuses to get on the scale by himself. So, she picks him up and steps on the scale with him. Their combined weight is 156 pounds. If Mrs. McFarland's weight is 12 more than twice that of Pino's, how much does Mrs. McFarland and Pino weigh? Write an equation and solve for both of their weights.

Solution

Define the variable: Let m = Pino's weight.

Mrs. McFarland's weight $= 12 + 2m$

Pino's weight + Mrs. McFarland's weight = total weight

$$m + 12 + 2m = 156$$

$$3m + 12 = 156 \qquad \text{Combine like terms.}$$

$$3m + 12 - 12 = 156 - 12 \qquad \text{Add } -12 \text{ to both sides.}$$

$$3m = 144 \qquad \text{Divide by the coefficient of } 3m.$$

$$\frac{3m}{3} = \frac{144}{3}$$

$$m = 48$$

Plug in the solution for m to find Mrs. McFarland's weight:

$$2m + 12 = 2(48) + 12 = 96 + 12 = 108$$

Explain your Solution

Pino weighs 48 pounds and Mrs. McFarland weighs 108 pounds.

Example 4 Rohan is saving up to buy his mother a birthday present for $82. He already has saved $34. He gets $4 for every chore he does around the house. How many chores will he have to do to have enough for his mother's present?

Solution

Define the variable: Let c = the number of chores Rohan needs to do.

If you are not sure about the expression, create a table and plug in numbers that make sense.

# of chores	Already Saved + 4c 34 + 4c	Explanation
2	34 + 4(2) = 42	If he completes two chores, Rohan will save $42.
5	34 + 4(5) = 54	If he completes five chores, Rohan will save $54.
10	34 + 4(10) = 74	If he completes ten chores, Rohan will save $74.
c	34 + 4c	

Write your equation and solve for the number of chores Rohan will have to do.

Already saved + amount earned from chores = total for the birthday present

$$34 + 4c = 82$$
$$34 + 4c - 34 = 82 - 34$$
$$4c = 48$$
$$\frac{4c}{4} = \frac{48}{4}$$
$$c = 12$$

Articulate your solution in a sentence: Rohan will need to complete 12 chores in order to have enough for his mother's $82 birthday present.

 **PRACTICE**

Directions: For each problem, write an equation and then solve the problem. Be sure to write a sentence to explain what your solution means.

1. Fifteen subtracted from the product of −2 and x equals 35 less than −7 times x.

2. Negative 24 equals the quotient of the sum of −4x and 8, and 3.

3. Negative ten is equal to one-half x less than three.

4. Fourteen is equal to the product of −2 and the sum of −x and 8.

5. The quotient of 45x and −5 is equal to −3 times the quantity of 1 less than 4x.

6. The sum of two consecutive numbers is 505. What are both numbers?

7. The sum of four consecutive odd numbers is 80. What are all 4 numbers?

8. Gaby opened up her math textbook and both pages add up to 197. What pages did she open her book up to?

9. At the movie theater, adult tickets cost $8.50 and children's tickets cost $4.25. If there were three adults and the total bill was $55.25, how many children did they chaperone?

10. The difference between two numbers is 12. If the second number is three less than one-half times the first, what are both numbers?

11. If the value of an unknown number of nickels is $1.35, how many nickels are there?

12. If the value of an unknown number of quarters is $11.75, how many quarters are there?

13. The perimeter of an equilateral triangle is 21 units. How long is each side of the triangle?

14. Chloe earns $6.50 per hour babysitting and receives a $25 allowance each week. How many hours did she babysit this week if she receives $70.50 total?

15. Abby is three times as old as Alice. Alice is twice as old as Anna. If their ages total 27, how old is each female?

16. The perimeter of an isosceles triangle is 52 inches. If the base is 16 inches, what is the length of each side?

(Answers are on pages 235–241.)

Lesson 3.3 Solving Algebraic Inequalities

Solving inequalities is almost like solving equations. With solving equations, there is one value (there are exceptions to this!) to make the mathematical statement true. With solving inequalities, there is a set of solutions or sometimes an infinite number of solutions to make the mathematical statement true. You can always plug in solutions and nonsolutions into your inequality to check your answer.

Graphing is a visual way to represent your solution.

Graph	Inequality	Explanation	Solutions for x	Nonsolutions for x
*Open circle on the 5 −5 0 5 10	$x < 5$	The number is less than 5.	4, 3, 0, −5, −10, and any number less than or equal to 4.	5, 10, and any number greater than 5.
*Open circle on the 5 −5 0 5 10	$x > 5$	The number is greater than 5.	6, 10, 100, and any number greater than or equal to 6.	5, 1, 0, −5, −1000, and any number less than or equal to 5.
*Closed or filled in circle on the 5 −5 0 5 10	$x \le 5$	The number is less than or equal to 5.	5, 4, 3, 0, −1, −5, any number less than but not including 6.	6, 10, 100, 1000, and any number greater than or equal to 6.
*Closed or filled in circle on the 5 −5 0 5 10	$x \ge 5$	The number is greater than or equal to 5.	5, 6, 10, 1000, and any number greater than or equal to 5.	4, 1, 0, −1, −5 and any number less than 5.

One trick to remember if the circle is open or closed is to think of these inequalities like pipes with water running through them. If the inequality sign has a line underneath like ≤ or ≥, there is water in the pipes and the circle is filled in or closed. If there is no line underneath the inequality like > or <, there is no water and the circle is open or not filled in.

Example 1 $x + 2 < 8$

$$x + 2 - 2 < 8 - 2$$
$$x < 6$$

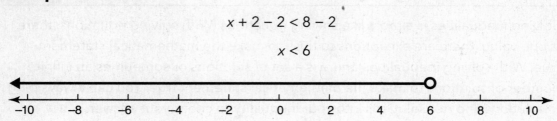

Plug in solutions and nonsolutions. Check your work using the table below.

Values of x	$x + 2 < 8$	True/False and Explanation
0	$0 + 2 < 8$ $2 < 8$	**True.** 2 is less than 8. 0 is part of the solution set that states that the value of x are all values less than 6.
6	$6 + 2 < 8$ $8 < 8$	**False.** 8 is not less than 8. 8 is equal to 8. 6 is not included in the solution set, and the graph indicates this with an open circle. For this inequality to be true, it would have to read $8 \leq 8$.
10	$10 + 2 < 8$ $12 < 8$	**False.** 12 is not less than 8. Locate 10 on the number line above and it will not be part of the solution set.

Example 2 $\frac{2}{3}x - \frac{3}{4} \leq -\frac{7}{12}$

$$\frac{2}{3}x - \frac{3}{4} + \frac{3}{4} \leq -\frac{7}{12} + \frac{3}{4}$$
$$\frac{2}{3}x \leq -\frac{7}{12} + \frac{9}{12}$$
$$\frac{2}{3}x \leq \frac{2}{12}$$
$$\frac{3}{2}\left(\frac{2}{3x}\right) \leq \left(\frac{2}{12}\right)\left(\frac{3}{2}\right)$$
$$x \leq \frac{1}{4}$$

Values of x	$\frac{2}{3}x - \frac{3}{4} \le -\frac{7}{12}$	True/False and Explanation
0	$\frac{2}{3}(0) - \frac{3}{4} \le -\frac{7}{12}$ $-\frac{3}{4} \le -\frac{7}{12}$ $-\frac{9}{12} \le -\frac{7}{12}$	**True.** $-\frac{3}{4}$ is less than $-\frac{7}{12}$ because it is further to the left on the number line. 0 is part of the solution set, which states that the values of x are all values less than or equal to $\frac{1}{4}$.
$\frac{1}{4}$	$\frac{2}{3}\left(\frac{1}{4}\right) - \frac{3}{4} \le -\frac{7}{12}$ $\frac{2}{12} - \frac{3}{4} \le -\frac{7}{12}$ $\frac{2}{12} - \frac{9}{12} \le -\frac{7}{12}$ $-\frac{7}{12} \le -\frac{7}{12}$	**True.** $-\frac{7}{12}$ is less than or equal to $-\frac{7}{12}$. The graph indicates this with a closed circle, which means $\frac{1}{4}$ is part of the solution set. For this solution to be false, it would have to read $\qquad -\frac{7}{12} < -\frac{7}{12}$
1	$\frac{2}{3}(1) - \frac{3}{4} \le -\frac{7}{12}$ $\frac{2}{3} - \frac{3}{4} \le -\frac{7}{12}$ $\frac{8}{12} - \frac{9}{12} \le -\frac{7}{12}$ $-\frac{1}{12} \le -\frac{7}{12}$	**False.** $-\frac{1}{12}$ is not less than $-\frac{7}{12}$ because $-\frac{1}{12}$ falls on the right-hand side of $-\frac{7}{12}$ on the number line, which means $-\frac{1}{12}$ is larger. Locate 1 on the number line and it will not be part of the solution set.

Example 3 $0.3x + 3.4 > 0.7x$

$$0.3x + 3.4 - 0.3x > 0.7x - 0.3x$$

$$3.4 > 0.4x$$

$$\frac{3.4}{0.4} > \frac{0.4x}{0.4}$$

$$8.5 > x$$

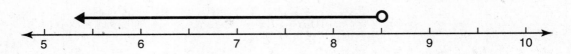

Values of x	$0.3x + 3.4 > 0.7x$	True/False and Explanation
0	$0.3x + 3.4 > 0.7x$ $0.3(0) + 3.4 > 0.7(0)$ $3.4 > 0$	**True.** 3.4 is greater than 0 because it is further to the right on the number line than 0. 0 is part of the solution set that states that the values of x are all values less than 8.5.
8.5	$0.3x + 3.4 > 0.7x$ $0.3(8.5) + 3.4 > 0.7(8.5)$ $2.55 + 3.4 > 5.95$ $5.95 > 5.95$	**False.** 5.95 is not greater than 5.95. 8.5 is not included in the solution set, and the graph indicates this with an open circle. For this inequality to be true, it would have to read $5.95 \geq 5.95$.
10	$0.3x + 3.4 > 0.7x$ $0.3(10) + 3.4 > 0.7(10)$ $3 + 3.4 > 7$ $6.4 > 7$	**False.** 6.4 is not greater than 7 because 6.4 falls on the left-hand side of 7 on the number line, which means 7 is larger. Locate 10 on the number line and it will not be part of the solution set.

Example 4 $-9x + 3.4 > -x - 7.2$

METHOD 1   Combine the like terms by adding $+9x$ to both sides of the inequality.

$$-9x + 3.4 + 9x > -x - 7.2 + 9x$$
$$3.4 > -7.2 + 8x$$
$$3.4 + 7.2 > -7.2 + 8x + 7.2$$
$$10.6 > 8x$$
$$\frac{10.6}{8} > \frac{8x}{8}$$
$$1.325 > x$$

METHOD 2   Combine the constants by adding $+7.2$ to both sides of the inequality.

$$-9x + 3.4 + 7.2 > -x - 7.2 + 7.2$$
$$-9x + 10.6 > -x$$
$$-9x + 10.6 + 9x > -x + 9x$$
$$10.6 > 8x$$
$$\frac{10.6}{8} > \frac{8x}{8}$$
$$1.325 > x$$

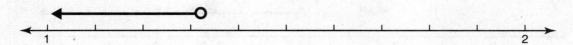

Values of x	$-9x + 3.4 > -x - 7.2$	True/False and Explanation
0	$-9x + 3.4 > -x - 7.2$ $9(0) + 3.4 > (0) - 7.2$ $3.4 > -7.2$	**True.** 3.4 is greater than -7.2 because it is further to the right on the number line than -7.2. 0 is part of the solution set that states that the values of x are all values less than 1.325.
1.325	$-9x + 3.4 > -x - 7.2$ $-9(1.325) + 3.4 > -(1.325) - 7.2$ $-11.925 + 3.4 > -1.325 - 7.2$ $-8.525 > -8.525$	**False.** -8.525 is not greater than -8.525. 1.325 is not included in the solution set, and the graph indicates this with an open circle. For this inequality to be true, it would have to read $-8.525 \geq -8.525$.
2	$-9x + 3.4 > -x - 7.2$ $-9(2) + 3.4 > -(2) - 7.2$ $-18 + 3.4 > -2 - 7.2$ $-14.6 > -9.2$	**False.** -14.6 is not greater than -9.2 because -14.6 falls on the left-hand side of -9.2 on the number line, which means -9.2 is larger. Locate 2 on the number line above, and it will not be part of the solution set.

Why do you flip the inequality sign when multiplying or subtracting by a negative?

Example 5

$$-2x \leq 10$$

$$\frac{-2x}{-2} \leq \frac{10}{-2}$$

$$x \geq -5$$

*Flip the sign when multiplying or dividing by a negative rational number.

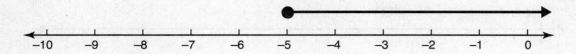

Values of x	$-2x \leq 10$	True/False and Explanation
0	$-2x \leq 10$ $-2(0) \leq 10$ $0 \leq 10$	**True.** 0 is less than 10 because it is further to the left on the number line. 0 is part of the solution set that states that the values of x are all values greater than or equal to -5.
-5	$-2x \leq 10$ $-2(-5) \leq 10$ $10 \leq 10$	**True.** 10 is less than or equal to 10. The graph indicates this with a closed circle, which means -5 is part of the solution set. For this solution to be false, it would have to read $-10 < -10$.
5	$-2x \leq 10$ $-2(5) \leq 10$ $-10 \leq 10$	**True.** -10 is less than 10 because -10 falls on the left-hand side of 10 on the number line, which means 10 is larger. Locate 5 on the number line above and it will be part of the solution set.
-10	$-2(-10) \leq 10$ $20 \leq 10$	**False.** 20 is not less than 10. It is to the right of 20 on the number line, which means 20 is larger than 10. Locate -10 on the number line above and it will not be part of the solution set.

Example 6 $\quad -\dfrac{2}{3}x \leq 15$

$$-\frac{3}{2}\left(-\frac{2}{3}x\right) \leq (15)\left(-\frac{3}{2}\right)$$

$$x \geq -\frac{45}{2} \text{ or } x \geq -22\frac{1}{2} \text{ or } x \geq -22.5$$

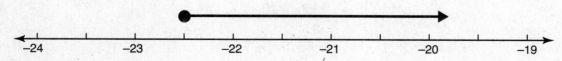

Values of x	$-\frac{2}{3}x \le 15$	True/False and Explanation
−30	$-\frac{2}{3}(-30) \le 15$ $20 \le 15$	**False.** 20 is not less than 15 because 20 is further to the right on the number line than 15. −30 is not part of the solution set that states that the values of x are all values greater than or equal to −22.5.
−22.5	$-\frac{2}{3}(-22.5) \le 15$ $15 \le 15$	**True.** 15 is less than or equal to 15. The graph indicates this with a closed circle, which means −22.5 is part of the solution set. For this solution to be false, it would have to read 15 < 15.
0	$-\frac{2}{3}(0) \le 15$ $0 \le 15$	**True.** 0 is less than 15 because 0 falls on the left-hand side of 15 on the number line, which means 15 is larger and 0 is smaller. Locate 0 on the number line and it will be part of the solution set.

Example 7 $0.3x + 3.4 > -0.7x$

$$0.3x + 3.4 - 0.3x > -0.7x - 0.3x$$

$$3.4 > -x$$

$$3.4(-1) > -x(-1)$$

$$-3.4 < x$$

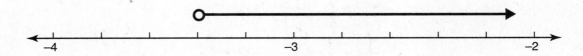

Values of x	$0.3x + 3.4 > -0.7x$	True/False and Explanation
0	$0.3(0) + 3.4 > -0.7(0)$ $3.4 > 0$	**True.** 3.4 is greater than 0 because it is further to the right on the number line than 0. 0 is part of the solution set that states that the values of x are all values greater than −3.4.
−3.4	$0.3(-3.4) + 3.4 > -0.7(-3.4)$ $-1.02 + 3.4 > 2.38$ $2.38 > 2.38$	**False.** 2.38 is not greater than 2.38. 2.38 is not included in the solution set, and the graph indicates this with an open circle. For this inequality to be true, it would have to read $2.38 ≥ 2.38$.
−10	$0.3(-10) + 3.4 > -0.7(-10)$ $-3 + 3.4 > 7$ $0.4 > 7$	**False.** 0.4 is not greater than 7 because 0.4 falls on the left-hand side of 7 on the number line, which means 7 is larger. Locate −10 on the number line and it will not be part of the solution set.

Example 8 $\dfrac{3}{4}x + 5 \le -\dfrac{3}{8}x - 7$

METHOD 1   Combine the like terms by adding −5 to both sides of the inequality.

$$\frac{3}{4}x + 5 - 5 \le -\frac{3}{8}x - 7 - 5$$

$$\frac{3}{4}x \le -\frac{3}{8}x - 12$$

$$\frac{3}{4}x + \frac{3}{8}x \le -\frac{3}{8}x - 12 + \frac{3}{8}x$$

$$\frac{6}{8}x + \frac{3}{8}x \le -12$$

$$\frac{9}{8}x \le -12$$

$$\frac{8}{9}\left(\frac{9}{8}x\right) \le -12\left(\frac{8}{9}\right)$$

$$x \le -\frac{32}{3} \text{ or } x \le -10\frac{2}{3}$$

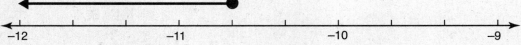

Values of x	$\frac{3}{4}x + 5 \le -\frac{3}{8}x - 7$	True/False and Explanation
-16	$\frac{3}{4}(-16) + 5 \le -\frac{3}{8}(-16) - 7$ $-12 + 5 \le 6 - 7$ $-7 \le -1$	**True.** -7 is less than -1 because -7 is further to the left on the number line than -1. -16 is part of the solution set that states that the values of x are all values less than or equal to $10\frac{2}{3}$.
$-\frac{32}{3}$	$\frac{3}{4}\left(-\frac{32}{3}\right) + 5 \le -\frac{3}{8}\left(-\frac{32}{3}\right) - 7$ $-8 + 5 \le 4 - 7$ $-3 \le -3$	**True.** -3 is less or equal to -3. The graph indicates this with a closed circle, which means $-\frac{32}{3}$ is part of the solution set. For this solution to be false, it would have to read: $-3 < -3$.
0	$\frac{3}{4}(0) + 5 \le -\frac{3}{8}(0) - 7$ $5 \le -7$	**False.** 5 is greater than -7 because 5 falls on the right-hand side of -7 on the number line, which means 5 is larger and -7 is smaller. Locate 0 on the number line and it will not be part of the solution set.

Example 9 $-0.2(-2x - 4) > -8$

METHOD 1   Distribute

$$-0.2(-2x - 4) > -8$$
$$-0.2(-2x) + (-0.2)(-4) > -8$$
$$0.4x + 0.8 > -8$$
$$0.4x + 0.8 - 0.8 > -8 - 0.8$$
$$0.4x > -8.8$$
$$\frac{0.4x}{0.4} > -\frac{8.8}{0.4}$$
$$x > -22$$

METHOD 2 Divide by −0.2 to both sides of the equality.

$$\frac{-0.2(-2x-4)}{-0.2} > \frac{-8}{-0.2}$$

$$-2x - 4 < 40$$

$$-2x - 4 + 4 < 40 + 4$$

$$-2x < 44$$

$$\frac{-2x}{-2} < \frac{44}{-2}$$

$$x > -22$$

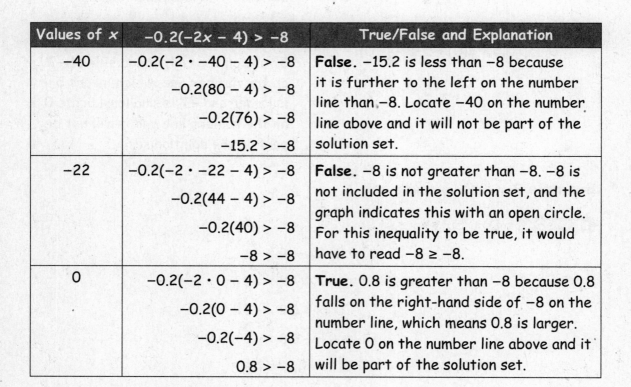

Values of x	$-0.2(-2x - 4) > -8$	True/False and Explanation
−40	$-0.2(-2 \cdot -40 - 4) > -8$ $-0.2(80 - 4) > -8$ $-0.2(76) > -8$ $-15.2 > -8$	**False.** −15.2 is less than −8 because it is further to the left on the number line than −8. Locate −40 on the number line above and it will not be part of the solution set.
−22	$-0.2(-2 \cdot -22 - 4) > -8$ $-0.2(44 - 4) > -8$ $-0.2(40) > -8$ $-8 > -8$	**False.** −8 is not greater than −8. −8 is not included in the solution set, and the graph indicates this with an open circle. For this inequality to be true, it would have to read −8 ≥ −8.
0	$-0.2(-2 \cdot 0 - 4) > -8$ $-0.2(0 - 4) > -8$ $-0.2(-4) > -8$ $0.8 > -8$	**True.** 0.8 is greater than −8 because 0.8 falls on the right-hand side of −8 on the number line, which means 0.8 is larger. Locate 0 on the number line above and it will be part of the solution set.

Example 10 $\frac{4}{5}(10x - 20) \leq -30$

METHOD 1 Distribute

$$\frac{4}{5}\left(\frac{10x}{1}\right) + \frac{4}{5}\left(-\frac{20}{1}\right) \leq -30$$

$$8x - 16 \leq -30$$

$$8x - 16 + 16 \leq -30 + 16$$

$$8x \leq -14$$

$$\frac{8x}{8} \leq -\frac{14}{8}$$

$$x \leq -\frac{7}{4}$$

METHOD 2 Multiply by the reciprocal of $\frac{4}{5}$.

$$\frac{5}{4}\left(\frac{4}{5}\right)(10x - 20) \leq -\frac{30}{1}\left(\frac{5}{4}\right)$$

$$10x - 20 \leq -\frac{75}{2}$$

$$10x - 20 + 20 \leq -\frac{75}{2} + 20$$

$$10x \leq -\frac{75}{2} + \frac{40}{2}$$

$$10x \leq -\frac{35}{2}$$

$$\left(\frac{10x}{1}\right)\left(\frac{1}{10}\right) \leq \left(-\frac{35}{2}\right)\left(\frac{1}{10}\right)$$

$$x \leq -\frac{7}{4}$$

METHOD 3 Multiply by the LCM of 5 and 1 to solve for the variable without performing fraction operations.

$$\frac{5}{1}\left(\frac{4}{5}\right)(10x - 20) \leq \left(-\frac{30}{1}\right)\left(\frac{5}{1}\right)$$

$4(10x - 20) \leq -150$. You can either divide by 4 on both sides or distribute on the left-hand side.

$$4(10x) + 4(-20) \leq -150$$

$$40x - 80 \leq -150$$

$$40x - 80 + 80 \leq -150 + 80$$

$$40x \leq -70$$

$$\frac{40x}{40} \leq -\frac{70}{40}$$

$$x \leq -\frac{7}{4}$$

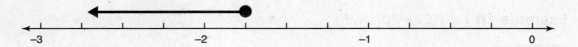

Values of x	$\frac{4}{5}(10x - 20) \leq -30$	True/False and Explanation
-2	$\frac{4}{5}(10 \cdot -2 - 20) \leq -30$ $\frac{4}{5}(-20 - 20) \leq -30$ $\frac{4}{5}(-40) \leq -30$ $-32 \leq -30$	**True.** -32 is less than -30 because -32 is further to the left on the number line than -30. -2 is part of the solution set that states that the values of x are all values less than or equal to $-\frac{7}{4}$.
$-\frac{7}{4}$	$\frac{4}{5}\left(10 \cdot -\frac{7}{4} - 20\right) \leq -30$ $\frac{4}{5}\left(-\frac{70}{4} - 20\right) \leq -30$ $\frac{4}{5}(-17.5 - 20) \leq -30$ $\frac{4}{5}(-37.5) \leq -30$ $-30 \leq -30$	**True.** -30 is less than or equal to -30. The graph indicates this with a closed circle, which means $-\frac{7}{4}$ is part of the solution set. For this solution to be false, it would have to read $-30 < -30$.
0	$\frac{4}{5}(10 \cdot 0 - 20) \leq -30$ $\frac{4}{5}(0 - 20) \leq -30$ $\frac{4}{5}(-20) \leq -30$ $-16 \leq -30$	**False.** -16 is greater than -30 because -16 falls on the right-hand side of -30 on the number line, which means -16 is larger and -30 is smaller. Locate 0 on the number line above and it will not be part of the solution set.

 **PRACTICE**

Directions: Solve each inequality and graph the solution on a number line.

1. $6 + 3x < 18$

2. $6 - 3x \geq 18$

3. $-6 + 3x \leq -18$

4. $-6 - 3x > -18$

5. $-\dfrac{1}{3}x < 2$

6. $-4x < -13$

7. $-4x - 1 \geq 12$

8. $-\dfrac{2}{3}x + \dfrac{5}{6} < \dfrac{11}{18}$

9. $-\dfrac{7}{8} + \dfrac{1}{4}x < -\dfrac{1}{2}$

10. $0.4 - 1.2x < -3.2$

11. $6x - 8 \geq -2x - 32$

12. $-3x - 11 \leq -16 - x$

13. $-\dfrac{2}{5}x + \dfrac{1}{3} \geq \dfrac{7}{5} - \dfrac{14}{15}x$

14. $\dfrac{11}{12}x - \dfrac{5}{6} \leq -\dfrac{2}{3}x + \dfrac{1}{2}$

15. $-0.7x - 3.9 > 1.8 - 0.5x$

16. $9.2 - x < -1.8 - 0.5x$

17. $-2\left(3x + \dfrac{1}{2}\right) \geq -0.2(-8 - 20x)$

(Answers are on pages 241–248.)

Lesson 3.4 Real-World Problems: Algebraic Inequalities

When solving word problems, translate the words into symbols and numbers.

<	>	≤	≥
Less than	Greater than	Less than or equal to	Greater than or equal to
Is fewer than	Larger than	At most	At least
Is below	More than	At the maximum	At the minimum
Is under	Above	Is no more than	No less than
Lower than	Higher than		
Beneath	Over		
	Exceeds		

Example 1 Write an inequality for each sentence. Then solve and graph the inequality.

The quotient of x and 3 is greater than the sum of negative x and 9.

$$\frac{x}{3} > -x + 9 \qquad \text{Multiply by the reciprocal of } \frac{1}{3}.$$

$$\left(\frac{3}{1}\right)\left(\frac{x}{3}\right) > 3(-x + 9) \qquad \text{Distribute 3.}$$

$$x > -3x + 27$$

$$x + 3x > -3x + 27 + 3x \qquad \text{Add +3x to both sides.}$$

$$4x > 27$$

$$\frac{4x}{4} > \frac{27}{4} \qquad \text{Divide by 4.}$$

$$x > 6.75$$

Check your answer by plugging solutions and nonsolutions into the original inequality.

Values of x	$\frac{x}{3} > -x + 9$	True/False and Explanation
9	$\frac{9}{3} > -9 + 9$ $3 > 0$	**True.** 3 is greater than 0 because 3 is further to the right on the number line than 0. 9 is part of the solution set that states that the values of x are all values greater than 6.75.
−9	$\frac{-9}{3} > -(-9) + 9$ $-3 > 9 + 9$ $-3 > 18$	**False.** −3 is less than 18 because it is farther to the left on the number line than 18. Locate −9 on the number line and it will not be part of the solution set.

Example 2 Michael's math test average needs to be at least 95 in order to get a new iPhone. If he scored a 92, 93, and 98 on the first three tests, what does he need to score on the fourth test in order to earn the iPhone?

Solution

Let x equal the score on the fourth test.

Write the inequality in words: Average ≥ 95.

Plug in the formula and plug in what you know from the problem:

$$\frac{\text{total}}{\text{number of tests}} \geq 95$$

$$\frac{92 + 93 + 98 + x}{4} \geq 95$$

$$\frac{4}{1}\left(\frac{92 + 93 + 98 + x}{4}\right) \geq (95)4$$

$$92$$

$$92 + 93 + 98 + x \geq 380$$

$$283 + x \geq 380$$

$$283 + x - 283 \geq 380 - 283$$

$$x \geq 97$$

Graph:

Articulate the solution in a sentence: Michael needs to score at least 97 to average 95 on all four math tests.

Example 3 Abby is saving up for a vacation that costs $600. She has already saved $20. If she earns $25 each week for mowing the lawn, how many more weeks will she need to wait to have enough saved up for her vacation?

Solution

Write the inequality in words: amount Abby needs to save ≥ 600.

Define your variable: Let n equal the number of lawns Abby has mowed.

To come up with the expression for the amount Abby needs to save, create a table and find a pattern.

# of Times Abby Has Mowed	Total Amount Abby Has Saved so Far
2	20 + 25(2) = 20 + 50 = 70
3	20 + 25(3) = 20 + 75 + 95
10	20 + 25(10) = 20 + 250 = 270
n	20 + 25n

Insert this expression into the original inequality and solve for n:

$$20 + 25n \geq 600$$

$$20 + 25n - 20 \geq 600 - 20$$

$$25n \geq 580$$

$$\frac{25n}{25} \geq \frac{580}{25}$$

$$n \geq 23.2$$

Interpret the solution and articulate it in a sentence. Do you round down or up? Plug the solution rounded up and down into the original inequality.

# of Times Abby Has Mowed	Saved ≥ 600 $20 + 25n \geq 600$	True or False?
23	$20 + 25(23) \geq 600$ $20 + 575 \geq 600$ $595 \geq 600$	**False**. If Abby mows 23 lawns, she will be $5 short of her goal.
24	$20 + 25(24) \geq 600$ $20 + 600 \geq 600$ $620 \geq 600$	**True**. If Abby mows 24 lawns, she will have enough for her goal.

Abby will need to mow at **least 24 more times** in order to have enough to go on vacation for $600.

Example 4   Leticia is at the local gym and needs to figure out which plan to sign up for. Her first option is to prepay $900 for three years of access and each subsequent month is $20. Her second option is to pay as she goes, and this will cost her $60 per month. After how many months will the first option be cheaper than the second one?

Solution

Let m equal the number of months she will be using the gym.

Write the inequality to represent the situation and solve:

$$\text{First option} < \text{second option}$$

$$900 + 20m < 60m$$

$$900 + 20m - 20m < 60m - 20m$$

$$900 < 40m$$

$$\frac{900}{40} < \frac{40m}{40}$$

$$22.5 < m$$

Interpret the solution in a sentence. Do you round up or down? Plug both solutions in the original inequalities.

# of Months	First Option < Second Option	True or False?
22	900 + 20(22) < 60(22) 900 + 440 < 1,320 1,340 < 1,320	False
23	900 + 20(23) < 60(23) 900 + 460 < 1,380 1,360 < 1,380	True

The first option will be less than the second option after **22 months**.

 PRACTICE

Directions: For each problem, write the inequality to represent the situation, graph, and explain the solution.

1. The sum of 8 and $2x$ is no less than 12.

2. The difference between $-4x$ and 12 is at most negative 25.

3. The product of -3 and $x + 2$ is more than its sum.

4. One-quarter of the sum of $8x$ and 12 is less than three-eighths.

5. 150% of the quotient of negative $24x$ and 4 is fewer than $2x$ less than 12.

6. Conor needs an average of at least 85 from his four English tests in order to keep his scholarship. He has already scored a 78, 92, and 83. What does he need to score on the fourth test?

7. Julia needs an average of no less than 90 from her five history quizzes in order to be exempt from the final exam. If she scored a 95, 82, 97, and 89 on the first four quizzes, what does she need to score on the fifth quiz?

8. Estella needs to maintain a 3.5 GPA from her five courses in order to apply for a fellowship she is interested in. What does she need from the fifth course if she scored the following from the first four courses: 2.9, 3.9, 3.4, and 3.6?

9. Maya is throwing her best friend a party and can spend up to $50. She has already spent $14 on balloons and $9 on the wall decorations. She is making her own centerpieces and has three to make. At most, how much can she spend on supplies for each centerpiece?

10. Uber charges a flat rate of $2.50 in addition to $1.15 per mile. How many miles did Orion travel if his bill came out to be more than $20?

11. Isabella is saving up to buy her mother a necklace for $225 including tax. She has already saved $75 and earns $15 for every time she walks her neighbors' dogs for one hour. How many times does she need to walk her neighbors' dogs to earn enough for her mother's necklace?

12. Kaitlyn has $125 in her piggy bank and needs $50 of it to purchase new clothes for school. She really wants to subscribe to Netflix, which costs $8 per month. How many months of Netflix can she afford?

13. Medina can stream up to 20 GB of data on her phone. If she goes over, she will be charged overage fees. She has already used 9.25 GB. If each movie uses 3.5 GB, how many movies can she watch without going over?

14. Katie signed up for the holiday fair and wants to sell boba drinks. She spent $85 on supplies and makes $2.75 on each drink she sells. At least how many drinks does she need to sell to start making a profit?

15. Karen is selling Girl Scout cookies and needs to sell at least 500 boxes in order to go on the national trip. She has already sold 345 boxes. With only two weeks left, at least how many boxes per day does she need to sell in order to meet her goal?

16. Jackie loves yoga and found a gym that offers unlimited yoga lessons for $185 per month. If she pays as she goes, each class costs $22 after an initial registration fee of $15. After how many classes does she need to take for the unlimited yoga plan to be more worthwhile?

17. Dennis leased an electric car and pays $190 per month for 12 months. It costs him $1 to charge the car for every 35 miles. He had the option of borrowing a friend's nonelectric car for $100 per month for 12 months. Gas would cost $2.59 for every 35 miles. After how many miles will the electric car be the cheaper option compared to the regular car?

18. Quinn received an $8,000 investment for her dog gift basket business. The investor wants $4.75 back for every basket she sells; this is known as a royalty. After how many dog gift baskets will she need to sell to not have to pay the investor anymore?

19. Bryan is at the arcade and can spend up to $25.00. He has already spent $2.75 on drinks and food. There are $1.25 and $1.50 arcade games. How many more $1.25 games can he play versus $1.50 games?

20. Jessica loves baking and decided to bake cupcakes for the holiday fair. She spent $46 total on supplies. If she sells the cupcakes for $2.50 each, she makes 75 cents back. If she sells the cupcakes for $3.00, she takes $1.25 back. How many less cupcakes will she need to sell if she prices them at $3.00 apiece?

(Answers are on page 249–261.)

Ratios and Proportional Relationships

The purpose of this standard is for students to analyze proportional relationships and use them to solve real-world and mathematical problems.

Standards

7.RP.A.1 Compute unit rates associated with ratios of fractions, including ratios of lengths, areas, and other quantities measured in like or different units.

7.RP.A.2 Recognize and represent proportional relationships between quantities.

7.RP.A.3 Use proportional relationships to solve multistep ratio and percent problems. Examples: simple interest, tax, markups and markdowns, gratuities and commissions, fees, percent increase and decrease, and percent error.

Sample Questions from the SBAC

The following are examples of question types that you will see on the SBAC Grade 7 Math test. We will cover them in this chapter.

This table shows a proportional relationship between the grams of peanuts and raisins in a bag of trail mix.

Grams of Peanuts	Grams of Raisins
14	4
21	6
35	10

Enter the number of grams of peanuts in a bag for every 1 gram of raisins.

←	→	↶	↷	⌫

1	2	3
4	5	6
7	8	9
0	.	-

Sara buys a sweater at a department store. The sweater costs $30. The store is having a 25% off sale on everything in the store.

Enter the amount of money, in dollars, Sara saves from the sale. Do not consider the sales tax.

1	2	3
4	5	6
7	8	9
0	.	-

An electrician is hired to install outdoor lighting. The electrician claims that the relationship between the number of hours worked and the total work fee is proportional. The fee for 5 hours of work is $225.

Select **all** combinations of values for the electrician's work hours and total work fee that support the claim that the relationship between the two values is proportional.

☐ 6 hours and $270

☐ 6.5 hours and $315

☐ 8 hours and $360

☐ 8.75 hours and $380

☐ 9.5 hours and $427.50

This graph shows a proportional relationship between the number of hours a factory is in operation and the number of gallons of water used.

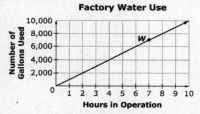

Factory Water Use

Select True or False for each statement about the graph.

	True	False
The factory uses 4 gallons of water when it is in operation for 4000 hours.	☐	☐
Point *W* represents the number of gallons of water used when the factory is in operation for 7 hours.	☐	☐
The factory uses 9000 gallons of water when it is in operation for 9 hours.	☐	☐

Alfonso went to Famous Sam's Appliance Store and purchased a refrigerator and a stove. The sale price of the refrigerator was 40% off the original price and the sale price of the stove was 20% off the original price.

Which statement must be true to conclude that Alfonso received a 30% overall discount on the refrigerator and the stove together?

Ⓐ The sale prices of the refrigerator and the stove were the same.

Ⓑ The original prices of the refrigerator and the stove were the same.

Ⓒ The sale price of the refrigerator was twice the sale price of the stove.

Ⓓ The original price of the refrigerator was twice the original price of the stove.

Select **all** tables that represent a proportional relationship between x and y.

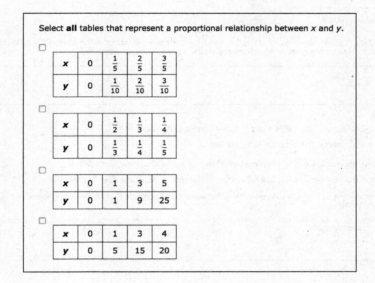

☐

x	0	$\frac{1}{5}$	$\frac{2}{5}$	$\frac{3}{5}$
y	0	$\frac{1}{10}$	$\frac{2}{10}$	$\frac{3}{10}$

☐

x	0	$\frac{1}{2}$	$\frac{1}{3}$	$\frac{1}{4}$
y	0	$\frac{1}{3}$	$\frac{1}{4}$	$\frac{1}{5}$

☐

x	0	1	3	5
y	0	1	9	25

☐

x	0	1	3	4
y	0	5	15	20

Lenny bought a motorcycle. He paid 12.5% in tax. The tax added $1437.50 to the price of the motorcycle.

What was the price of the motorcycle, not including the tax?

1	2	3
4	5	6
7	8	9
0	.	-

This graph shows a proportional relationship between the number of gallons of gasoline used (g) and the total cost of gasoline (c).

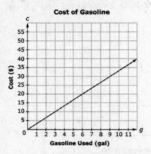

Find the constant of proportionality (r). Using the value for r, enter an equation in the form of $c = rg$ that represents the relationship between the number of gallons of gasoline used (g) and the total cost (c).

When playing basketball, Jan makes 4 out of every 10 shots she takes.

Select **all** the statements that describe Jan's situation.

☐ The ratio of the number of shots Jan makes to the number of shots she takes is 2:5.

☐ The ratio of the number of shots Jan makes to the number of shots she does not make is 2:3.

☐ The equation $4x = 10y$ shows the relationship between x, the number of shots Jan makes, and y, the number of shots she takes.

☐ The equation $6x = 4z$ shows the relationship between x, the number of shots Jan makes, and z, the number of shots she does not make.

Mary and Jerry are exercising on a track.

- Mary is walking at a rate of 3 miles per hour.
- Jerry starts jogging at a rate of 4 miles per hour after Mary has been walking for 15 minutes.
- Jerry jogs 2 miles as Mary continues walking, and they both stop at the same time.

Enter the **total** distance, in miles, that Mary walks around the track.

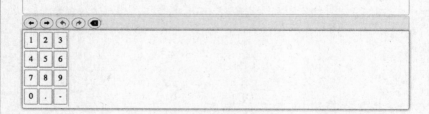

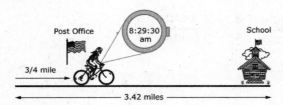

Emily leaves her house at exactly 8:25 a.m. to bike to her school, which is 3.42 miles away. When she passes the post office, which is $\frac{3}{4}$ mile away from her home, she looks at her watch and sees that it is 30 seconds past 8:29 a.m.

Post Office 8:29:30 am School

3/4 mile

3.42 miles

If Emily's school starts at 8:50 a.m., can Emily make it to school on time without increasing her rate of speed? Show and/or explain the work necessary to support your answer.

Lesson 4.1 Unit Rates

A **unit rate** compares the amount to its unit of measure. It can be written as a fraction or ratio where the denominator is one. These relationships are often described using words such as *per* or *for each*.

$$\frac{\$7.25}{\text{hour}} = \text{Minimum wage in the U.S. is \$7.25 per hour.}$$

Employees that make minimum wage make $7.25 for each hour.

A **complex fraction** is a fraction where the numerator, denominator, or both contain a fraction. Unit rates can also be expressed as a complex fraction where the numerator is a fraction and the denominator is one.

$$\frac{\frac{1}{3}\,\text{feet}}{\text{hour}} = \text{The snail traveled one-third mile per hour.}$$

Example 1   Dennis is running late for a meeting but needs to fill his water bottle. It takes him $\frac{1}{5}$ of a minute to fill $\frac{1}{4}$ of the water bottle. How much time will it take him to fill the whole thing?

Solution

METHOD 1   Equivalent fractions

Set up the proportion using information the problem gives you. Make sure the units in the numerator and the denominator match.

$$\frac{\frac{1}{5}\,\text{minute}}{\frac{1}{4}\,\text{bottle}} = \frac{?}{1\,\text{bottle}}$$

Multiplying by 1 does not change the value of the fractions. $\frac{1}{4}$ fits into one whole four times. Thus, you multiply by $\frac{4}{4}$.

$$\frac{\frac{1}{5} \text{ minute}}{\frac{1}{4} \text{ bottle}} \cdot \frac{4}{4} = \frac{\frac{4}{5} \text{ bottle}}{1 \text{ bottle}}$$

METHOD 2   Cross-multiply

Set up the proportion using information the problem gives you. Make sure the units in the numerator and the denominator match.

$$\frac{\frac{1}{5} \text{ minute}}{\frac{1}{4} \text{ bottle}} = \frac{x}{1 \text{ bottle}}$$

Cross-multiplying means setting the product of the numerator of the left and the denominator of the right equal to the product of the denominator of the left and numerator of the right.

$$\left(\frac{1}{5}\right)(1) = \frac{1}{4}x$$

$$\frac{1}{5} = \frac{1}{4}x$$

Multiply by the reciprocal of $\frac{1}{4}$

$$\left(\frac{4}{1}\right)\left(\frac{1}{5}\right) = \left(\frac{1}{4}x\right)\left(\frac{4}{1}\right)$$

$$\frac{4}{5} = x$$

METHOD 3   Tape diagram

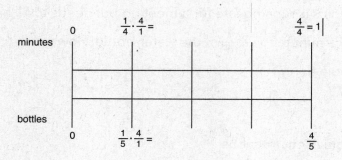

Explain your solution using a sentence: It takes Dennis $\frac{4}{5}$ minute to fill up one water bottle.

Example 2 Comparing unit rates, better deal?

Mrs. Jones is buying dog food for her dog Reggie. She can buy a 22-pound bag for $51.99, a 10-pound bag for $31.99, or a 4-pound bag for $18.67. She prefers a 4-pound because it would take up less room in her small apartment. What should she buy and why?

Solution

Find the unit rate for each option and compare them.

$$\frac{\$51.99}{22 \text{ pounds}} = \frac{x}{1 \text{ pound}}; x \approx \$2.36/\text{pound}$$

$$\frac{\$31.99}{10 \text{ pounds}} = \frac{x}{1 \text{ pound}}; x \approx \$3.19/\text{pound}$$

$$\frac{\$18.67}{4 \text{ pounds}} = \frac{x}{1 \text{ pound}}; x \approx \$4.67/\text{pound}$$

She should buy the 22-pound bag and make room in her apartment because she will save $2.31 per pound with this option. She is basically getting 11 pounds of the 22 pounds for free if she chooses this option.

Example 3 The local trampoline park charges each person $14 for the first hour and then $5.50 for each additional hour. How much did Annalise and Kevin spend if they played from 10:30 A.M. to 1:30 P.M.?

Solution

Create a table to organize the information.

Total number of hours from 10:30 to 1:30 is 3 hours.

Cost per Person	Hours	Costs
$14 for the first hour	1 hour	$14
$5.50 for each additional hour	2 hours	2(5.50) = 11
Total	3 hours	14 + 11 = 25

It costs Kevin $25 to play from 10:30 to 1:30 P.M. Therefore, it costs Annalise and Kevin $50 total.

Example 4   Hank and Henry are driving from Mountain View to Lake Tahoe. They started off driving 67 miles per hour for 1.5 hours and hit some traffic. Now they are driving at 42 miles per hour. The total distance from Mountain View to Lake Tahoe is 237 miles. How long will it take for them to complete their journey?

Solution

Distance before traffic:

$$\frac{67 \text{ miles}}{1 \text{ hour}} = \frac{x}{1.5 \text{ hour}}; x = 100.5 \text{ miles}$$

Distance left to drive: Total − distance already traveled = 237 − 100.5 = 136.5 miles

Time left on their trip. Cross-cancel to solve for x:

$$\frac{42 \text{ miles}}{1 \text{ hour}} = \frac{136.5 \text{ miles}}{x}$$

$$42x = 1(136.5)$$

$$\frac{42x}{42} = \frac{136.5}{42}$$

$$x = 3.25$$

Explain your solution using a sentence. At a rate of 42 miles per hour, it will take Hank and Henry 3.25 hours to drive 136.5 miles.

 PRACTICE

Directions: Solve the following problems using unit rates.

1.   Jane is baking dog treats and uses $\frac{1}{8}$ cup of peanut butter to make $\frac{1}{16}$ of a muffin pan. How many cups of peanut butter are needed to make a full muffin pan of dog treats?

2.   Cindy is trying to use $\frac{1}{4}$ stick of unsalted butter to make $\frac{1}{8}$ of a pecan pie. How much unsalted butter does she need to make the whole pie?

3. Mr. Sproule can paint $\frac{3}{10}$ of the baby's room using $\frac{3}{7}$ gallon of paint. How many gallons of paint will he need to paint the entire room?

4. Shelly would like a massage and is looking at two companies. Massage place A charges $55 for $\frac{1}{2}$ of an hour. Massage place B charges $80 for $\frac{3}{4}$ of an hour. Which is a better deal and by how much? What other factors should she consider other than the price?

5. Peter and Irene are trying to blow up their inflatable mattresses for camping. Peter can blow up $\frac{3}{10}$ of the mattress after 2 minutes. Irene can blow up $\frac{2}{9}$ of the mattress after 2.5 minutes. Who can blow up their mattress the fastest?

6. Company A charges $19.47 for 36 rolls of toilet paper. Company B charges $27.40 for 48 rolls of toilet paper. Which is a better deal? How much do you save? What are some reasons you would pay for the more expensive brand?

7. The local grocery is selling one banana for 50 cents, a dozen for $4, or two dozen for $7. You only need four bananas. Which is the better deal? Would you buy more bananas for less even though you do not need them all? If so, what would you do with the extra?

8. The local grocery store sells one dozen bags of chips for $4. The local convenience store sells two bags of chips for $1. Which is a better deal? Why do you think one establishment or the other charges more?

9. Use the fractions $\frac{2}{3}$ and $\frac{4}{5}$ to create a word problem involving unit rates.

10. Use the fractions $\frac{3}{7}$ and $\frac{2}{9}$ to create a word problem involving unit rates.

11. The distance from Dallas, Texas to Denver, Colorado is approximately 795 miles. Cary drives 68 miles an hour for 1.5 hours. He drives another 74 miles per hour for 4.5 hours. What is his average speed? At this rate, how much longer will it take him to get to Denver?

12. The sidewalk outside Kevin's house is 36 inches wide. The average garden snail can crawl at a rate of 0.55 inches per minute. If Kevin wants to watch the garden snail crawl across the sidewalk, assuming the snail crawls in a straight line and does not stop, how long will Kevin be watching the snail for?

13. The distance from Francesco's home to his office is 5.4 miles. He bikes 14 mph for 6 minutes and 18 mph for 4 minutes. What is his average speed thus far? How many miles does he have left to bike? If he bikes at 16 mph for the rest of his commute, how much longer will it take him to get to work?

14. Toby, a French Bulldog, spotted a squirrel and started chasing it. The squirrel was just 30 feet ahead and started running at a rate of 19 miles per hour. Toby ran at a rate of 20 miles per hour. Did Toby catch up to the squirrel? If so, how long did it take him to catch up?

15. The longest commercial flight in the world is from Singapore to Newark, New Jersey. What is the average speed if the distance is approximately 9,500 miles and the flight is about 19 hours long?

16. A parking lot in San Francisco charges $25 for the first two hours and $6.50 for each additional hour. How much would Mac pay if he parked from 9 A.M. until 4 P.M.?

17. An hourly car rental service charges $35 per year for membership and $9 per hour for renting a four-door sedan. If Patrick's bill for the year was $349, how many total hours did he use the car rental service for the year?

18. The initial charge for a taxi in New York is $2.50 for the first 0.2 mile. If each additional 0.2 mile costs $1.85, how much would it cost to travel 0.9 miles?

19. In San Francisco, taxis cost $3.50 for the first 0.2 miles and 0.55 for each additional 0.2 mile. The distance from the Palace of Fine Arts to Union Square is 3.3 miles. How much would it cost to travel in a taxi?

20. A local frozen yogurt shop charges $2.99 for the frozen yogurt and $0.29 for each additional topping. If Jane wants to take her daughter Annalise and a handful of her daughter's friends for an afternoon treat and can only spend up to $20, how many different combinations of friends can Annalise invite assuming they all get the same number of toppings?

(Answers are on pages 261–269.)

Lesson 4.2 Constant of Proportionality

A **proportional relationship** between two quantities is one in which the rate of change is constant or one in which the ratio of one quantity to the other is constant.

A **rate of change** is a rate that describes how one quantity changes in relation to another quantity.

The constant ratio between two quantities is called the **constant of proportionality**. If x is directly proportional to y, then $k = \dfrac{y}{x}$ or $y = kx$. The graph will always start at the origin or (0, 0) and is always a straight line.

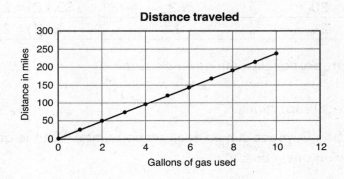

If x is inversely proportional to y, then $xy = k$ or $y = \dfrac{k}{x}$.

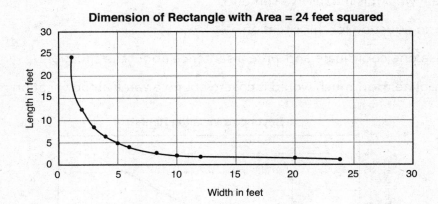

Width	Length	$xy = k$
1	24	1(24) = 24
2	12	2(12) = 24
3	8	3(8) = 24
4	6	4(6) = 24
5	4.8	5(4.8) = 24
6	4	6(4) = 24
8	3	8(3) = 24
10	2.4	10(2.4) = 24
12	2	12(2) = 24
20	1.2	20(1.2) = 24
24	1	24(1) = 24

The constant of proportionality can never be zero.

Example 1   Direct Proportion

For Superbowl 2016, Beyonce stayed at a vacation rental. Use the graph below to answer the following questions:

A. Does this situation represent a direct proportion? If so, what is the constant of proportionality?

B. Explain what this means in a sentence.

C. Write an equation for this situation.

D. Choose one coordinate and write a sentence about the situation.

E. Extrapolate: How much would it cost to spend a week at the vacation rental?

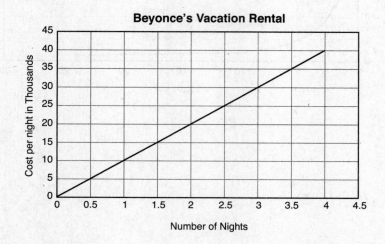

Beyonce's Vacation Rental
Cost per night in Thousands
Number of Nights

Solution

A. Does this graph start at the origin or (0, 0)?   **Yes.**

Is it a straight line?   **Yes.**

Is the quotient of y and x always the same number?   **Yes.**

Coordinates (x, y)	$\frac{y}{x} = k$
(1.5, 15)	$\frac{15}{1.5} = 10$
(2.5, 25)	$\frac{25}{2.5} = 10$
(3, 30)	$\frac{30}{3} = 10$
(4, 40)	$\frac{40}{4} = 10$

If you can say *yes* to the three questions above, this is a direct proportion. If you get at least one *no* to the answers, then it is not a direct proportion.

Another way to create the table is displayed below.

To find the constant of proportionality, create a table with coordinates from the graph and find what number you need to multiply the x by to get your y.

x: # of Nights	Calculations for the Constant	y: Cost (in Thousand Dollars)
1	$1 \cdot 10 = 10$	10
2	$2 \cdot 10 = 20$	20
3	$3 \cdot 10 = 30$	30
4	$4 \cdot 10 = 40$	40
5	$5 \cdot 10 = 50$	50
x	$x \cdot 10 = 10x$	$10x$

Unit rate = constant = $k = 10$

B. The cost of the vacation rental is $10,000 per night

C. $y = 10x$

Total cost = 10(number of nights)

D. The total cost for five nights of stay is $50,000.

E. $y = 10x = 10(7) = 70$

Total cost for seven nights is $70,000.

Example 2   Inverse Proportion

This concept is not part of the standards but is explained to show the contrast between direct and inverse proportions.

For Super Bowl 2016, Beyonce stayed at a vacation rental. Use the graph to answer the following questions:

A. What is the constant of proportionality (k)?

B. Explain what this means in a sentence.

C. Write an equation for this situation.

D. Choose one coordinate and write a sentence about the situation.

E. How much would it cost if 20 people split the costs for one night?

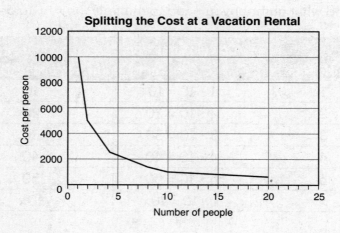

Solution

A. To find the constant of proportionality for the inverse proportion, create a table with the coordinates and find the relationship between the independent and dependent variables. Constant = k = 10,000

Number of People	Cost per Person	Calculations for the Constant
1	10,000	$1 \cdot 10{,}000 = 10{,}000$
2	5,000	$2 \cdot 5{,}000 = 10{,}000$
4	2,500	$4 \cdot 2{,}500 = 10{,}000$
8	1,250	$8 \cdot 1{,}250 = 10{,}000$
10	1,000	$10 \cdot 1{,}000 = 10{,}000$
20	500	$20 \cdot 500 = 10{,}000$
x	y	$xy = 10{,}000$

B. The vacation rental costs $10,000 per night. The cost per person is inversely proportionate to the number of people splitting the costs for the vacation rental.

C.
$$xy = 10{,}000$$
$$(\text{Number of people})(\text{Costs per person}) = 10{,}000$$

D. Coordinates (10, 1,000)

If ten people stay at the vacation rental, they each pay $1,000. Collectively, their cost per night at the vacation rental is $10,000 per night.

E.
$$xy = 10{,}000$$
$$20y = 10{,}000$$
$$y = 500$$

If 20 people stay at the vacation rental, each person pays $500 per night for his or her stay. Collectively, they will pay $10,000 per night to stay at the vacation rental.

 **PRACTICE**

Directions: For problems 1–5, determine if it is a directly proportional relationship. If it is, do the following:

A. Find the constant of proportionality and explain what the constant means.

B. Create an equation for the situation.

C. Find a coordinate not on the table and explain what it means.

1. The data below represents the amount of money charged for the purchase of each DVD.

x = # of DVDs	2	3	4	7
y = Total cost	38	57	76	133

2. The data below represents the amount of money charged per person by a bike rental shop.

x = Hours	2	3	4
y = Cost (Dollars)	20	27.50	35

3. The data below represents the cost of dog daycare for each day.

x = Number of days	1	5	7	10
y = Total cost	29	145	175	250

4. The data below represents circumferences and diameters of various circles.

x = Diameter (cm)	10	2	7	13
y = Circumference (cm)	31.416	6.283	21.991	40.841

5. The data below represents the distance an electric car can travel in the time it takes to charge the car.

x = Number of charges	2	4	5	7
y = Distance (miles)	250	500	625	875

Directions: For numbers 6–10, find the constant of proportionality of each situation and explain what it means. Create an equation and graph to represent each situation.

6. It took Arya 8.5 minutes to clean two white boards and 17 minutes to clean the next four.

7. At a competitive eating contest, one of the competitors ate 50 hot dogs in 12 minutes.

8. A cheetah escaped from the zoo and ran 122 miles in 2 hours.

9. Jeff is a personal trainer and earned $810 in one week after working with 18 clients.

10. Jane's favorite snack are mochi balls that are filled with fruit and cake. She purchased five of them for $22.50.

Directions: For numbers 11–15, find the constant of proportionality of each situation if it represents a direct proportion. Explain what the constant means. Then create an equation to represent the graph and answer the additional questions for each.

11. How many inches are in 30 centimeters?

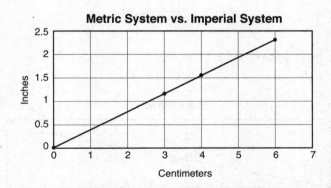

Metric System vs. Imperial System

Centimeter	Inches
0	0
3	1.1811
4	1.5748
6	2.3622

12. The average dinner per person in London is approximately 30 British pounds. How much is this in U.S. dollars?

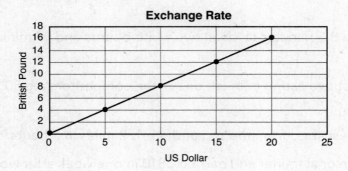

13. What does the coordinate (4, 1,000) mean?

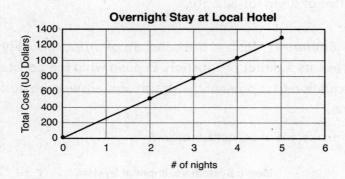

14. Why would the graph start at (0, 50)?

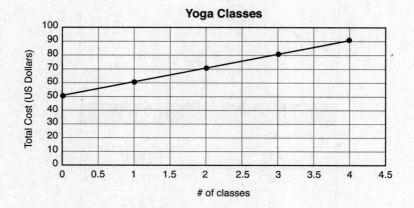

15. What does the coordinate (5, 2,875) mean? How far did the commercial aircraft travel in 12 hours? How long will it take to travel 71,875 miles?

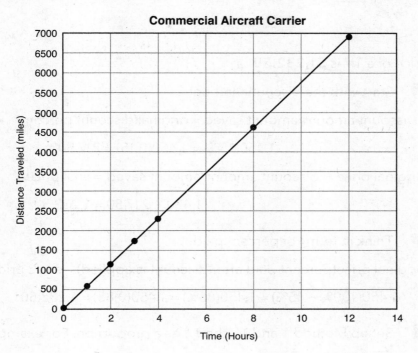

Commercial Aircraft Carrier

(Answers are on pages 269–273.)

Lesson 4.3 Percent Decrease: Discounts and Markdowns

Percent decrease is a measure of percent of change, which is the extent to which something loses value.

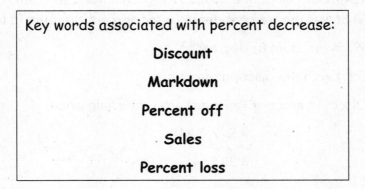

Key words associated with percent decrease:

Discount

Markdown

Percent off

Sales

Percent loss

Example 1 It is Labor Day weekend! TVs that normally cost $1,450 are 15% off. How much does a TV cost after the discount is applied?

Solution

The final price of a TV is **$1,232.50**.

METHOD 1 Start with the discount amount

Discount amount/amount saved = original(discount percent)

$$1,450(15\%) = 1,450(0.15) = 217.50$$

Original price − discount amount/amount saved = final price

$$1,450 - 217.50 = 1,232.50$$

METHOD 2 Think in terms of percent paid

Original price(percent paid after discount is applied) = sales price

$$1,450(100\% - 15\%) = 1,450(85\%) = 1,450(0.85) = 1,232.50$$

METHOD 3 Set up Method 1 and Method 2 as a proportion. For example,

$$\frac{\text{paid}}{\text{original}} = \frac{85\%}{100\%} = \frac{\text{amount paid}}{1,450}$$

$$(85\%)(1,450) = (100\%)(\text{amount paid})$$

$$(0.85)(1,450) = (1)(\text{amount paid})$$

$$1,232.50 = \text{amount paid}$$

Example 2 A popular cell phone cost $599 when it first came out. One year later, it costs $245. What was the percent decrease or percent discount in the price?

The answer is 59.1% discount or decrease.

METHOD 1 Start with the discount amount

STEP 1 Discount amount = original amount − sale price

$$= 599 - 245$$

$$= 354$$

STEP 2   Discount amount = original amount (discount percent in decimal form)

354 = 599 (discount percent in decimal form)
set up equation

$\dfrac{354}{599}$ = discount percent in decimal form
then divide both sides by 599.

0.591 = discount percent in decimal form/divide

59.1% = discount percent/convert to percents

METHOD 2   Think in terms of a fraction: part/whole

Start with the discount amount: 354

Think in terms of

$$\dfrac{\text{part}}{\text{whole}} = \dfrac{\text{decrease}}{\text{original}} = \dfrac{354}{599} = 0.591 = 59.1\%$$

METHOD 3   Proportion

$$\dfrac{\text{decrease}}{\text{original}} = \dfrac{599 - 245}{599} = \dfrac{354}{599} = \dfrac{x}{100\%}$$

Cross-multiply to solve for x: (100%)(354) = (599)(decrease percent)

Example 3   Grant purchased a football for $47.50 after a 15% discount. What was the original price and how much did Grant save?

The original price was **$55.88**. Grant saved **$8.38**.

METHOD 1   Equation

Original cost(percent paid) = sale price

Original cost(100% − 15%) = 47.50

$$\text{Original cost} = \dfrac{47.50}{100\% - 15\%} = \dfrac{47.5}{85\%} = \dfrac{47.5}{0.85} = 55.88$$

Amount saved = 55.88 − 47.50 = 8.38

METHOD 2   Proportion

$$\dfrac{\text{paid}}{\text{original}} = \dfrac{47.50}{\text{original}} = \dfrac{100\% - 15\%}{100\%}$$

(47.5)(100%) = (85%)(original cost)

(47.5)(1) = (0.85)(original cost)

$$\dfrac{47.5}{0.85} = 55.88 = \text{original cost}$$

 **PRACTICE**

Directions: Solve the following by using percent decrease and discounts.

1. 58 is what percent less than 60?

2. What is the percent decrease from 25 minutes to 10 minutes?

3. Find the cost of a $148 tablet after a 15% discount.

4. The sale price of a video game was $45 after a 10% discount. What was the original price?

5. The sale price of basketball shoes was $120 after a 30% discount. What was the original price of the shoes?

6. Eric buys a video game for $56. He went back to the store two weeks after and noticed it was marked down 25%. How much money would he have saved if he waited to purchase the video game? Should the store give Eric the difference? Explain why or why not.

7. After the year 2000, six northern white rhinos were left in the world. There are now two northern white rhinos. What is the population decrease of these rhinos from 2000 until 2016?

8. According to the Environmental Protection Agency, the average air quality index (AQI) in New York in September was 51. In August, the average AQI was 54. Was the change an increase or decrease? What was the percent of change?

9. A clothing company is having a Labor Day Weekend sale. Which is a better deal? 10% off of $50, 15% off of $75, or 20% off of $100?

10. The average gas price in northern California in 2015 was $3.80. In 2016, the average gas price was $2.45. What was the percent decrease in gas prices? What do you think contributed to the decrease?

11. A portable music device used to cost about $250. Now they are worth about $30. What is the percent decrease? Why do you think they are worth less now?

12. Megan purchased a winter jacket for $278. The following month, it was on sale at 10% off. The month after that, it was further discounted at 15% off. How much could she have saved if she waited?

13. For problem 12, why is taking 25% off of $278 incorrect?

14. Complete the following table and explain the patterns and relationships between each column.

#	Item	Original Price	Sale Price	Amount Saved	Percent Saved	Percent Paid	Percent of the Original
1	Jeans	$98			20%		100%
2	Tickets for a concert		$135			90%	
3	Cell phone	$650	$487.50				
4	Pet food		$32.50			65%	
5	Laptop			$210	15%		

(Answers are on pages 273–278.)

Lesson 4.4 Percent Increase: Tax, Markups, Gratuity, Commissions, and Simple Interest

Percent increase is a measure of percent change, which is the extent to which something gains value.

Key words associated with percent increase:

Tax

Markup

Gratuity/tip

Commission

Simple interest

Royalty fee/royalty percent

Interest

Example 1   Simone orders take-out for $45.00. What is the final price after an 8.5% tax?

The answer is **$48.83**.

METHOD 1   Find the tax amount first.

STEP 1   Tax amount = original amount(tax percent)

$$= (45)(8.5\%)$$

$$= (45)(0.085) = 3.825$$

STEP 2   Total including tax = total without tax + tax amount

$$= 45 + 3.825$$

$$= 48.825$$

METHOD 2   Think about what percent Simone paid of the original.

To think about the one-step method, work backward from the two-step method:

$$45 + 3.825 = 48.825$$

$$45(100\%) + 45(8.5\%) = 48.825$$

$$45(100\% + 8.5\%) = 48.825$$

$$45(108.5\%) = 48.825$$

$$45(1.085) = 48.825$$

Example 2   It costs a publisher $9 to print a book. If they sell it for $19.95, what is the percent markup?

The answer is a **121% markup**.

METHOD 1   Multi-step

STEP 1   Markup amount = 19.95 − 9 = 10.95

STEP 2   Markup percent = $\dfrac{\text{markup}}{\text{original}} = \dfrac{10.95}{9} = \dfrac{\text{markup}}{100\%}$

$$10.95(100\%) = 9 \text{ (markup percent in decimal form)}$$

$$\frac{10.95(1)}{9} = 1.21 = \text{markup percent in decimal form}$$

$$121\% = \text{markup percent}$$

METHOD 2   One-step

Wholesale cost(1 + markup percent in decimal form) = retail price

9(1 + markup percent in decimal form) = 19.95

$$1 + \text{markup percent in decimal form} = \frac{19.95}{9} = 2.21$$

markup percent in decimal form = 2.21 − 1 = 1.21

markup percent = 121%

Example 3   A bank is offering 1.75% simple interest on a savings account. If you deposit $500, how much interest will you earn in two years?

The answer is **$17.50** in interest.

Simple interest = PRT

Simple interest = (500)(1.75%)(2) = 17.50

Simple interest = the interest money created in dollars

P = the principal starting amount of money

R = the interest rate per year

T = the time the money is invested, borrowed, in years

 PRACTICE

Directions: Solve the following by using percent increase, tax, markups, gratuity, commissions, and interest.

1. What is the percent increase from 12 to 24?

2. What is the percent increase from 12 to 12?

3. What is the percent increase from 12 to 16?

4. What is the final price of a $98 pair of shoes after an 8.5% tax?

5. What was the original price on a pair of pants that costs $78 after a 160% markup?

6. Kelly deposits $50 into a savings account. How much will she earn in interest after one year if the simple interest rate is 2.25%?

7. What is the final bill of a $78 dinner after a 20% tip?

8. If the total cost of groceries is $214 including an 8.5% tax, what was the cost before tax?

9. An entrepreneur needs to pay 3% royalties for every blanket sold. If each blanket sells for $20 and his cost to make the blanket is $3.75, how much does he make on the sale after he pays royalties?

10. Jim is asked to sell the new type of cell phone for $600 each. For each insurance policy he sells with the phone, he receives a 10% commission. How much commission will he receive if he sells 12 phones in one day?

11. A popular German board game cost $34 last year and now it costs $56. What is the percent increase?

12. If the total for dinner costs $245 after an 8.5% tax and 15% tip were included, what was the original price of the bill?

13. What is the total dinner bill that costs $29 after a 7.5% tax and 20% tip? Will you get the same answer if you apply the tip and then the tax or the tax first and then the tip?

14. Kelly deposits $50 into a savings account. If the simple interest rate is 2.25%, how long will she need to keep her savings in there if she wants to earn $60 in simple interest?

15. Last year's popular cell phone is now selling for $375 with an additional 15% off. What is the final price after the discount and an 8.5% tax is applied?

16. Complete the following table and explain the patterns and relationships between each column.

#	Item	Original Number	Amount Increase	Total After Increase	Percent of Original	Percent Increase	Percent of Total After Increase
1	60 minute massage	$125			100%	20% tip	120%
2	Total bill from dinner	$80	$6.80				
3	Wholesale price of a basketball		$14			70% markup	
4	Score on a math test			88			110%
5	Weight of cereal in a box		4	22.5 oz		25%	

(Answers are on pages 279–284.)

Geometry

Geometry is the branch of mathematics that is concerned with the properties and relations of points, lines, surfaces, and solids. In other words, it is really all about shapes and their properties. In the common core seventh grade math curriculum, you will dig deeper into properties of angles and the properties of three-dimensional solids.

Standards

7.G.A.1 Solve problems involving scale drawings of geometric figures, including computing actual lengths and areas from a scale drawing and reproducing a scale drawing at a different scale.

7.G.A.2 Draw (freehand, with ruler and protractor, and with technology) geometric shapes with given conditions. Focus on constructing triangles from three measures of angles or sides, noticing when the conditions determine a unique triangle, more than one triangle, or no triangle.

7.G.A.3 Describe the two-dimensional figures that result from slicing three-dimensional figures, as in plane sections of right rectangular prisms and right rectangular pyramids.

Solve real-life and mathematical problems involving angle measure, area, surface area, and volume.

7.G.B.4 Know the formulas for the area and circumference of a circle and use them to solve problems; give an informal derivation of the relationship between the circumference and area of a circle.

7.G.B.5 Use facts about supplementary, complementary, vertical, and adjacent angles in a multistep problem to write and solve simple equations for an unknown angle in a figure.

7.G.B.6 Solve real-world and mathematical problems involving area, volume, and surface area of two- and three-dimensional objects composed of triangles, quadrilaterals, polygons, cubes, and right prisms.

Sample Questions From the SBAC

The following are examples of the question types that you will see on the SBAC Grade 7 Math test. We will cover them in this chapter.

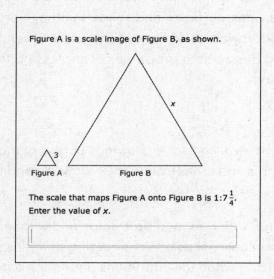

Figure A is a scale image of Figure B, as shown.

Figure A   Figure B

The scale that maps Figure A onto Figure B is $1:7\frac{1}{4}$.
Enter the value of *x*.

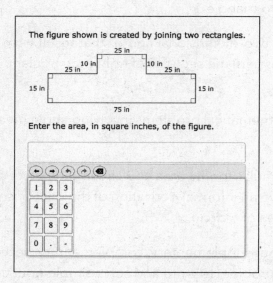

The figure shown is created by joining two rectangles.

Enter the area, in square inches, of the figure.

The circumference of a circle is approximately 37.7 centimeters.

Enter the radius of the circle, in centimeters. Round your answer to the nearest whole number.

←	→	↰	↱	⌫

1	2	3
4	5	6
7	8	9
0	.	-

A company makes two sizes of boxes shaped like rectangular prisms. The large box is 16 inches tall, 10 inches wide, and 10 inches long. The drawing shows the dimensions of the small box.

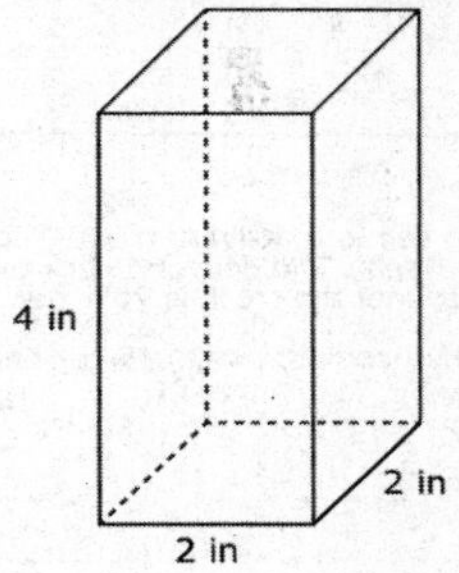

4 in

2 in

2 in

Part A
What is the maximum number of small boxes that can fit inside the large box?

Part B
The company plans to increase the width and length of the large box by 4 inches each to create a new larger box. How many more of the small boxes will be able to fit inside this new larger box compared to the original large box?

Part A _____

Part B _____

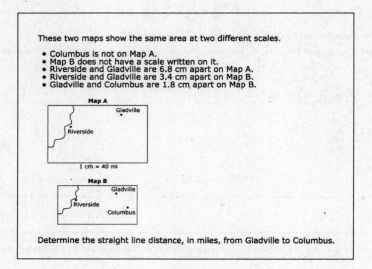

These two maps show the same area at two different scales.

- Columbus is not on Map A.
- Map B does not have a scale written on it.
- Riverside and Gladville are 6.8 cm apart on Map A.
- Riverside and Gladville are 3.4 cm apart on Map B.
- Gladville and Columbus are 1.8 cm apart on Map B.

Map A

Gladville

Riverside

1 cm = 40 mi

Map B

Gladville

Riverside

Columbus

Determine the straight line distance, in miles, from Gladville to Columbus.

Johnny uses a wheelbarrow to move planting soil to a delivery truck. The volume of planting soil that fits in the wheelbarrow measures 2 feet by 3 feet by 1.5 feet. The delivery truck measures 11 feet by 8 feet and is 6 feet tall. Johnny puts planting soil in the delivery truck until the truck is 70% full.

What is the minimum number of times Johnny needs to use the wheelbarrow until the delivery truck is 70% full?

1	2	3
4	5	6
7	8	9
0	.	-

Lesson 5.1 Scale Drawings

Since it is not always possible to draw on paper the actual size of real-life objects such as a house or a building, scale drawings are used to represent real objects with accurate sizes reduced or enlarged by a certain amount known as the scale. In other words, scale drawings make it easy to see large or small things on paper.

The scale gives the ratio that compares the measurements of the drawing or model to the measurements of the real factor. Scale factor is a scale written as a ratio without units in simplest form.

What patterns do you notice about scale factor as it relates to the original being enlarged or reduced? Fill in the table and check your answers below.

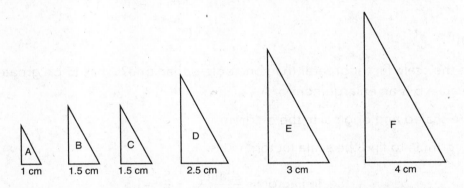

Original	Scaled	Is the Scaled Larger or Smaller?	Scale Factor = $\dfrac{\text{scaled diagram}}{\text{original}}$	What Percent Increase or Decrease Is the Scaled from the Original?
A	F	Larger	$\dfrac{4}{1} = 4$	$\dfrac{4-1}{1} = 3 = 300\%$ increase
B	E	Larger	$\dfrac{3}{1.5} = 2$	$\dfrac{3-1.5}{1.5} = \dfrac{1.5}{1.5} = 1 = 100\%$ increase
C	F	Larger	$\dfrac{4}{1.5} \approx 2.67$	$\dfrac{4-1.5}{1.5} = \dfrac{2.5}{1.5} \approx 1.67 \approx 167\%$ increase
C	D	Larger	$\dfrac{2.5}{1.5} \approx 1.67$	$\dfrac{2.5-1.5}{1.5} = \dfrac{1}{1.5} \approx 0.67 \approx 67\%$ increase
B	C	Larger	$\dfrac{1.5}{1.5} = 1$	$\dfrac{1.5-1.5}{1.5} = \dfrac{0}{1.5} = 0 = 0\%$ increase
F	A	Smaller	$\dfrac{1}{4} = 0.25$	$\dfrac{4-1}{4} = \dfrac{3}{4} = 0.75 = 75\%$ decrease
E	A	Smaller	$\dfrac{1}{3} \approx 0.33$	$\dfrac{3-1}{3} = \dfrac{2}{3} \approx 0.67 \approx 67\%$ decrease
D	B	Smaller	$\dfrac{1.5}{2.5} = 0.6$	$\dfrac{2.5-1.5}{2.5} = \dfrac{1}{2.5} = 0.4 = 40\%$ decrease

If the scaled diagram is larger than the original, then the scale factor is *greater* than one. If the scaled diagram is smaller than the original, then the scale factor is *less* than one. If there is no change from the scaled diagram to the original, then the scale factor is 1.

Example 1   In the diagram below, rectangle A has been enlarged to produce rectangle B. Find the scale factor and percent increase.

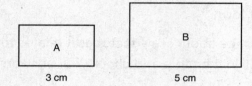

3 cm   5 cm

Solution

Think. Is the scale factor greater than one or less than one? It has to be greater than one because B is an enlargement of A.

Label the scaled and original in the diagram.

Use the formula to find the scale factor:

$$\text{Scale Factor} = \frac{\text{scaled}}{\text{original}} = \frac{5}{3} = 1.\overline{6}$$

The percent increase from Figure A to Figure B = 166.$\overline{6}$% − 100% = 66.$\overline{6}$%.

The length of Figure B is a 66.$\overline{6}$% increase of Figure A.

Example 2   Maia is painting pictures for her parents. The first painting is 24 inches by 36 inches. She wants the size of the second painting to be 25% smaller than the first. What is the scale factor and what are the dimensions of the second painting?

Solution

Draw a picture:

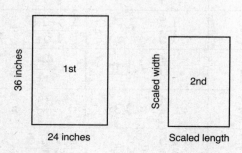

Think. Is the scale factor going to be *less* than one or *greater* than one? Less than one because the scaled object is a reduction or smaller than the original.

$$\text{Scale Factor} = 100\% - 25\% = 75\% = 0.75$$

To find the dimensions of the second painting, use the formula

$$\text{Scale Factor} = \frac{\text{scaled diagram}}{\text{original}}$$

Scaled Length	Scaled Width
$0.75 = \dfrac{\text{scaled length}}{24}$	$0.75 = \dfrac{\text{scaled length}}{36}$
$24(0.75) = \dfrac{\text{scaled length}}{24}\left(\dfrac{24}{1}\right)$	$36(0.75) = \dfrac{\text{scaled length}}{36}\left(\dfrac{36}{1}\right)$
$18 = \text{scaled length}$	$27 = \text{scaled length}$

The dimensions of the second painting are 18 inches by 27 inches.

Example 3 The scale of a map in California is 1 inch : 50 miles. On the map, the distance between Los Angeles to San Francisco is 8 inches. What is the actual distance between Los Angeles to San Francisco?

Solution

Set up a proportion using the given scale.

$$\frac{\text{distance on map}}{\text{actual distance}} = \frac{1 \text{ inch}}{50 \text{ miles}} = \frac{8 \text{ inches}}{\text{actual distance}}$$

Solve for the actual distance.

$$\frac{\text{distance on map}}{\text{actual distance}} = \frac{1 \text{ inch}}{50 \text{ miles}} \cdot \frac{8}{8} = \frac{8 \text{ inches}}{\text{actual distance}}$$

$$\text{actual distance} = \mathbf{400} \text{ miles}$$

The distance between Los Angeles to San Francisco is **400** miles.

 **PRACTICE**

Directions: Use the information given to answer each question.

1. Use the diagram below to answer the following questions in the table.

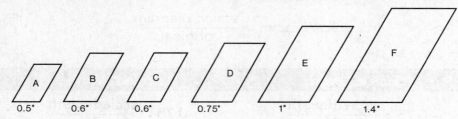

0.5" 0.6" 0.6" 0.75" 1" 1.4"

Complete the table.

Original	Scaled	Is the Scaled Larger or Smaller Than the Original? Should the Scale Factor Be Greater or Less Than One?	Scale Factor	Percent Reduction or Enlargement?
A	F			
F	A			
B	C			
E	B			
D	F			
F	B			
E	A			

2. Noirin is knitting matching hats for herself and her daughter. Her hat has a circumference of 58.7 centimeters. What is the circumference of her daughter's hat if she uses a scale factor of 0.8?

3. Thomas is making copies and needs to reduce an image to fit on an 8.5 inch by 11 inch piece of paper. The original image is 17 inches by 14 inches. If he uses a scale factor of 0.7, will the image fit? If not, what does the scale factor need to be in order to fit?

4. Arya is making copies and needs to enlarge a chart onto an 8.5 inch by 11 inch piece of paper. The original chart is 2.5 inches by 4.75 inches. Her scale factor is 1.4. Will her chart fit the paper? If not, what does her scale factor need to be in order to maximize the space on the paper?

5. Nico is making a blueprint of his bedroom that is the shape of a rectangle. His bedroom is 140 feet by 185 feet. What is one possible scale he can work with so that his blueprint fits on a sheet of 11 inches by 17 inches sheet of paper?

6. Joanne is a landscape architect and wants to redesign her yard. What are the dimensions of her actual yard if her blueprint is shown in the diagram below and she used a scale factor of 1 inch to 8 feet?

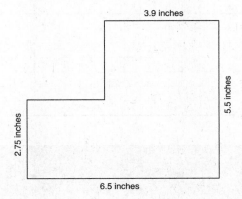

7. On a map, 1 inch represents 250 kilometers. How many inches would there be between two towns if they are 1,100 kilometers apart?

8. An architect is making a scale model of the Eiffel Tower, which is 984 feet tall. How tall is the scale model if the scale is 1 inch : 41 feet?

9. On a map, 0.25 inches represents 10 miles. How far apart are Dallas and Houston if they are 6 inches apart on the map?

10. Using the map below, what is the distance between the two towns if the scale is 1 inch? Use a ruler to measure the distance on the map.

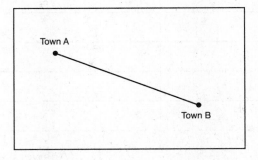

11. Use the grid paper below to draw enlargements and reductions of the original. Label each scaled diagram and fill in the table below. The original figure is A.

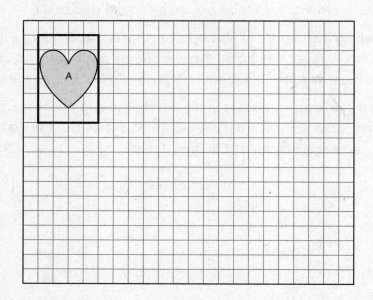

Label the Scaled Diagram	Scale Factor	Is the Scaled Getting Larger or Smaller?	What Is the Percent Increase or Reduction?	Length	Width
A (original)	NA	NA	NA	6	4
B	0.5				
C	0.25				
D	0.75				
E	1				
F	1.25				
G	1.5				
H	2				
I	3				
J	2.5				

(Answers are on pages 285–288.)

Lesson 5.2 Geometric Constructions

Constructions in geometry means to draw shapes, angles, or lines accurately. For these constructions you need to use a protractor, compass, ruler, and pencil. This year, you will focus on constructing triangles.

Here are some basic skills of geometric construction you will need to know in order to construct triangles.

Arcs—An **arc** is part of a circumference of a circle or other curve. When drawing an arc, you will be given the radius of each circle. For example, create an arc with a radius of 4 cm from point *X*.

STEP 1 Draw point *X*.

STEP 2 Use your protractor and ruler to draw an arc such that any point along the arc to point *X* is 4 cm.

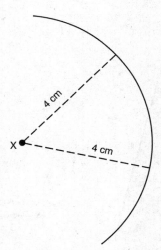

Angle—**Angle** is the space (usually measured in degrees) between two intersecting lines or surfaces at or close to the point where they meet. Parts of an angle include the vertex and rays. The **vertex** is the point where the two rays or line segments meet. The **ray** is part of the line that starts at one point and continues in one direction.

To draw an angle with a given degree, try this example: Construct the following angle m∠*BAC* = 75°.

STEP 1 Construct ray $\vec{AB}$ using a ruler. It can be any length that is reasonable for the space on your paper.

STEP 2 From point *A*, construct an angle that measures 75°. The 0° on your protractor needs to line up with ray $\vec{AB}$. Draw a mark where the angle 75° is.

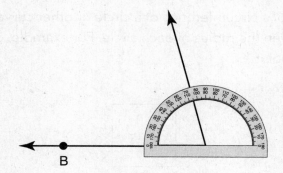

STEP 3 Draw a ray from point *A* to where your mark for where 75° is. Label this ray $\vec{AC}$.

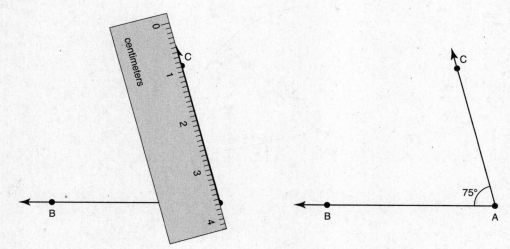

Perpendicular Bisector—A **perpendicular bisector** is a line segment, line, or ray that intersects a given segment at a 90° angle and passes through the segment's midpoint. Construct a perpendicular bisector for line segment $\overline{AB}$, which measures 6 cm.

STEP 1 Draw line segment $\overline{AB} = 6$ cm.

STEP 2 Draw your first arc from point *A*. Set the radius to more than one-half of the line segment and less than the entire line segment. In other words, the radius should be set to greater than 3 cm and less than 6 cm in order for the other arc in Step 3 to intersect the one you will draw in Step 2. This one is set to 5 cm. Draw the arc above and below the line segment.

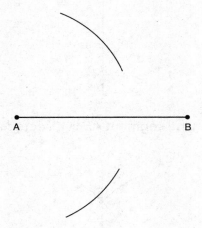

STEP 3 From point *B*, draw two arcs with the same radius used in Step 2.

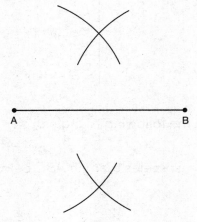

STEP 4 Label the two intersections point *C* and point *D*. Use a straightedge to create line segment $\overline{CD}$. Line segment $\overline{CD}$ is your perpendicular bisector for line segment $\overline{AB}$.

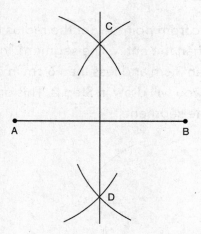

STEP 5 Check your work. Line segment $\overline{AB}$ is bisected and half of line segment $\overline{AB}$ = 3 cm.

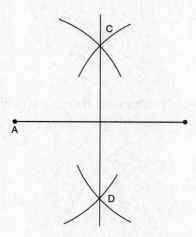

Use these skills to construct the following triangles:

Example 1 Construct the isosceles triangle *ABC* below.

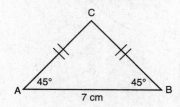

Solution

METHOD 1   Draw the triangle by constructing a perpendicular bisector.

STEP 1   Draw line segment $\overline{AB}$ that is 7 centimeters long.

STEP 2   Construct the perpendicular bisector of line segment $\overline{AB}$.

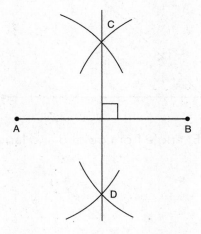

STEP 3   Use a straightedge to connect line segments $\overline{AC}$ and $\overline{BC}$ to create isosceles triangle *ABC*.

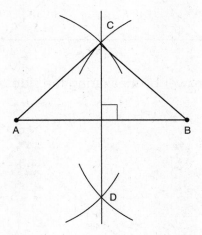

STEP 4   Check your answer by measuring the two angles that are congruent.

METHOD 2 Draw the triangle by constructing the angles

STEP 1 Draw line segment $\overline{AB}$ that is 7 centimeters long.

STEP 2 Construct a 45° angle from point A.

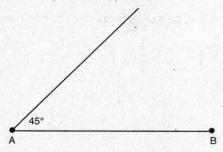

STEP 3 Construct a 45° angle from point B and label their point of intersection point C.

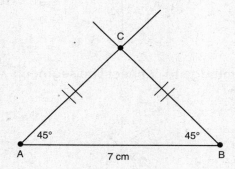

STEP 4 Check your answer by measuring the sides that are congruent.

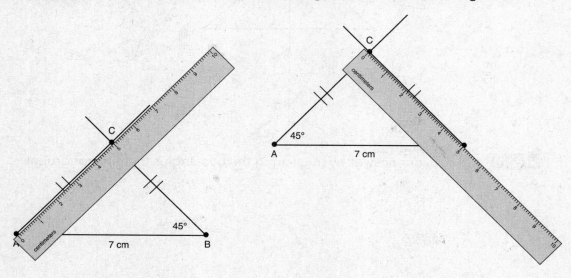

Example 2   Construct triangle *DEF* with $\overline{DE}$ = 5 cm, m∠*DEF* = 135°, and *DF* = 8.5 cm.

Solution

STEP 1   Construct line segment $\overline{DE}$ = 5 cm.

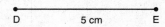

STEP 2   From point *E*, construct m∠*DEF* = 135° (you will label point *F* in Step 3).

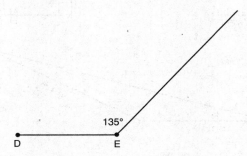

STEP 3   From point *D*, draw an arc that has a radius of 8.5 cm. Make sure it is long enough to intersect where you constructed ∠135°. Label the intersection point *F*.

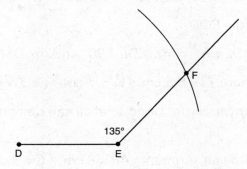

STEP 4   Use a straightedge to connect point *D* and point *F* to create line segment *DF*.

 **PRACTICE**

1. Construct a copy of the following triangles:

   A.

   B.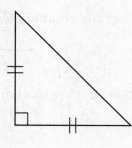

   C.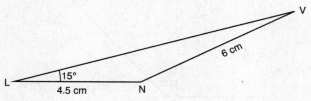

2. Construct a triangle whose sides are twice as long as the sides of the given triangle.

   A. Triangle *XYZ* where $\overline{XY}$ = 3 cm, $\overline{ZY}$ = 5 cm, and m∠*ZXY* = 120°.

   B. Equilateral triangle *PQR*

   C. Right triangle *MDL* where m∠*MDL* = 90° and m∠*DML* = 25°.

   D. Triangle *TJW* where $\overline{TJ}$ = 5.5 cm, $\overline{TW}$ = 7 cm, and $\overline{JW}$ = 3.5 cm.

3. Determine how many triangles or none at all can be constructed from the following:

   A. Triangle *ABC* with line segments $\overline{AB}$ = 8 cm, $\overline{AC}$ = 3 cm, and $\overline{BC}$ = 4 cm.

   B. Triangle *ABC* with line segments $\overline{AB}$ = 5 cm, $\overline{BC}$ = 4 cm, and m∠*BCA* = 50°.

   C. Triangle *ABC* with m∠*BAC* = 105° and m∠*ABC* = 75°.

   (Answers are on pages 289–290.)

Lesson 5.3 Slicing

A **cross-section** is the 2-D shape we get when we cut through a 3-D object. Three-dimensional shapes can have more than one cross-section, that may or may not be the same shape, depending on how you cut them.

Example 1   Using the table below, determine the 2-D shape that would be produced if the 3-D shape were sliced.

3-D Shape that Is Sliced by a Dotted Line	2-D Shape Produced

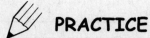 **PRACTICE**

1. Determine the 2-D shape that would be produced if the 3-D shape were sliced below.

	A	B	C
D			
E			
F			
G			

(Answers are on page 291.)

Lesson 5.4 Angles

Angles are measured in degrees and radians, which is a measure of circularity, or rotation. Here are some angle properties.

Term	Definition	Example
Complementary Angles	Two angles whose sum is 90°.	 $m\angle 1 + m\angle 2 = 90°$
Supplementary Angles	Two angles whose sum is 180°.	 $m\angle 1 + m\angle 2 = 180°$
Vertical Angles	Also known as opposite angles, are two angles that are opposite of each other when two lines intersect.	 Pairs of opposite angles: $\angle 1$ and $\angle 3$, $\angle 2$ and $\angle 4$ Therefore, $\angle 1 \cong \angle 3$ and $\angle 2 \cong \angle 4$
Adjacent Angles	Two angles that share a common side and a common vertex and do not overlap.	 Common side is $\overleftrightarrow{BD}$ Common vertex is $\angle B$

Term	Definition	Example
Transversal Line	A line that intersects two or more other lines.	
Alternate Interior Angles	Angles that are formed when a transversal passes through two lines. When the two lines are parallel, these angles within the parallel lines are congruent.	 Pairs of alternate interior angles: ∠2 and ∠8, ∠3 and ∠5 Since the lines a and b are parallel, ∠2 ≅ ∠8 and ∠3 ≅ ∠5. Pairs of alternate interior angles: ∠2 and ∠8, ∠3 and ∠5

Term	Definition	Example
Alternate Exterior Angles	Angles that are formed when a transversal passes through two lines. When the two lines are parallel, these angles outside the parallel lines are congruent.	Pairs of alternate exterior angles: ∠1 and ∠7, ∠4 and ∠6 Since the lines a and b are parallel, $\angle 1 \cong \angle 7$ and $\angle 4 \cong \angle 6$. Pairs of alternate exterior angles: ∠1 and ∠7, ∠4 and ∠6
Corresponding Angles	Angles that are formed when a transversal passes through two lines. When the two lines are parallel, the angles that are on both sides of the transversal line are congruent.	Pairs of corresponding angles: ∠1 and ∠5, ∠2 and ∠6, ∠4 and ∠8, and ∠3 and ∠7 . Since the lines a and b are parallel, $\angle 1 \cong \angle 5$, $\angle 2 \cong \angle 6$, $\angle 4 \cong \angle 8$, and $\angle 3 \cong \angle 7$.

Type of Polygon	Sum of Angles in the Polygon	Example
Scalene Triangle	180°	100° + 30° + 50° = 180°
Isosceles Triangle	180°	20° + 2(80°) = 180° 20° + 80° + 80° = 180°
Equilateral Triangle	180°	3(60°) = 180° 60° + 60° + 60° = 180°
Quadrilateral	360°	100° + 65° + 55° + 140° = 360°

Type of Polygon	Sum of Angles in the Polygon	Example
Trapezoid	360°	$100° + 80° + 115° + 65° = 360°$
Isosceles Trapezoid	360°	$2(65°) + 2(115°) = 360°$ $65° + 65° + 115° + 115° = 360°$
Parallelogram	360°	$2(60°) + 2(120°) = 360°$ $60° + 60° + 120° + 120° = 360°$ *Opposite angles in a parallelogram are congruent.
Square or Rectangle	360°	$4(90°) = 360°$ $90° + 90° + 90° + 90° = 360°$

Example 1 Write an equation to find the value of *x* and then solve for *x*.

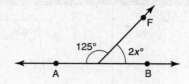

Solution

Supplementary angles add up to 180°.

$$125 + 2x = 180$$

$$125 + 2x - 125 = 180 - 125$$

$$2x = 55$$

$$\frac{2x}{2} = \frac{55}{2}$$

$$x = 27.5$$

Example 2 In the diagram below, m∠1 = 126°. Find the measure of each numbered angle and write the relationship for each pair of angles.

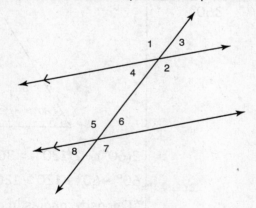

Solution

m∠2 = 126°

m∠3 = 54°

m∠4 = 54°

m∠5 = 126°

m∠6 = 54°

m∠7 = 126°

m∠8 = 54°

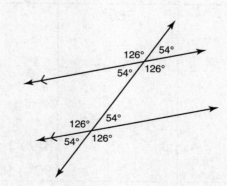

Relationship of the angles:

Pairs of opposite angles, vertical angles ≅

∠1 and ∠2
∠3 and ∠4
∠5 and ∠7
∠6 and ∠8

Pairs of alternate interior angles that are ≅

∠4 and ∠6
∠2 and ∠5

Pairs of alternate exterior angles that are ≅

∠1 and ∠7
∠3 and ∠8

Pairs of corresponding angles that are ≅

∠1 and ∠5
∠4 and ∠8
∠3 and ∠6
∠2 and ∠7

Example 3   Given: Triangle ABC is an isosceles triangle where m∠ABC is 30°. Find the measure of each angle and identify the property associated.

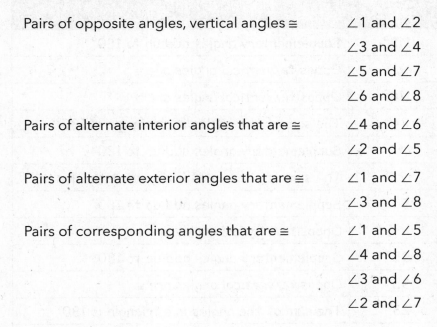
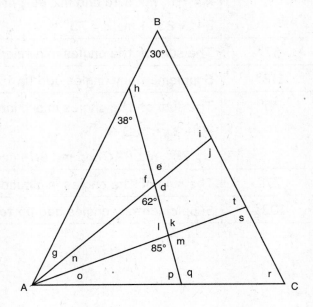

The Measure of _____	Is _____	Because _____.
∠d	118°	Supplementary angles add up to 180°
∠e	62°	Opposite/vertical angles are ≅
∠f	118°	Opposite/vertical angles are ≅
∠g	24°	The sum of the angles in a triangle is 180°
∠h	142°	Supplementary angles add up to 180°
∠i	126°	The sum of the angles in a quadrilateral is 360°
∠j	54°	Supplementary angles add up to 180°
∠k	85°	Opposite/vertical angles are ≅
∠l	95°	Supplementary angles add up to 180°
∠m	95°	Opposite/vertical angles are ≅
∠n	23°	The sum of the angles in a triangle is 180°
∠o	28°	The sum of the angles in a triangle is 180° $30 + 2x = 180$ $x = 75°$, $m\angle BAC$ and $m\angle BCA$ are also 75° $24° + 23° + m\angle o = 75°$
∠p	67°	The sum of the angles in a triangle is 180°
∠q	113°	Supplementary angles add up to 180°
∠r	75°	The sum of the angles in a triangle is 180° $30 + 2x = 180$ $x = 75°$, $m\angle BAC$ and $m\angle BCA$ are also 75°
∠s	77°	The sum of the angles in a quadrilateral is 360°
∠t	103°	Supplementary angles add up to 180°

PRACTICE

1. Angles A and B are complementary angles. Angles A and C are supplementary angles. Find the m∠B and m∠C.

m∠A	m∠B	m∠C
36°		
89°		
95°		
12°		

2. Given: $\overline{AB}$ is a straight line and m∠CDE = 90°. Write an equation to represent the diagrams below. Then find the value of x in each.

A.

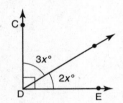

B.

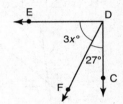

C.

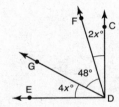

D.

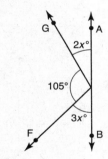

E.

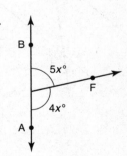

F.

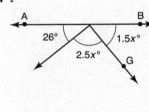

G.

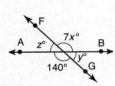

H.

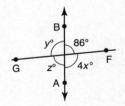

I.

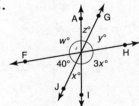

J.

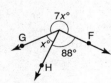

K.

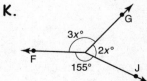

L.

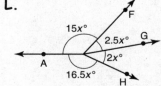

3. In each diagram, find the measure of the numbered angles and write the relationship for each pair of angles.

A. m∠1 = 78°

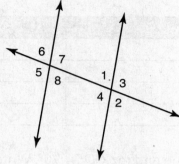

B. m∠1 = 136°

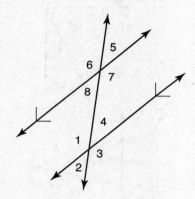

4. Find the value of each unknown variable and the measure of each angle.

A.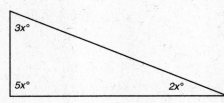

B.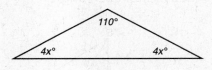

C.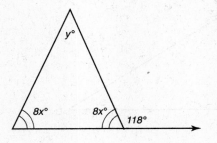

D.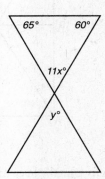

E.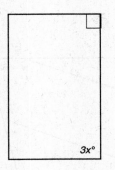

F.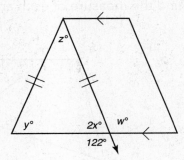

G.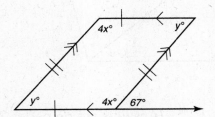

H.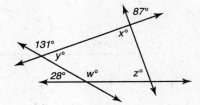

5. Triangle *ABC* is a right triangle where m∠*BAC* is a right angle. Find the measure of each angle.

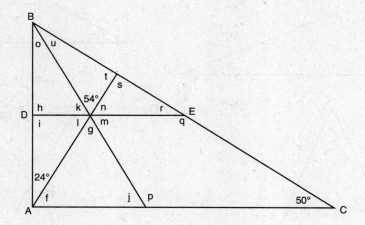

6. Given: In parallelogram *ABCD*, m∠*ECF* = 62° and $\overline{DE}$ and $\overline{AF}$ are parallel. Find the measure of each angle.

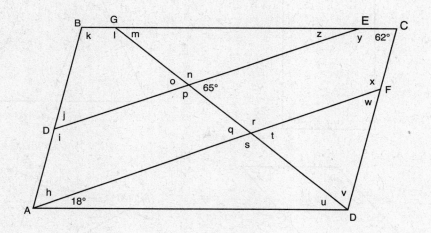

(Answers are on pages 291–300.)

Lesson 5.5 Circles: Circumference and Area

A **circle** is a round plane figure whose boundary, the circumference, consists of points equidistant from the fixed point, the center. The **radius** is the straight line from the center to the circumference of a circle. The **diameter** is a straight line that passes from side to side through the center of the circle. The diameter is double the radius ($d = 2r$). The radius is half the diameter $\left(r = 0.5d \text{ or } r = \dfrac{d}{2}\right)$.

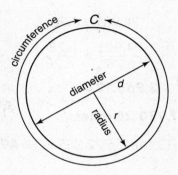

Circumference = $2\pi r$

The **circumference** of a circle is the distance around the edge of the circle. Keywords that indicate the circumference of a circle: perimeter, border, boundary, edge, rim, revolution, rolls, and fringe.

Area = πr^2

Where did the formula come from? Draw a circle and cut it into 16 wedges. Arrange the wedges so they resemble a rectangle.

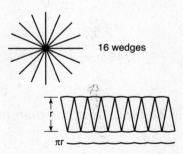

16 wedges

Area of circle = area of rectangle = $\pi r(r) = \pi r^2$

Example 1   The circumference of Earth is 24,901 miles. What is the radius, diameter, and area? Use 3.14 for π.

Solution

Circumference = $2\pi r$

Plug in the circumference and solve for the radius:

$$24{,}901 = 2(3.14)r$$

$$24{,}901 = 6.28r$$

$$\frac{24{,}901}{6.28} = \frac{6.28r}{6.28}$$

$$\mathbf{3{,}965.13} = r$$

Diameter = $2r$ = 2(3,965.13) = **7,930.26 miles**

Area = πr^2 = (3.14)(3,965.13)^2 = (3.14)(15,722,255.92) = **49,367,883.58 miles^2**

Example 2   What is the diameter of a crop circle if the area is 484π?

Solution

Area= πr^2

Plug in the area and first solve for the radius:

$$484\pi = \pi r^2$$

$$\frac{484\pi}{\pi} = \frac{\pi r^2}{\pi}$$

$$484 = r^2$$

$$\sqrt{484} = \sqrt{r^2}$$

$$22 = r$$

The radius of the crop circle is **22 feet**. Thus, the diameter is (2)(22) = **44 feet**.

PRACTICE

1. Fill in the table.

	2 cm	12 m	100 in
Radius (r)	1 cm	12 m	50 in.
Diameter (d)			
Circumference = 2πr	Find the circumference of each circle.		
Use 3.14 for π			
Use 3 for π			
Use π			
Area = πr²	Find the circumference of each circle.		
Use 3.14 for π			
Use 3 for π			
Use π			

2. Fill in the table given the circumference.

Radius (r)			
Diameter (d)			
Circumference = 2πr			
Use 3.14 for π	2(3.14)(4) = 25.12	2(3.14)(0.25) = 75.36	2(3.14)(25) = 157
Use 3 for π			
Use π			
Area = πr²			
Use 3.14 for π			
Use 3 for π			
Use π			

3. Fill in the table given the area of the circle.

Radius (r)			
Diameter (d)			
Circumference = $2\pi r$			
Use 3.14 for π			
Use 3 for π			
Use π			
Area = πr^2			
Use 3.14 for π	$3.14(0.5)^2 = 0.785$	$3.14(3)^2 = 28.26$	$3.14(1.1)^2 = 3.7994$
Use 3 for π			
Use π			

4. Rohan just learned how to ride a unicycle. How far did Rohan cycle if the diameter of the unicycle wheel is 36 inches and he made six revolutions with the wheel without falling?

5. Letitia is decorating the edge of her circular picture frame. How much lace will she need if the diameter of the picture frame is 8.5 inches?

6. High Roller, the world's largest Ferris wheel in Las Vegas, Nevada, is 550 feet tall. If the diameter is 540 feet, how many feet will you have to travel if you go from the top of the Ferris wheel to the bottom?

7. Mochi, the Goldendoodle played fetch with his owner. His owner kicked the ball and the ball traveled 30 feet. How many times did it roll if the diameter of the ball is 0.75 feet?

8. The outer circumference of the Colosseum is 545 meters. What is its diameter? Use 3 for π.

9. What is the diameter of a pancake with an area of 314 square inches?

10. Julia is building a circular garden. How many square feet of soil does she need if her garden has a diameter of 14 feet? Use 3 for π.

11. An ant mill is when blind army ants become disoriented and march in circles. The circumference of one of the ant mills is 650 square feet. Assuming half of the entire circle is covered with ants, how many square feet of ants is this? Use 3.14 for π.

12. A local pizza shop charges $9.99 for a large pizza that is 14 inches in diameter, $7.99 for a medium pizza that is 12 inches in diameter, and $5.99 for a small pizza that is 10 inches in diameter. Which is the best deal? Use 3.14 for π.

(Answers are on pages 300–303.)

Lesson 5.6 Area of Composite Figures

Composite figures are figures or shapes that can be divided into more than one of the basic figures or shapes. It is important to first think about how to find the area of these shapes by thinking of the shapes themselves, then use the formulas to plug in to find your solution. See the examples below.

Example 1 Find the area of the composite figure. Show your work in more than one way.

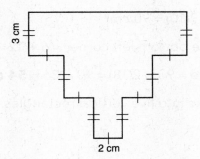

METHOD 1 Split the composite figure into three horizontal rectangles.

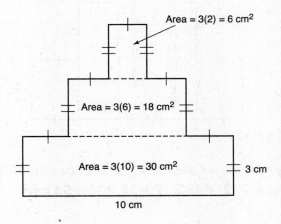

Total area of the figure = 30 + 18 + 6 = 54 cm²

METHOD 2   Find the difference between the area of the big rectangle and the two identical figures. See the picture on how the figure is split.

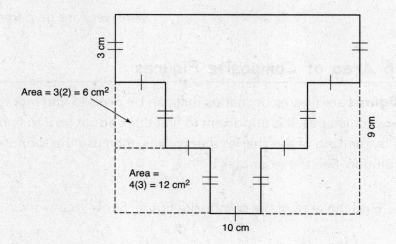

Area of the big rectangle = 9(10) = 90 cm²

Area of the rectangles in the bottom left corner = 6 + 12 = 18

Area of the composite figure = 90 − 2(18) = 90 − 36 = **54 cm²**

METHOD 3   Split the figure into five vertical rectangles. See the diagram below.

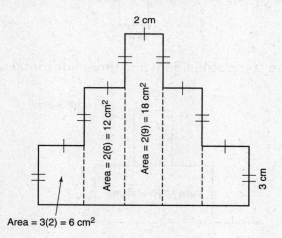

The rectangles on the outer layer are identical to each other. Therefore, the total area of the figure = 2(6) + 2(12) + 18 = 12 + 24 + 18 = **54 cm²**

Example 2   Find the area of the shaded region.

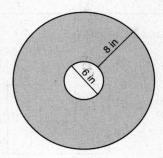

Solution

Write your equation in words first:

Area of the shaded region = area of big circle − area of small circle

Find the area of each separately:

Area of the big circle = πr^2 = (3.14)(11^2) = 379.94 in.^{2}

Area of the small circle = πr^2 = (3.14)(3^2) = 28.26 in.^{2}

Area of the shaded region = 379.94 − 28.26 = **351.68 in.^{2}**

PRACTICE

1. Find the area of the composite figures.

A.

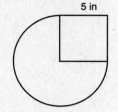

5 in

B.

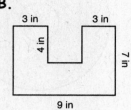

3 in   3 in

4 in

7 in

9 in

C.

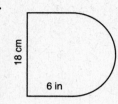

18 cm

6 in

D.

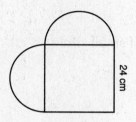

24 cm

E.

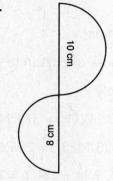

10 cm

8 cm

F.

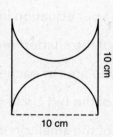

10 cm

10 cm

G.

11 in

36 in

H.

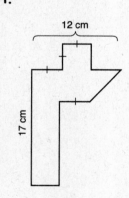

12 cm

17 cm

I.

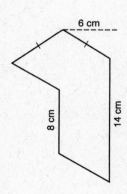

6 cm

8 cm

14 cm

J.

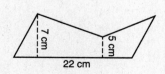

7 cm

5 cm

22 cm

K.

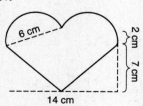

6 cm

2 cm

7 cm

14 cm

L.

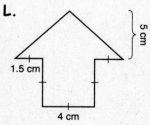

5 cm

1.5 cm

4 cm

2. Find the area of the shaded region.

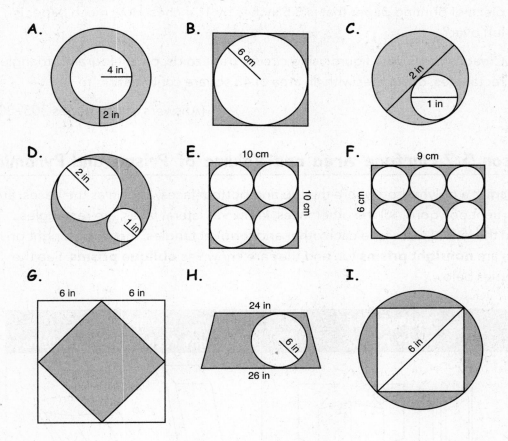

A.

4 in

2 in

B.

6 cm

C.

2 in

1 in

D.

2 in

1 in

E.

10 cm

10 cm

F.

9 cm

6 cm

G.

6 in   6 in

H.

24 in

6 in

26 in

I.

6 in

3. The shape of Neal's garden is such that two isosceles triangles share a base of 4 feet. The height of one triangle is 5 feet and the height of the other is 6 feet. What is the area of his garden?

4. A standard track is in the shape of two semicircles and one rectangle. The straight path is approximately 84 meters while the distance along the curve of one of the semicircles is approximately 116 meters. What is the area of the inside of the tracks? How much would it cost to fill in the inside of the track with grass if grass costs $2.75 per square meter?

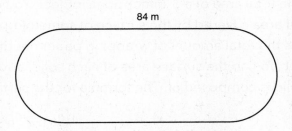

84 m

5. Orion is making a paper snowflake and cuts a perfect circle from a regular piece of printing paper that is 8.5 inches by 11 inches. How much paper is left over?

6. Create a composite figure using circles, trapezoids, parallelograms, triangles, rectangles, or squares with an area of 48 square centimeters

(Answers are on pages 303–306.)

Lesson 5.7 Surface Area and Volume of Prisms and Pyramids

A **prism** is a polyhedron where the top and bottom faces, known as the bases, are congruent polygons. All the other faces, known as lateral faces, are rectangles. When the lateral sides face each other and form rectangles, they form a right prism. There are **nonright prisms** too and they are known as **oblique prisms**. See the examples below.

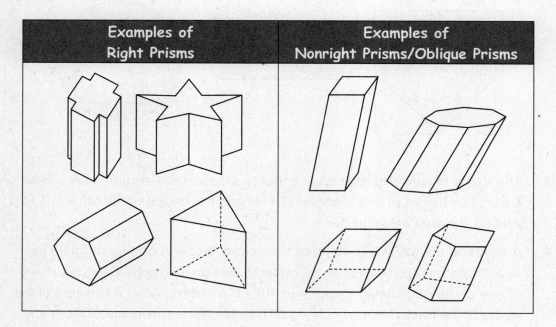

Surface Area is the total area of a 3-dimensional object. You can also think of it as the amount of area covered by the surface of something. You can think of the surface area as the total amount of wrapping paper needed to cover a 3-dimensional object. To find the surface area of each solid, add up the area of each polygon the solid is composed of. The formula for the surface area of right prisms is $SA = 2B + LA$ where B is the base area and LA is the lateral area. For the lateral area, look at the shape of the area and find the sum of each polygon.

Volume is the measure of the amount of space inside a solid figure. It can also be known as capacity. Units of volume include: cubic centimeters (cm^3), cubic meters (m^3), liters, cubic inches ($in.^3$), cubic feet ($ft.^3$), pints, gallons, and fluid ounces.

To calculate the volume of any right prism, multiply the base of the prism times the height. Notice the base of the prism is different from the base of a polygon as in a trapezoid or triangle. The base of the prism is the area of the base and is also referred to in the formula with a capital B. The height and the base make a 90° angle, and the height is also the distance between the two parallel, congruent bases in a right prism.

The volume of a prism is $V = Bh$, where B is the base area and h is the height. Note that the base area of a 3-D solid is indicated with a capital B. The lower base b is used for the length of the base of a 2-D polygon. Imagine stacking the base of your prism until you reach your desired height.

Look at the nets of each right prism below. Identify the prism and write what 2-D objects each net is composed of to find the surface area.

Net of 3-D Solid	3-D Solid	Classify
		Triangular Prism

Total Surface Area = 2(base) + Lateral Area = 2B + LA

Total Surface Area = 2(area of triangle) + 3(area of rectangles)

Total Surface Area = 2(area of triangle) + big rectangle

Volume = Bh = area of triangle(height)

Net of 3-D Solid	3-D Solid	Classify
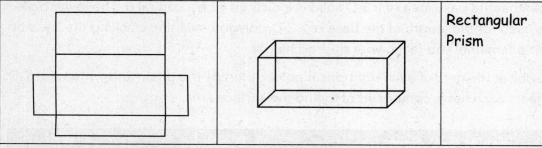		Square Prism

Total Surface Area = 2(base) + Lateral Area = 2B + *LA*

Total Surface Area = 2(area of square) + 4(area of rectangle)

Total Surface Area = 2(area of square) + big rectangle

Volume = *Bh* = Area of square(height)

		Rectangular Prism

Total Surface Area = 2(base) + Lateral Area = 2B + *LA*

Total Surface Area = 2(side rectangles) + 2(bottom rectangles) + 2(front rectangles)

Volume = *Bh* = area of rectangle(height)

		Trapezoidal prism
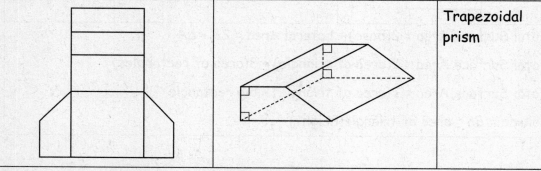		

Surface Area = 2(Base) + Lateral Area = 2B + *LA*

Surface Area = 2(area of trapezoid) + area of bottom rectangle + area of left rectangle + area of top rectangle + area of right rectangle

Volume = *Bh* = area of trapezoid(height)

Net of 3-D Solid	3-D Solid	Classify
		Cube

Surface Area = 6(area of square)

Volume = Bh = area of square(height)

Volume = length(width)(height) = side(side)(side) = s^3

Net of 3-D Solid	3-D Solid	Classify
		Hexagonal Prism

Surface Area = $2B$ + LA = 2(area of hexagon) + 6(area of rectangles)

Volume = Bh = area of hexagon(height)

The volume for any pyramid is always area of base (height of prism)/3. This is because if you take the volume of any right prism and break it into three parts, it would equal the volume of the pyramid with the same height and base. Note there is a difference between the height of a prism and slant height. The height of a prism is the same as the height of a pyramid. In a prism, the height is the distance between the two bases of a prism. In a pyramid, the height is the distance between the top of the pyramid and the base. The height makes a 90° angle with the base. The slant height is the hypotenuse of the right triangle formed by the height and half of the base length. See the picture below. You will need to use the slant height to find the area of triangles in a pyramid.

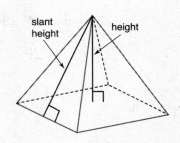

Triangular Pyramid

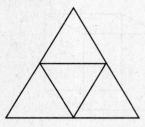 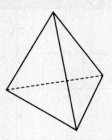

Total Surface Area = base + Lateral Area = B + LA

Total Surface Area = area of triangle + 3(area of three triangles)

*If the base is an equilateral triangle, then the triangles in the lateral area are all congruent. If the base is an isosceles triangle, then two of the triangles in the lateral area will be congruent. If the base is a scalene triangle, then all three triangles will have different areas.

$$\text{Volume} = \frac{Bh}{3} = \frac{(\text{Area of triangle})(\text{height of prism})}{3}$$

Square Pyramid

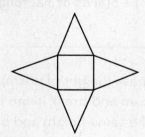 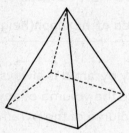

Total Surface Area = base + Lateral Area = B + LA

Total Surface Area = area of square + 4(area of triangle)

Since all the sides in a square are congruent, the four triangles in the Lateral Area are congruent.

$$\text{Volume} = \frac{Bh}{3} = \frac{(\text{Area of square})(\text{height of prism})}{3}$$

Rectangular Pyramid

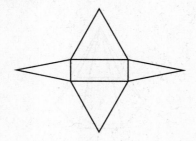 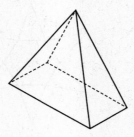

Total Surface Area = base + Lateral Area = B + LA

Total Surface Area = area of triangle + 2(area of front triangles) + 2(area of side triangle)

*Since opposite sides in a rectangle are congruent, the front and back triangle in the lateral area are congruent. The left and right triangles in the lateral area are congruent.

$$\text{Volume} = \frac{Bh}{3} = \frac{(\text{Area of rectangle})(\text{height of prism})}{3}$$

Pentagonal Pyramid

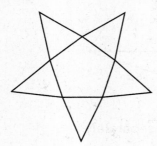 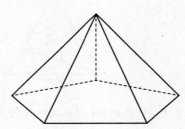

Total Surface Area = base + Lateral Area = B + LA

Total Surface Area = area of pentagon + 5(area of triangle)

*If the pentagon is a regular pentagon, then all the triangles in the lateral area are congruent.

$$\text{Volume} = \frac{Bh}{3} = \frac{(\text{Area of pentagon})(\text{height of prism})}{3}$$

Hexagonal Pyramid

 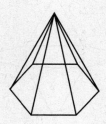

Total Surface Area = base + Lateral Area = $B + LA$

Total Surface Area = area of hexagon + 6(area of triangle)

*If the hexagon is a regular pentagon, then all the triangles in the lateral area are congruent.

$$\text{Volume} = \frac{Bh}{3} = \frac{(\text{Area of hexagon})(\text{height of prism})}{3}$$

Example 1 Find the surface area of the triangular prism.

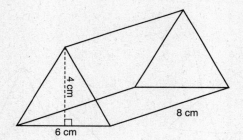

METHOD 1 Find the area of each side or face separately.

Area of the triangle = $0.5bh = 0.5(6)(4) = 12$ cm^2

Area of the rectangle = $bh = 8(6) = 48$ cm^2

Surface Area = 2(area of triangles) + 3(area of rectangles)

$$2(12) + 3(48) = 24 + 144 = \textbf{168 cm}^2$$

METHOD 2   Find the Lateral Area by seeing it as a rectangle.

LA = area of rectangle = bh = 18(8) = 144

Surface Area = 2(area of triangle) + LA = 2(12) + 144 = 24 + 144 = **168 cm²**

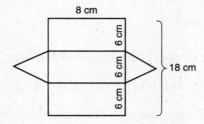

Example 2   A hexagonal prism has a surface area of 148 inches squared. The base area is 32 inches squared and the height is 4 inches. What is the lateral area, base dimensions of the lateral area, and area of each rectangular face?

Solution

METHOD 1   Find the Lateral Area first and then find the area of each rectangular face.

To find the Lateral Area, work backward using this formula:

Surface Area = 2(area of hexagon base) + LA

$$148 = 2(32) + 4b$$

$$148 - 64 = 2(32) + 4b - 64$$

$84 = 4b$ (the Lateral Area is 84 cm²)

$$\frac{84}{4} = \frac{4b}{4}$$

$$21 = b$$

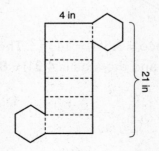

Since the Lateral Area is in the shape of a rectangle, the dimensions of the lateral area are 21 inches by 4 inches and the area is 84 cm².

To find the area of each rectangular face, take the lateral area and divide by 6 since there are six congruent rectangles that make up the lateral area. Each rectangular face = $\frac{84}{6}$ = **14 in.²**.

METHOD 2 Find the area of each rectangular face first, then find the Lateral Area.

Work backward by solving for the length of the rectangular face.

Surface Area = 2(area of hexagon base) + 6(area of each rectangular face)

$$148 = 2(32) - 6(4b)$$

$$148 - 64 = 2(32) - 6(4b) - 64$$

$$84 = 24b$$

$$\frac{84}{24} = \frac{24b}{24}$$

$$3.5 = b$$

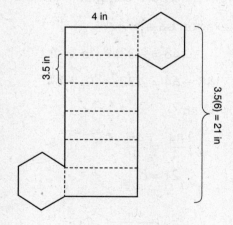

The area of each rectangular face = 3.5(4) = 14 in.². The dimensions of the Lateral Area are 21 inches by 4 inches and the area is 4(21) = **84 square inches**.

Example 3 The volume of a hexagonal pyramid is 880 cubic centimeters. What is the surface area if the height of the pyramid is 8 centimeters, the slant height is 12.6 centimeters, and each side of the hexagon is 11.25 centimeters?

Solution

First, find the area of the base that is in the shape of a hexagon. Start with the formula and plug in the information provided. Then solve for the area of the base.

$$\text{Volume} = \frac{Bh}{3} = \frac{(\text{Area of hexagon})(\text{height of prism})}{3}$$

$$880 = \frac{8B}{3}$$
$$3(880) = \left(\frac{8B}{3}\right)\left(\frac{3}{1}\right)$$
$$2{,}640 = 8B$$
$$\frac{2{,}640}{8} = \frac{8B}{8}$$
$$330 = B$$

To find the Surface Area, start with the formula, plug in the information provided, and solve.

Remember: The height of the triangle is the slant height.

Surface Area = base + Lateral Area = area of hexagon + 6(area of triangles)

$$330 + 6\left(\frac{bh}{2}\right) = 330 + 3(11.25)(12.6) = 330 + 425.25 = \mathbf{755.25}$$

The Surface Area of the hexagonal pyramid is **755.25** square centimeters.

Example 4 A triangular prism has a height of 12 feet. The triangular base has a base of 3 feet and a height of 9 feet. What is the base area and the volume of the triangular prism?

Solution

Write the formula: $V = Bh = (\text{area of triangle})(\text{height})$

$$\text{Area of the triangle} = \frac{bh}{2} = \frac{3(9)}{2} = \frac{27}{2} = 13.5 \text{ ft.}^2$$

Plug the numbers back in to the formula to find the volume.

$$V = 13.5(12) = \textbf{162 ft.}^3$$

The volume of the triangular prism is **162 ft.^{3}**.

Example 5   The volume of a trapezoidal prism is 490 cubic inches. The trapezoidal base has a height of 8 inches and the sum of the two bases is 24.5 inches. Find the height of the trapezoidal base.

Solution

Write the formula: $V = Bh = $ (area of trapezoid)(height)

Find the base area: base area = area of a trapezoid = $\dfrac{(b_1 + b_2)h}{2} = \dfrac{(24.5)8}{2} = 98$ ft.^{2}

Plug the numbers back into the formula to find the height:

$$490 = 98h$$

$$\frac{490}{98} = \frac{98h}{98}$$

$$\textbf{5} = h$$

The height of the trapezoidal base is **5 inches**.

 PRACTICE

1. In the figure below, each cube measures 1 cm by 1 cm by 1 cm. Find the surface area of the figure.

2. A triangular prism has a surface area of 260.6 square centimeters. Find its lateral area, base area, height of the triangular, and area of each rectangular face. The height of the prism is 18 cm, and one side of the equilateral traingle is 4.5 cm.

3. A gift box is shaped in the form of a triangular prism. The dimensions of the base are 8 cm, 8 cm, and 11.3 cm. The height of the prism is 17 cm. How much wrapping paper is needed for this gift box?

4. A triangular prism has a scalene triangle as its base. What is the height of the triangular base if the surface area is 204 square centimeters, each side of the scale triangle measures 3 and 4 cm, the base of the triangle is 8 cm, and the height of the prism is 12 cm?

5. Nicole has an aquarium in the shape of a trapezoidal prism. How much glass was used to make the fish tank? The bases of the prism are not covered in glass. (See figure below for dimensions of the fish tank.)

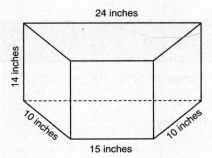

6. A pentagonal prism has a base area of 139.36 square feet. The height of the prism is 18 feet, and one side of the pentagonal base is 9 feet. What is its lateral area and surface area?

7. Most #2 pencils are in the shape of a hexagonal prism. The length of a pencil is 7.5 inches and each side of the hexagonal base measures 0.0833 inches. How much paint is needed to paint a box of 24 pencils? (*Hint: just find the lateral area.*)

8. A local bakery received an order for two rectangular sheet cakes. The dimensions of the first are 18 inches by 24 inches by 4 inches. The dimensions of the second are 25% less than the first. How much frosting is needed to cover both cakes separately?

9. Thomas and Tony are building a teepee and need to figure out how much cloth they will need to purchase. The teepee is in the shape of a pentagonal pyramid. The slant height is 9 feet, and one side of the pentagonal base is 4 feet. The fabric they are looking at costs $6.50 for every 18 square feet. How much will it cost them to cover their teepee with this fabric?

10. The volume of a square pyramid is 147 cubic feet. What is the length of the base if the height is 9 feet?

11. A rectangular pyramid has a height of 11 inches and a volume of 220 cubic inches. What are the possible dimensions of the base?

12. What is the volume of a square pyramid if the surface area is 176 square feet, the height of the prism measures 12 feet, and one of the triangular faces of the lateral area measures 28 square feet?

13. What is the surface area of a rectangular pyramid if the volume measures 372 cubic inches and the height of the pyramid is 18 inches?

14. Fill in the table below.

3-D Solid	Formula for Volume	Volume (cm^3)	Base (cm^2)	Height (cm)
Triangular Prism	$V = Bh$ = (area of triangle)(height)	48		4
Triangular Prism	$V = Bh$ =	208	16	
Rectangular Prism	$V = Bh$ =		8	12
Rectangular Prism	$V = Bh$ =	114		7.6
Trapezoidal Prism	$V = Bh$ =	256	16	
Pentagonal Prism	$V = Bh$ =		25	15
Pentagonal Prism	$V = Bh$ =	247		19
Hexagonal Prism	$V = Bh$ =	486	27	
Hexagonal Prism	$V = Bh$ =	558		9
Cylinder	$V = Bh$ =		20	30
Cylinder	$V = Bh$ =	108		9

15. A rectangular prism has a volume of 288 cubic inches and a height of 8 inches. What are the possible dimensions of the base area?

16. A jewelry store received a shipment of bracelets. Each bracelet is packaged in a hexagonal prism, which has a base area of 1.875 square inches and a height of 1.5 inches. The shipment came in a rectangular box with dimensions 48 inches by 24 inches by 12 inches. What is the maximum number of bracelets the jewelry store received in this shipment?

17. An aquarium is in the shape of a trapezoidal prism. The tank has a volume of 48 cubic inches with a height of 6 inches. What is the height of the base area if the sum of the bases of the trapezoid is 5 inches?

18. A hexagonal prism has a volume of 276 cubic centimeters. What are possible dimensions of its base area and height?

19. If it costs $91.50 to paint 267 square feet, how much would it cost to paint the barn below, not including the roof?

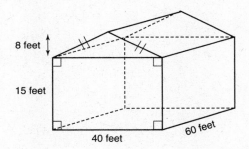

20. Two square pyramids share the same base. Each side of the base is 6 inches. The top pyramid has a height of 5 inches and a slant height of 6.5 inches. The bottom pyramid has a height of 2 inches and a slant height of 3.25 inches. What is the solid's volume and surface area?

21. Lana is in woodshop class and cuts a triangular prism hole through a piece of wood measuring 12 inches by 6 inches by 8 inches. What is the volume of her piece of wood now if the triangular has a base of 10.5 square inches?

(Answers are on pages 306–314.)

Statistics and Probability

Statistics is a branch of mathematics dealing with the collection, analysis, interpretation, presentation, and organization of data. It can be used to gain information about a population by examining a sample of the population. Generalizations about a population from a sample are valid only if the sample is representative of that population.

There are two main types of statistics: **descriptive** and **inferential**. Descriptive statistics uses the data to provide descriptions of the population, either through numerical calculations or graphs or tables. Inferential statistics makes inferences and predictions about a population based on a sample of data taken from the population in question.

Data can be classified as categorical (qualitative) and numerical (quantitative). **Categorical data** is the statistical data type consisting of categorical variables or of data that has been converted into that form, for example, as grouped data. Categorical data represents characteristics such as color, a person's gender, etc. Numerical data are values or observations that can be measured. These numbers can be placed in ascending or descending order such as weight or height.

A statistic is a fact or piece of data from a study of a large quantity of numerical data. In this chapter, you will be organizing, analyzing, and interpreting the data represented to see how data influences or does not influence your thinking.

Probability is the extent to which something is probable; the likelihood of something happening or being the case. In mathematics, probability is the extent to which an event is likely to occur, measured by the ratio of the favorable cases to the whole number of cases possible. There are two main types of probability: theoretical vs. experimental. **Theoretical probability** is what is expected to happen whereas **experimental probability** is what actually happens. For example, consider the sum of two six-sided fair dice.

How are these two related? Probability theory enables us to find the consequences of a given ideal world, while statistical theory enables us to measure the extent to which our world is ideal. In other words, statistics are used to quantify *observations* of phenomena whose behavior is *predicted* by probability.

Standards

7.SP.A.1 Understand that statistics can be used to gain information about a population by examining a sample of the population; generalizations about a population from a sample are valid only if the sample is representative of that population. Understand that random sampling tends to produce representative samples and support valid inferences.

7.SP.A.2 Use data from a random sample to draw inferences about a population with an unknown characteristic of interest. Generate multiple samples (or simulated samples) of the same size to gauge the variation in estimates or predictions. *For example, estimate the mean word length in a book by randomly sampling words from the book; predict the winner of a school election based on randomly sampled survey data. Gauge how far off the estimate or prediction might be.*

7.SP.B.3 Informally assess the degree of visual overlap of two numerical data distributions with similar variability, measuring the difference between the centers by expressing it as a multiple of a measure of variability. *For example, the mean height of players on the basketball team is 10 cm greater than the mean height of players on the soccer team, about twice the variability (mean absolute deviation) on either team; on a dot plot, the separation between the two distributions of heights is noticeable.*

7.SP.B.4 Use measures of center and measures of variability for numerical data from random samples to draw informal comparative inferences about two populations. *For example, decide whether the words in a chapter of a seventh-grade science book are generally longer than the words in a chapter of a fourth-grade science book.*

7.SP.C.5 Understand that the probability of a chance event is a number between 0 and 1 that expresses the likelihood of the event occurring. Larger numbers indicate greater likelihood. A probability near 0 indicates an unlikely event, a probability around 1/2 indicates an event that is neither unlikely nor likely, and a probability near 1 indicates a likely event.

7.SP.C.6 Approximate the probability of a chance event by collecting data on the chance process that produces it and observing its long-run relative frequency, and predict the approximate relative frequency given the probability. *For example, when rolling a number cube 600 times, predict that a 3 or 6 would be rolled roughly 200 times, but probably not exactly 200 times.*

7.SP.C.7 Develop a probability model and use it to find probabilities of events. Compare probabilities from a model to observed frequencies; if the agreement is not good, explain possible sources of the discrepancy.

7.SP.C.7.A Develop a uniform probability model by assigning equal probability to all outcomes, and use the model to determine probabilities of events. *For example, if a student is selected at random from a class, find the probability that Jane will be selected and the probability that a girl will be selected.*

7.SP.C.7.B Develop a probability model (which may not be uniform) by observing frequencies in data generated from a chance process. *For example, find the approximate probability that a spinning penny will land heads up or that a tossed paper cup will land open-end down. Do the outcomes for the spinning penny appear to be equally likely based on the observed frequencies?*

7.SP.C.8 Find probabilities of compound events using organized lists, tables, tree diagrams, and simulation.

Sample Questions from the SBAC

The following are examples of question types that you will see on the SBAC Grade 7 Math test. We will cover them in this chapter.

A principal wants to know if students at a particular high school are in favor of a new dress code at their school. The principal is not able to ask the opinion of every student at the school, so she needs to select an appropriate sample of the students to represent the high school.

Select which sample of students the principal should choose.

Ⓐ Students randomly selected from a list of all students at the school.

Ⓑ Students sitting at randomly selected tables in the library.

Ⓒ Students she selects from the hallway between classes.

Ⓓ Students selected by the teachers.

A bag contains 16 marbles. There are 5 blue, 9 yellow, and 2 red marbles. One marble is selected at random.

Determine whether each statement correctly describes the likelihood of an event based on the given bag of marbles. Select True or False for each statement.

	True	False
It is impossible that a green marble will be selected.	☐	☐
It is unlikely that a yellow marble will be selected.	☐	☐
It is certain that a blue marble will be selected.	☐	☐
It is unlikely that a red marble will be selected.	☐	☐

Lesson 6.1 Random Sampling Methods

In statistics, quality assurance and survey methodology sampling has to do with the selection of a subset of individuals from within a statistical population to estimate characteristics of the whole population. Two advantages of sampling are that the cost is lower and data collection is faster than measuring the entire population.

Types of Sampling Methods

- Simple Random Sampling (SRS)
- Stratified Sampling
- Cluster Sampling
- Systematic Sampling
- Multistage Sampling (in which some of the methods above are combined in stages)

For the examples below, consider this scenario: The administration of a junior high consisting of 700 seventh and eighth graders would like to know how long their students spend on homework each night. They would like to get a random sample that best represents their population.

Sampling Method	Definition	Example
Simple Random Sampling	The basic sampling technique where a select group of subjects (sample) for study represents a larger group (a population). Each individual is chosen entirely by chance and each member of the population has an equal chance of being included in the sample.	All the students' names are inserted in a database and 100 names are randomly drawn. This sample is random because each student has an equal chance of being chosen.
Stratified Sampling	This method divides the population into groups by characteristics called strata.	The student population is separated into males and females. A random sample of 50 is then taken from each of these strata.
Cluster Sampling	This method divides the population into groups—usually geographically. These groups are called blocks or clusters. The clusters are randomly selected, and each element in the selected clusters are used.	The student population is asked to go to their homerooms. There are 24 homerooms total for 700 students. Four students from each homeroom are then chosen at random to make up the random sample of 96 to represent the population.
Systematic Sampling	The elements in the population are counted off and every x number is sampled to produce the random sample.	Each student is assigned a number. Every seventh student is surveyed for a random sample of 100 to represent the population.

Convenient sampling is a nonprobability sampling technique where subjects are selected because of their convenient accessibility and proximity to the researcher. For example, in the previous situation, convenient sampling would be if the principal sends a survey on to the student body. Since the data collected would only be from students that choose or volunteer to respond to the survey, this would not represent the entire population.

 PRACTICE

Directions: Determine what type of sampling method is used for each scenario below. Then determine if this sampling method was representative of the population. If not, suggest another sampling method. Are there other sampling methods that would also represent the population?

1. To determine which snack to add to the lunch menu, every fifth student that purchased a snack on Monday was surveyed.

2. Georgia is conducting a science fair project about carbon footprints in her neighborhood. Since it is not feasible to interview every household, she decides to interview one house from every block.

3. Nora wants to see how many people in her community purchase organic products, so she surveys every tenth customer that walks out of her neighborhood grocery store.

4. Laila is in the student leadership group and needs to make 700 spirit buttons for the entire student body. Since she is not able to check every 700 buttons to make sure they come out right, she checks every 25th button instead.

5. Kevin, who is in third grade, wants to know how many students at his elementary school have a cell phone. He decides to randomly select 10 students from each grade level, kindergarten through fifth grade.

(Answers are on pages 314–315.)

Lesson 6.2 Making Inferences from Random Samples

An **inference** is a conclusion reached based on evidence and reasoning. You can draw inferences about a population by analyzing the data collected from random samples. The idea is that the random sample represents the population.

Example 1   For every 100 purses a manufacturer produces, 6 are defected. How many are expected to be defected if 500 purses are produced?

Let d = number of defective purses in the population

METHOD 1   Use a proportion.

$$\frac{\text{defective purses in sample}}{\text{size of sample}} = \frac{\text{defective purses in sample}}{\text{size of population}}$$

$$\frac{6}{100} = \frac{d}{500}$$

$$\frac{6}{100} \cdot \frac{5}{5} = \frac{d}{500}$$

$$d = 30$$

Based on the sample, you can predict that 30 out of the 500 purses produced will be defective.

METHOD 2   Use percentages.

Find the percent of defects from the sample: $\frac{6}{100} = 0.06 = 6\%$

Use this percent to predict the number of defects in the population:

6% of the 500 purses are defective, therefore, 6% of 500 = 0.06(500) = 30

PRACTICE

Directions: Use inferences and random sampling to answer the following questions.

1. Annie is trying to gauge for building a new community park. She randomly surveys 50 people and finds that 27 of them were planning on voting *yes*. Assuming the survey is valid, how many people would vote *yes* for the community park if there are 8,000 people in the town?

2. A local shoe store sold 245 size 8 women's shoes out of all the 450 female shoes sold last month. They need to place a minimum order of 3,000 women's shoes. Based on the data, what is the most reasonable number of size 8 shoes they should place for the next order?

3. Carter is trying to figure out how quickly the population of feral cats is growing in the city. He tagged 30 cats last January. This January, he found 40 cats and 8 of them were tagged. What is the best estimate for the population of feral cats this year?

4. Ben is planning on making hot dogs for the holiday fair and is trying to see how many he would sell. He sold 7 hot dogs to 30 students that walked by during lunch one day. If there are 745 students at his school, how many hot dogs should he plan to sell?

5. Eve is trying to figure out how much of each cupcake to prepare for the school bake sale. She surveyed students of their preferences and the survey results are below.

Type of cupcake	Chocolate	Vanilla	Red Velvet	Carrot Cake	Peanut Butter	Lemon
Frequency	8	9	6	3	3	2

If she is expected to sell 500 cupcakes, how much of each flavor will she sell?

6. Brady is helping out at his school's snack shop. Out of every 25 students, 11 of them purchase Ramen Noodles for lunch. If about 200 students visit the snack shop every day, what is the best estimate for the number of Ramen Noodle cups sold every day? If the school purchases Ramen Noodle cups for 22 cents apiece and sells each cup for $1, how much does the school make every day just on the Ramen Noodle cups?

(Answers are on pages 315–318.)

Lesson 6.3 Measures of Central Tendency and Variability

There are three main measures of central tendency: *mode*, *median*, and *mean*. Each of these measures describes a different indication of the typical or central value in the distribution. It answers the question: Where does the center of the data tend to fall, or lie?

The most common measures of the spread of the data, or variability are the range, interquartile range (IQR), variance, and standard deviation. **Range** is the variation between the upper and lower limits of a data set. The **interquartile range** is the difference between the upper (Q3) and lower (Q1) quartiles, and describes the middle 50% of the values when ordered from least to greatest. The IQR is often seen as a better measure of the spread than the range because it is not affected by outliers. **Variance** measures how far each number in the set is away from the mean. **Standard deviation** is a number used to tell how measurements for a group are spread out from the mean (average) or expected value. In this chapter, we will focus on mean absolute deviation (MAD). This number tells us the average distance between each data value between the mean.

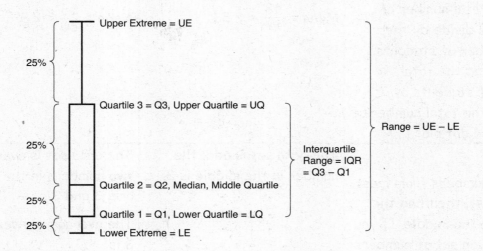

Example 1 Mrs. Cullimore is trying to analyze the test scores from her two math classes: one taught in the morning and one taught in the afternoon. She then looked at and compared the measures of central tendency and variability for the two classes. What inferences can she draw from this data?

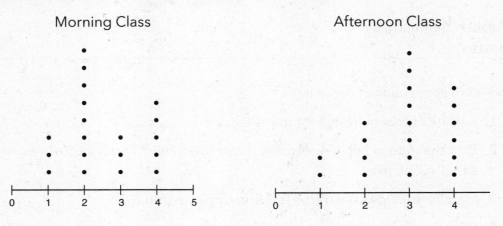

To find the measures of central tendency, use the table below.

Measures of Central Tendency	Morning Class	Afternoon Class
Mean Also known as the average. Find the total number of points and divide by the total number of students. You can find the total number of students by counting the total number of dots in the dot plot.	Total points = $3(1) + 8(2) + 3(3) + 5(4) = 48$ Mean = $\frac{48}{19} \approx 2.53$	Total points = $2(1) + 4(2) + 8(3) + 6(4) = 58$ Mean = $\frac{58}{20} = 2.9$
Median List the numbers from least to greatest, then find the number in the middle. If you have an even set of numbers, take the average of the two. The median is also your Q2, which splits your data in half.	The data set is odd; the number in the middle is 2.	The data set is even; the two numbers in the middle are: 3 and 3. The average between 3 and 3 is $\frac{3+3}{2} = \frac{6}{2} = 3$
Mode The number that occurs the most.	2	3

To find the measures of variability:

1. List the numbers from least to greatest.

2. Split the data in two halves using the median, which is also known as your Q2. Label your halves.

3. Identify your lower extreme (LE) and upper extreme (UE).

4. Q1 = the median of the lower half, Q3 = the median of the upper half. The three quartiles divide your data into four equal sections.

Morning Class   Afternoon Class

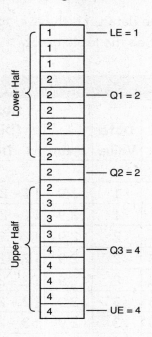
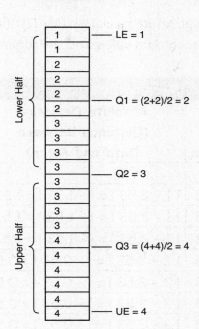

Morning Class

Morning Class

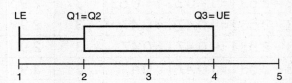

Afternoon Class

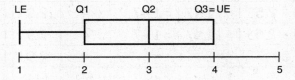

5. The interquartile range (IQR) = Q3 − Q1 = 4 − 2 = 2

6. The mean absolute deviation (MAD) of the data set is the average distance between each data value and the mean. See the table below.

#	Morning Class			Afternoon Class		
	Data Value	Mean	Absolute Deviation (Distance Between Data and Mean)	Data Value	Mean	Absolute Deviation (Distance Between Data and Mean)
1	1	2.53	| 1 − 2.53 | = | − 1.53 | = 1.53	1	2.9	| 1 − 2.9 | = | − 1.9 | = 1.9
2	1	2.53	| 1 − 2.53 | = | − 1.53 | = 1.53	1	2.9	| 1 − 2.9 | = | − 1.9 | = 1.9
3	1	2.53	| 1 − 2.53 | = | − 1.53 | = 1.53	2	2.9	| 2 − 2.9 | = | − 0.9 | = 0.9
4	2	2.53	| 2 − 2.53 | = | − 0.53 | = 0.53	2	2.9	| 2 − 2.9 | = | − 0.9 | = 0.9
5	2	2.53	| 2 − 2.53 | = | − 0.53 | = 0.53	2	2.9	| 2 − 2.9 | = | − 0.9 | = 0.9
6	2	2.53	| 2 − 2.53 | = | − 0.53 | = 0.53	2	2.9	| 2 − 2.9 | = | − 0.9 | = 0.9
7	2	2.53	| 2 − 2.53 | = | − 0.53 | = 0.53	3	2.9	| 3 − 2.9 | = | 0.1 | = 0.1
8	2	2.53	| 2 − 2.53 | = | − 0.53 | = 0.53	3	2.9	| 3 − 2.9 | = | 0.1 | = 0.1
9	2	2.53	| 2 − 2.53 | = | − 0.53 | = 0.53	3	2.9	| 3 − 2.9 | = | 0.1 | = 0.1
10	2	2.53	| 2 − 2.53 | = | − 0.53 | = 0.53	3	2.9	| 3 − 2.9 | = | 0.1 | = 0.1
11	2	2.53	| 2 − 2.53 | = | − 0.53 | = 0.53	3	2.9	| 3 − 2.9 | = | 0.1 | = 0.1
12	3	2.53	| 3 − 2.53 | = | 0.47 | = 0.47	3	2.9	| 3 − 2.9 | = | 0.1 | = 0.1
13	3	2.53	| 3 − 2.53 | = | 0.47 | = 0.47	3	2.9	| 3 − 2.9 | = | 0.1 | = 0.1
14	3	2.53	| 3 − 2.53 | = | 0.47 | = 0.47	3	2.9	| 3 − 2.9 | = | 0.1 | = 0.1
15	4	2.53	| 4 − 2.53 | = | 1.47 | = 1.47	3	2.9	| 3 − 2.9 | = | 0.1 | = 0.1
16	4	2.53	| 4 − 2.53 | = | 1.47 | = 1.47	4	2.9	| 4 − 2.9 | = | 1.1 | = 1.1
17	4	2.53	| 4 − 2.53 | = | 1.47 | = 1.47	4	2.9	| 4 − 2.9 | = | 1.1 | = 1.1
18	4	2.53	| 4 − 2.53 | = | 1.47 | = 1.47	4	2.9	| 4 − 2.9 | = | 1.1 | = 1.1
19	4	2.53	| 4 − 2.53 | = | 1.47 | = 1.47	4	2.9	| 4 − 2.9 | = | 1.1 | = 1.1
20	NA	2.53	17.59	4	2.9	| 4 − 2.9 | = | 1.1 | = 1.1
Total	38	NA		58	NA	13.8
MAD			$\frac{17.59}{19} \approx 0.926$			$\frac{13.8}{20} = 0.69$

What inferences can she draw from the data?

1. On average, the scores for the morning class are 0.926 away from the mean. On average, the scores for the afternoon class are 0.69 units away from the mean. Since the MAD for the morning class is higher, that means the scores for the morning class are less consistent and have more variability. This also means that the spread of the data is larger in the morning class than the afternoon class.

2. For the morning and afternoon class, 50% of the data lie between 2 and 4. This does not tell us much about the data and the differences between them.

3. Since the mean for the afternoon class is higher, this means that students on averages score higher on the test than students in the morning class.

 PRACTICE

1. Below are the scores for the 2016 Olympics Women's Gymnastics All-Around Final Results. Create a dot plot to represent the data. Find the measures of central tendency (mean, median, and mode), measures of variability (range, IQR, and MAD), and draw conclusions by making qualitative inferences about the population.

Position	Gymnast	Country	Score
1	Simone Biles	United States	62.198
2	Aly Raisman	United States	60.098
3	Aliya Mustafina	Russia	58.665
4	Shang Chunsong	China	58.549
5	Elsabeth Black	Canada	58.298
6	Wang Yan	China	58.032
7	Jessica Brizeida Lopez-Arocha	Colombia	57.966
8	Asuka Teramoto	Japan	57.965
9	Eythora Thorsdottir	Netherlands	57.632
10	Giulia Steingruber	Switzerland	57.565

2. Below are the scores for the 2016 Olympics Men's 100-meter sprint scores. Create a dot plot to represent the data. Find the measures of central tendency (mean, median, and mode), measures of variability (range, IQR, and MAD) and draw conclusions by making qualitative inferences about the population

Rank	Participant	Result
G	Usain Bolt (JAM)	9.81
S	Justin Gatlin (USA)	9.89
B	Andre De Grasse (CAN)	9.91
4	Yohan Blake (JAM)	9.93
5	Akani Simbine (RSA)	9.94
6	Ben Youssef Meite (CIV)	9.96
7	Jimmy Vicaut (FRA)	10.04
8	Trayvon Bromell (USA)	10.06

3. Below are the fastest times for the top 10 runners for the 100-meter sprint at a local middle school. Create a dot plot to represent the data. Find the measures of central tendency (mean, median, and mode), measures of variability (range, IQR, and MAD), and draw conclusions by making qualitative inferences about the population.

12.44
12.5
12.84
13.18
12.26
14.27
14.32
15.08
15.16
15.32

Compare the measures of central tendency and variability. What factors do you think contribute to the differences? If you took the top runner's score from the middle school and place it with the Olympic 2016 scores, how would that affect the measures of tendency and variability? If you took Usain Bolt's score and mixed it in with the top scores from the middle school, how would his score affect the measures of central tendency and variability?

4. Death Valley in Nevada is the hottest and driest place in North America. Below is the mean temperature from the last 20 years. Create a dot plot to represent the data. Compare the measures of central tendency and variability from 2007–2016 and 1997–2006. What factors do you think contribute to these changes?

Year	Mean Temperature (°F)	Year	Mean Temperature (°F)
2016	79.2	2006	75.1
2015	78.1	2005	74.4
2014	80.4	2004	78.6
2013	81.0	2003	72.7
2012	78.5	2002	78.5
2011	76.4	2001	74.9
2010	73.2	2000	79.9
2009	75.5	1999	70.2
2008	77.6	1998	69.3
2007	79.3	1997	75.1

5. The North Pole is located at the center of the Northern Hemisphere. Create a dot plot to represent the data. Compare the measures of central tendency and variability from the last 10 years to 2007–2016 and 1970–1979. What factors do you think contribute to these changes?

Year	Mean Temperature (°F)	Year	Mean Temperature (°F)
2016	4.4	1979	-12.4
2015	-8.3	1978	-4.3
2014	4.6	1977	5.9
2013	-3.6	1976	-13.7
2012	-28.6	1975	-21.9
2011	-7.8	1974	-20.4
2010	-14.1	1973	-24.9
2009	-13.9	1972	-18.3
2008	-15.7	1971	-34.8
2007	-11.9	1970	-17.8

6. Palo Alto, California is the heart of the Silicon Valley. Create a box plot to represent the data. Compare the measures of central tendency and variability for the price per square foot for houses sold between the years 1998–2001 and 2016. What factors do you think contribute to these changes?

1998–2001	2016
174	2,058
231	1,343
242	1,314
252	1,366
281	1,746
308	1,665
328	2,186
330	1,437
331	1,792
343	1,545
361	1,655
362	1,127
369	1,109
	2,016
	1,619
	1,251
	1,802
	1,371
	1,454
	1,898

7. Atherton is the richest zip code in California. Below is the price per square foot for houses sold between January through March 2017. Create a dot plot to represent the data. Compare the measures of central tendency and variability to that of Palo Alto from January through March 2017. What conclusions can you draw from the data?

Price per Square Foot
1,939
1,891
1,721
1,683
1,675
1,648
1,611
1,521
1,471
1,460
1,459
1,432
1,429
1,402
1,359
1,322
1,301
1,199
1,170
1,147
1,119
1,102
1,003

(Answers are on pages 318–330.)

Lesson 6.4 Understanding Probability

Probability is the extent to which something is probable or likely to occur. It is the likelihood of something happening or being the case. It is measured by the ratio of the favorable cases to the whole number of cases possible. See the figure and table below for examples.

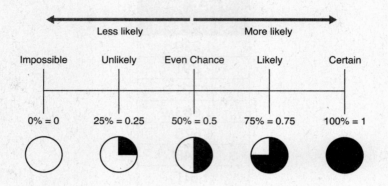

Probability	Example
0% = Impossible	1. It is impossible to roll a number higher than six on a six-sided die. 2. Since the bag does not contain a red marble, there is zero chance I will choose a red marble.
25% = Unlikely	1. Since the bag contains 15 yellow marbles and 5 blue marbles, it is unlikely I will choose a blue one without looking. 2. With over 500 raffle tickets that were sold, it is unlikely I will win if I only purchased 2. 3. It is unlikely that I will roll a sum of 2 if I roll two dice. 4. I have never been late to school. It is unlikely I will be late to school tomorrow.
50% = Even Chance	1. There is an even chance of flipping a heads or tails on a two-sided coin. 2. On a true/false exam, there is a 50% chance I will get the answer right. 3. Since the bag contains 10 yellow marbles and 10 blue marbles, there is a 50% chance I can choose a yellow marble without looking.

Probability	Example
75% = Likely	1. Since the bag contains 15 yellow marbles and 5 blue marbles, it is likely or a good chance I will choose a yellow marble without looking. 2. If there is a blizzard tomorrow and temperatures drop below freezing, it is likely there will be ice on the bridges. 3. As you drive toward higher elevation, there is a good chance your ears will pop.
100% = Certain	1. I am certain the sun will rise in the east and set in the west every day. 2. Since the bag contains 10 green marbles, there is a 100% chance I will choose a green marble.

 PRACTICE

Directions: Use the information provided to answer the questions. Tell whether the event is impossible, is unlikely, has an even chance, is likely, or is certain. Then approximate or calculate the probability. To calculate the probability, use the formula:

$$P(\text{event}) = \frac{\text{number of favorable events}}{\text{total number of possible events}}$$

For questions 1–6, use the spinner below.

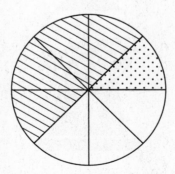

1.   What are the chances the spinner will end on a dotted, striped, or white space?

2.   What are the chances the spinner will land on the striped space?

3.   What are the chances the spinner will land on the dotted or white space?

4.   What are the chances the spinner will land on a solid space?

5.   What are the chances the spinner will land on the striped or white space?

6.   What are the chances the spinner will land on the dotted space?

For questions 7–11, use the following information.

Each deck has 52 cards and is composed of 26 red cards, 26 blue cards, and 13 of each suit: clubs, diamonds, hearts, and spades. Each suit consists of the numbers 1 through 10 and a jack, queen, and king. Each card is chosen at random and put back in the original deck for the next question.

7.   What are the chances of choosing a red card?

8.   What are the chances of choosing a spade?

9.   How likely is it that an ace is chosen?

10.   How likely is it that a jack, queen, or king is chosen?

11.   What are the chances of choosing a zero?

For questions 12–16, use the following information.

In a gumball machine, there are 25 stickers, 50 gumballs, 2 watches, and 23 bouncy balls.

Create a table to organize the information and find the probability of each event in the table.

12.   What are the chances of getting a watch?

13.   What is the likelihood of getting a gumball, sticker, or bouncy ball?

14. What are the chances of getting a keychain?

15. What the chances of getting a sticker or bouncy ball?

16. What are the chances of getting a sticker?

Create your own scenarios for the following probabilities:

17. 0	**20.** 0.4	**23.** 0.75	**26.** 1
18. 0.1	**21.** 0.5	**24.** 0.9	
19. 0.25	**22.** 0.6	**25.** 0.99	

(Answers are on pages 330–333.)

Lesson 6.5 Probability Models

There are two types of probability: **theoretical** and **experimental**. **Theoretical probability** is the likelihood of an event happening based on all the possible outcomes. The ratio for the probability of an event "P" occurring is $P(\text{event}) =$ number of favorable outcomes divided by the number of possible outcomes. **Experimental probability** is the ratio of the number of times an event occurs to the total number of trials the activity is performed.

The **sample space** is the range of values of a random variable or the set of all outcomes. The probabilities sum to 1.

In statistics, the **frequency** is the number of times a particular value for a variable has been observed to occur. The **absolute frequency** or **observed frequency** describes the number of times a particular value for a variable has been observed to occur. A **relative frequency** describes the number of times a particular variable has been observed to occur in relation to the total number of values for that variable. Relative frequency applies to situations that can be repeated over and over again.

Simple events are events where one experiment happens at a time and it will have a single outcome. The probability of simple events is denoted by $P(E)$ where E is the event. The probability will lie between 0 and 1. The sum of all simple events is equal to 1.

$$\text{Probability of an event} = P(\text{event}) = \frac{\text{number of successful/favorable outcomes}}{\text{total number of possible outcomes}}$$

For example, consider a die that has six sides numbered 1 through 6. The sample space is rolling a 1, 2, 3, 4, 5, or 6. There are six equally possible outcomes.

The theoretical probability of rolling each number is as follows:

Number Rolled	Theoretical Probability of Rolling the Number: $P(\text{event}) = \dfrac{\text{favorable outcomes}}{\text{total number of possible outcomes}}$	Explanation
1	$P(\text{rolling a 1}) = \dfrac{1}{6} \approx 0.167 \approx 16.7\%$	The theoretical probability of rolling a 1 is approximately 0.167.
2	$P(\text{rolling a 2}) = \dfrac{1}{6} \approx 0.167 \approx 16.7\%$	Theoretically, there is a 16.7% chance of rolling a 2.
3	$P(\text{rolling a 3}) = \dfrac{1}{6} \approx 0.167 \approx 16.7\%$	The theoretical probability of rolling a 3 is approximately 0.167.
4	$P(\text{rolling a 4}) = \dfrac{1}{6} \approx 0.167 \approx 16.7\%$	Theoretically, there is a 16.7% chance of rolling a 4.
5	$P(\text{rolling a 5}) = \dfrac{1}{6} \approx 0.167 \approx 16.7\%$	The theoretical probability of rolling a 5 is approximately 0.167.
6	$P(\text{rolling a 6}) = \dfrac{1}{6} \approx 0.167 \approx 16.7\%$	Theoretically, there is a 16.7% chance of rolling a 6.

Below is the experimental probability of rolling each number. The simple event is rolling a die because the die in this experiment is rolled 25 times. The sum of the relative frequency of rolling the die is 1.

Number Actually Rolled	Absolute Frequency (Observed Frequency)	Relative Frequency
1	3	$\dfrac{3}{25} = 0.12$
2	4	$\dfrac{4}{25} = 0.16$
3	5	$\dfrac{5}{25} = 0.2$
4	3	$\dfrac{3}{25} = 0.12$
5	4	$\dfrac{4}{25} = 0.16$
6	6	$\dfrac{6}{25} = 0.24$
Total	25	$\dfrac{25}{25} = 1$

The long-term frequency approaches the probability of the outcome. In other words, the relative frequency can be used to predict long-term proportions of times the outcome will occur. In the previous example, if the dice is rolled 500 more times, the relative frequencies of each number rolled will approach and be closer to 0.167 or 16.7%.

A probability model is used to assign probabilities to outcomes of a chance process by examining the nature of the process. For example, the probability model below is a relative frequency histogram for the experimental probability of rolling the die.

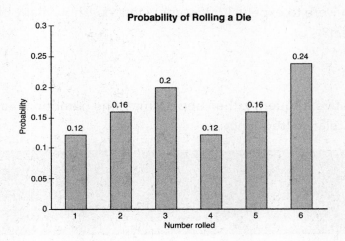

One type of probability model is called the **uniform probability model** where the probability is constant or the same for each event. In the example below, the probability for rolling any number 1 through 6 is approximately 0.167. In other words, theoretically there is a 16.7% chance that any of the numbers are rolled.

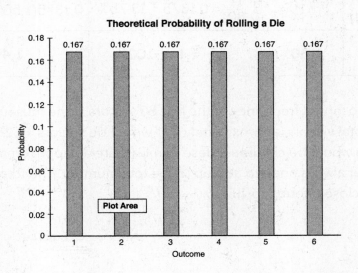

Approximating the relative frequency means that the frequency is approximated based on the relative frequency of the experiment. Consider the next example. Below is the observed frequency of the first 80 visitors at a museum.

Visitor Type	Observed Frequency
Seniors	23
Adults	46
Children (<12 years old)	11
Total	80

If the museum were to expect 1,500 visitors that day, how many of each visitor would they expect?

Solution

First find the relative frequency, then approximate the number of each type of visitor using the relative frequency.

Visitor Type	Observed Frequency	Relative Frequency	Approximating the Number of Each Number Based on the Relative Frequency
Seniors	23	$\frac{23}{80} = 0.2875 = 28.75\%$	$0.2875(1,500) = 431.25$
Adults	46	$\frac{46}{80} = 0.575 = 57.5\%$	$0.575(1,500) = 862.5$
Children (<12 years old)	11	$\frac{11}{80} = 0.1375 = 13.75\%$	$0.1375(1,500) = 206.25$
Total	80	$\frac{80}{80} = 1 = 100\%$	1,499

Based on the observed frequency of the first 80 visitors, if the museum were to expect 1,500 total visitors, approximately 431 would be seniors, 862 would be adults, and 206 would be children. These numbers are an approximation and therefore do not always need to add up to the total number. The total adds up to 1,499, which is close enough to 1,500.

PRACTICE

Directions: Use the information provided to answer the questions.

1.   A quarter has two sides: heads and tails

   A. What is the sample space?

   B. Is the probability model in part A uniform? Why or why not?

   C. What is the theoretical probability of flipping a coin and having it land on heads or tails? Construct a probability model for flipping the coin.

   D. You flip a coin 50 times. It lands on heads 23 times and tails 27 times. Find the relative frequency of both events and construct a probability model for the experimental probability of flipping the coin.

   E. Based on your relative frequency, how many times will the coin land on heads or tails if you flip it 200 more times?

   F. What is the long-term frequency of this situation?

2.   A bag contains 3 red marbles, 7 blue marbles, 4 green marbles, and 6 yellow marbles.

   A. What is the probability of selecting each colored marble? Construct a probability model for selecting each colored marble.

   B. Is the probability model in part A a uniform one? Why or why not?

   C. Jenna randomly draws a marble from the bag and returns it once the color is recorded. She repeats this process 50 times. Find the approximate frequency of each color she picked and construct a probability model to represent her experiment.

   D. What does the long-term frequency mean in this situation?

   E. What are external factors that could explain the discrepancy between the theoretical and experimental probability of these events?

3.   Two dice are rolled. Each die is numbered 1–6.

   A. What is the sample space?

   B. What is the probability that each sum is rolled? Tally up the frequency of each sum and find the probability of each sum. Construct a probability model.

Sum of the Dice	Number of Favorable Events	Probability of Each Event
2	1	
3	2	
4	3	
5	4	
6	5	
7	6	
8	5	
9	4	
10	3	
11	2	
12	1	
Total	36	

C. Is the probability model in part B a uniform one?

D. Amelia, Kelly, Ryan, and Angelia are playing a board game where they record each sum that is rolled. The table below shows the results of the event. Find the relative frequency of each sum rolled and construct a probability model.

Sum of the Dice	Observed Frequency	Relative Frequency
2	1	
3	2	
4	3	
5	4	
6	9	
7	8	
8	6	
9	5	
10	6	
11	1	
12	0	
Total	45	

E. What does the long-term frequency mean in this situation?

F. What are external factors that could explain the discrepancy between the theoretical and experimental probability of these events?

4. Mrs. Massaro works with a small group of eight students. Each day, she chooses a volunteer at random to be the teacher assistant.

A. What is the sample space?

B. What is the theoretical probability of each student being chosen? Construct a probability model for each student's name being drawn.

C. Is the probability model in part B a uniform probability model?

D. Mrs. Massaro randomly draws the students' names every day and returns each name back to the bag once it has been recorded. The table below shows the results for the last 30 days. Find the relative frequency of each student and construct a probability model to represent the data.

Student	Observed Frequency	Relative Frequency
Zach	3	
Sonia	6	
Jason	2	
Medha	3	
Niel	5	
Andrew	4	
Hinako	5	
Evo	2	
Total	30	

E. What does the long-term frequency mean in this situation?

F. What are external factors that could explain the discrepancy between the theoretical and experimental probability of these events? Approximate the probability using relative frequency.

5. The table shows the relative frequency of how the students commuted to school on a particular day. There were 340 students at the school on that day.

Type of Transportation	Relative Frequency
Walk	0.25 = 85
Bike	0.3 = 102
Car—No Carpool	0.35 = 119
Car—Carpool	0.1 = 34
Total	1 = 340

   A. How many students were there for each category?

   B. How many more students biked than walked?

   C. How many more students rode in a car but did not carpool?

6. The table shows the relative frequency of how many customers ordered different kinds of drinks at the local boba (bubble drink) store. There were 900 customers that day.

Type of Drink	Relative Frequency
Original Milk Tea with Boba	0.42
Thai Ice Tea with Boba	0.26
Other	0.32
Total	1

   A. How many customers ordered each type of drink?

   B. How many more customers ordered the original milk tea than the Thai iced tea?

(Answers are on pages 333–339.)

Lesson 6.6 Probability of Compound Events

A **compound event** is one in which there is more than one possible outcome. Determining the probability of a compound event involves finding the sum of the probabilities of the individual events, and, if necessary, removing any overlapping probabilities.

You can use organized lists, tables, tree diagrams, or simulations.

Example 1   At the local frozen yogurt store, you can choose from the following flavors: chocolate, vanilla, or strawberry and one of the following toppings: sprinkles, mochi, or blueberries. Draw a tree diagram to represent the following combinations of frozen yogurt you can get if you choose one flavor and one topping. What is the probability of choosing chocolate and mochi?

Solution

The answer is **1/9**.

First, create a tree diagram with all of the options. Remember to label each column. The last column is your outcome.

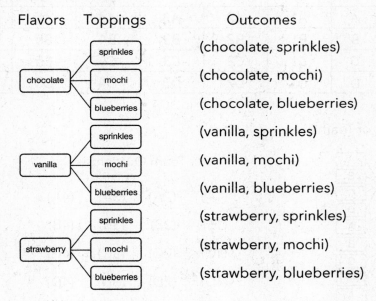

Next, count the total number of outcomes and check the outcome the problem is looking for. In this case, there is only one combo of chocolate and mochi.

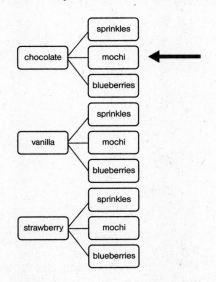

Example 2   Students choose their teams by first randomly selecting a letter from letters A through D. Then they roll a six-sided fair die. Kaia has a friend on team D6. Draw a table or a tree diagram to represent all the possible teams. What is the probability she will be on her friend's team?

Solution

There is a **1/24 chance** Kaia will be on her friend's team.

Letters	Each Side of the Die					
	1	2	3	4	5	6
A	A1	A2	A3	A4	A5	A6
B	B1	B2	B3	B4	B5	B6
C	C1	C2	C3	C4	C5	C6
D	D1	D2	D3	D4	D5	D6

Number of Teams

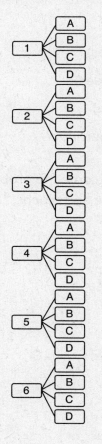

Team Outcomes

(1A)   (2A)   (3A)   (4A)

(1B)   (2B)   (3B)   (4B)

(1C)   (2C)   (3C)   (4C)

(1D)   (2D)   (3D)   (4D)

 **PRACTICE**

Directions: Use probability to answer the following questions.

1. Stella is trying to choose a name for her new puppy. She likes the consonants K, S, T, and M, and the vowels A, E, and U as her second letter. Her friend Nico is trying to guess the name of the puppy. What is the probability he will guess a name that starts with a K or has an A as the second letter?

2. A fair coin is tossed three times. What is the probability it will land on either all heads or all tails?

3. A fair coin is tossed four times. What is the probability it will land on at least two heads?

4. Two six-sided fair dice are rolled. What is the probability they will land on a sum that is greater than 8?

5. Two six-sided fair dice are rolled. What is the probability they will land on an even sum?

6. Jenna's little brother is only 2 and is choosing his own hat and T-shirt. What is the probability he will choose matching hats and T-shirts if he has a red, green, orange, and blue hat and the same color shirts?

7. Amelia wants to order a cake for her best friend Kelly and is not sure what flavor to order. She can choose a chocolate, strawberry, lemon, or vanilla cake with the following toppings: strawberries, cookies, or sprinkles. What are the odds Amelia will pick her friend's favorite combination?

8. Angelina is ordering monogram beach towels but does not want the same color as her sister. She can choose between red, orange, yellow, blue, green, or purple beach towels with gray, black, or white letters. She can also choose to add decorative polka dots, stripes, or checkered patterns at the end of her towel. What are the odds that she will choose the exact same custom design as her sister?

9. Create your own problem that has a solution of one-half.

10. Create your own problem that has a solution of one-eighth.

(Answers are on pages 339–342.)

Practice Test

CHAPTER

7

Computer-Adaptive Test

Directions: On the actual SBAC Grade 7 Math exam, the instructions will inform you about the rules and navigation of the test. These instructions include the fact that you cannot skip questions, and all questions on one page must be answered before moving on to the next page. In addition, you will be able to flag or mark a question to review later or before submitting your test. Good luck!

1. Honeybees consume about 8.4 pounds of honey to secrete one pound of wax. It takes about 2.6 pounds of wax to construct about 100,000 cells of a honeycomb. Enter the pounds of honey the honeybees need to construct 100,000 cells.

2. Bryan is trying to figure out his final score on an exam. He got 20 problems correct that were worth 3.5 points each, 7 problems correct that were worth 5 points each, and only showed one method on 9 of the problems and knows he will be deducted 1.25 points each for those. For 3 of the problems, he found the solution but could not think of the equation so he will be deducted 0.75 points each for those problems. Write a numerical expression for this situation. If the exam is out of 110, enter his score to the nearest percent.

3. Simplify the following expression:

$-4(3x - 2y) - 0.1(5y - 20x) - \frac{3}{4}(12x - y)$

4. The sum of 5 consecutive odd numbers is 205. Enter an equation and solve for the five numbers.

5. What is the original cost of a printer if the total cost including tax is $269.54? The sales tax is 8.25%.

- ○ A. $22.91
- ○ B. $249.00
- ○ C. $246.63
- ○ D. $498.65

6. Jane is trying to pack a care package for her brother. She wants to include books that weigh 4.5 pounds total. Each item of clothing weighs about 6.25 ounces. She needs to stay under nine pounds or she will be charged an additional fee. Select the number of pieces of clothing she will include without going over the weight limit? One pound = 16 ounces.

   O A. 8
   O B. 9
   O C. 10
   O D. 11

7. Triangle B is a scaled image of Triangle A. The dimensions of Triangle A are 3 cm, 4 cm, and 5 cm, and the dimensions of Triangle B are 12 cm, 16 cm, and 20 cm. What is the scale factor?

   O A. 4
   O B. $\frac{1}{4}$
   O C. 5
   O D. 3

8. How many triangles can be created from the following information: $AB = 4$ cm and $AC = 5$ cm?

   O A. 0
   O B. 1
   O C. 2
   O D. 3

9. Kirill is working on a science project and is trying to figure out the rate of evaporation. If his water was reduced by 60% to 400 mL, how much water did he start with?

   O A. 640 mL
   O B. 560 mL
   O C. 1000 mL
   O D. 840 mL

10. Evaluate and enter the solution: $-0.2 - (-0.02) - \frac{1}{2} \div -2(-0.2) + 20\%$.

11. $-\frac{12}{28} \div \left(-\frac{6}{12}\right) \div \left(-\frac{5}{10}\right) = $ _____.

Directions: For the following problems, write an expression and draw a number line to represent each scenario.

12. Kate picks and cleans up after her disobedient puppy for $\frac{1}{6}$ hour each day. How many hours has she lost after one week?

13. For a science experiment, Camila needs $3\frac{1}{2}$ cups of salt. She only has $1\frac{7}{8}$ cups. How many cups is she short?

14. A chocolate bar has 98 calories. Three-tenths of it is sugar. How many calories of sugar does it have?

15. Ellen has a rain catcher and caught $3\frac{1}{2}$ inches of rain on Monday. She lost $\frac{3}{8}$ inch due to condensation. She got another $2\frac{5}{6}$ inches and lost another $\frac{2}{3}$ inch. How much water is left in her rain catcher?

16. Annalise is building a $\frac{1}{480}$ scale model shipping container out of building blocks. If the actual shipping container is 1,200 feet, how long is her model?

17. It takes Jeshua $\frac{7}{8}$ gallons of gas to and from school. If an average tank can hold 13 gallons, how many trips can he make before he needs to get gas?

Directions: For each problem, write an expression to represent the situation and then solve.

18. Kevin receives donations for his dog rescue center. He received seven donations at $25 each. With the funds, he purchased two dog beds at $42 each. He received three more donations at $20 each. Write an expression to show the total he has left and then solve. _____.

19. Chloe's credit card bill is deducted from her checking account each month. From January through June, her deductions are as follows: −134.34, −210.90, −325.12, −125.76, −253.24, −97.00. On average, how much does she charge on her credit card each month? _____.

20. Jake emptied his piggy bank and has 52 nickels, 67 pennies, 37 quarters, and 14 dimes. Does he have enough for two movie tickets at $7.50 each? How much is he over or under? _____.

21. Abby is grading her math quiz. She gets 2.5 points for each problem she answers correctly, −1.5 point for each problem she answers incorrectly, and −2.25 points for each problem she skips. If she got 12 problems correct, 3 problems incorrect, and skipped 1 problem, how many points did she get on her math quiz? _____.

22. Kaitlyn's snail crawled 0.25 inches the first day, 0.8 inches the second day, 1.32 inches the third, and 1.05 inches the fourth. On average, how many inches did Kaitlyn's snail crawl each day? _____.

23. Isabella wants to bake cookies for her class. She needs 2.5 cups of chocolate chips for each batch. She plans on making three batches but only has 4.25 cups at home.

A. How many cups is she short? [ ]

B. Each bag of chocolate chips contains $3\frac{3}{4}$ cups of chocolate chips. How many more bags will she need? How many cups will she have left over after she uses what she needs from the bag? _____.

24. What is the largest number you can create from the following numbers using one set of parentheses and each operation once: 2, 3, 4, 5? _____.

25. What is the smallest number you can create from the following numbers using one set of parentheses and each operation once: 2, 3, 4, 5? _____.

26. Create your own problem with a solution of 1. Include at least one decimal, percent, fraction, integer, and all the operations. _____.

27. What is halfway between $\frac{1}{2}$ and $\frac{1}{4}$? [ ]

28. What is halfway between $-\frac{3}{4}$ and $-\frac{5}{6}$? [ ]

29. The sum of 4 consecutive odd numbers is 80.

What are all 4 numbers? _____.

30. The sum of 3 consecutive even numbers is 48.

What are all 3 numbers? _____.

31. Henry's frisbee costs $1.45 more than his squeaky ball. If the total cost was $4.75, what was the cost of each? _____ and _____.

32. The perimeter of a rectangle is 36 inches. If the length is one less than four times the width, what is the length and width? _____.

(Answers are on pages 343–351.)

Performance Task

Directions: On the actual SBAC Grade 7 Math exam, the instructions will inform you about the rules and navigation of the test. These instructions include the fact that you cannot skip questions, and all questions on one page must be answered before moving on to the next page. In addition, you will be able to flag or mark a question to review later on before submitting your test.

1. Kirsten makes a soy latte every morning before going to work and uses one cup of soy milk. She buys three half gallons (1.89 liters) for $8.99. How much does she spend on soy milk in one year? There are 365 days in a year and 4 cups in one liter.

2. Kassy is at an arcade and paid $0.75 for a 3-token game and $1.25 for a 5-token game. Does this situation represent a direct proportion? If so, find the constant of proportionality, which means an equation for the situation, and find out how much she would spend if she used 24 more tokens.

3. Find the missing angles in the quadrilateral given. *AB* is parallel to *EF* and *EF* is parallel to *DC*.

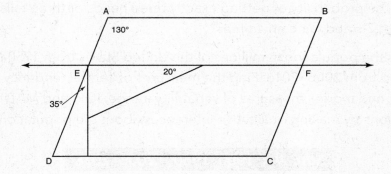

4. The width of a rectangle is two-fifths of its length. Find the area if the perimeter is 44.8 cm. Write your equations to support the situation and solve algebraically.

5. The volume of a square pyramid is 864 cm^3. What are the dimensions of the base area if the height is 18 cm?

6. Kaia is filling the triangular prism below with candy for a friend's birthday. How much wrapping paper and candy does she need?

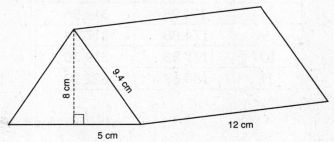

7. Three congruent circles fit inside a larger circle shown below. Find the area and perimeter of the shaded region.

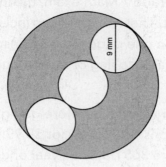

9 mm

8. The local indoor playground has a snack bar and the owner is trying to figure out how much of each item to stock for the children. The past Saturday, there were 145 children. Of the 145 children, 47 ordered pizza, 32 ordered hot dogs, and 66 ordered chicken fingers. What is the relative frequency of each order? If the owner expects about 1,800 children to come in each month, how much of each item should he have ready?

9. What is the probability of getting exactly three heads or three tails when flipping a 2-sided fair coin 4 times?

10. Below is the population in millions of the United States from 1950 through 1960 and from 2006–2016. Find the measures of central tendency (mean, median, and mode), measures of variability (range, IQR, and MAD) and draw conclusions by making qualitative inferences about the population.

Data #	1950-1960	2006-2016
1	152.27	298.38
2	154.88	301.23
3	157.55	304.09
4	160.18	306.77
5	163.03	308.11
6	165.93	310.45
7	168.90	312.76
8	171.98	314.96
9	174.88	317.34
10	177.83	319.70
11	180.67	321.93

(Answers are on pages 352–357.)

Answers Explained

Chapter 1 Rational Numbers

Lesson 1.1: Integer Operations

1.1A: Adding and Subtracting Positive and Negative Integers
Practice, pages 13–14

1. $-18 + 6 = \mathbf{-12}$

2. $-23 + 36 = \mathbf{13}$

3. $-19 + -28 = \mathbf{-47}$

4. $-102 + -234 = \mathbf{-336}$

5. $-19 - (-25) = -19 + 25 = \mathbf{+6}$

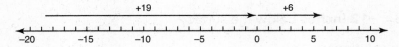

6. $-123 - (-432) = -123 + 432 = \mathbf{309}$

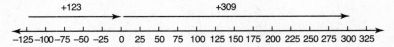

7. $-7 - (-9) - 10 = -7 + 9 + (-10) = \mathbf{-8}$

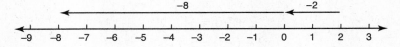

8. $8 - (-11) - 19 = 8 + 11 + (-19) = 8 + 11 + (-19) = \mathbf{0}$

9. $-19 - (25) + 14 - 82 = -19 + (-25) + 14 + (-82) = \mathbf{-112}$

10. $-12 - 18 - (-25) = -12 + (-18) + 25 = -30 + 25 = \mathbf{-5}$

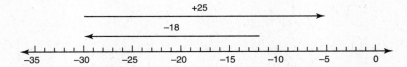

11. −345 + 168 = **−177 feet** below sea level

12. −789 − 231 = −789 + (−231) = **−1,020 feet** below sea level

13. 108 − (−15) = 108 + 15 = **123 degrees**

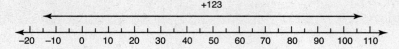

14. −4 + 12 = **8 degrees warmer**

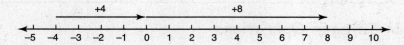

15. The golfer's total score is **−10**.

    −4 + (−5) + (−1) = −10

16. 23 − 16 + 3 − 7 = **3 yards change**

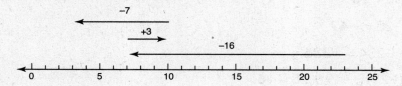

17. −15 + 3 = **−12 inches** below the surface

18. Possible solutions:

$$8 + (−3) = 5$$
$$4 − (−1) = 5$$
$$2 − (−3) = 5$$
$$3 − (−2) = 5$$

19. Answers will vary.

$$2 + −3 = −1$$
$$2 − (−3) = 5$$
$$−3 + 2 = −1$$
$$−3 − 2 = −5$$

20. Answers will vary. Possible solution: −10 + 20 + (30) + −40 = 0

1.1B: Multiplying and Dividing Positive and Negative Integers

Practice, pages 16–17

1. $(-3)(-5) = $ **15**
2. $(-3)(5) = $ **–15**
3. $15 \div (-3) = $ **–5**
4. $(11)(-11) = $ **–121**
5. $28 \div -4 = $ **–7**
6. $(-15)(-15) = $ **225**
7. $-100 \div (-5) = $ **20**
8. $(-1)(-1)(-1) = $ **–1**
9. $(-1)(-1)(-1)(-1) = $ **1**
10. $(-2)(-3)(-5)(-6)(-1) = $ **–180**
11. Jade received a total deduction of **6 points** for not showing her work.

    $-1(6) = $ **–6**

    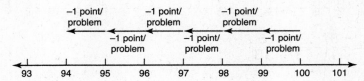

12. Tammy has **$21 less** in her wallet after she pays for the Starbucks drinks.

    $-3(7) = $ **–21**

13. Jeshua's cell phone bill will cost him **$1,380.00** for one year.

    $-115(12) = $ **–1,380**

14. Eric descends **24.5 ft.** per hour. $-98 \div 4 = $ **–24.5**

15. Tasmin descended **24 feet** in 1 hour.

    $5 \text{ min}(12) = 60 \text{ min}, 1 \text{ hour}$

    $-2(12) = $ **–24**

    Each arrow segment represents a 2 foot descent every 5 minutes.
    5 minutes goes into 60 minutes 12 times. Therefore, 2 foot descent occurs 12 times.

16. After 4 hours, Zoe's scarves will be sold for **$9**. $13 - 4(1) = $ **9**

17. Answers will vary. $-48 \div 6 = \textbf{-8}$

-48 can be divided into 6 equal groups. There are -8 units in each group.

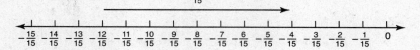

18. Possible answers: $-2(4)$, $4(-2)$, $1(-8)$, $-1(8)$

19. Possible answers: $(-12)(-1)(-1)$, $3(4)(-1)$, $1(3)(-4)$, $(-6)(1)(2)$

20. Possible answers: $(24)(1)(1)(-1)$, $(24)(-1)(-1)(-1)$, $2(-2)(-2)(-3)$, $4(-6)(-1)(-1)$

Lesson 1.2: Fraction Operations

Practice, pages 20–21

1. $-\dfrac{3}{5} \div -\dfrac{6}{15} = -\dfrac{3}{5}\left(-\dfrac{15}{6}\right) = \dfrac{\textbf{3}}{\textbf{2}}$

2. $-\dfrac{4}{5} - \left(-\dfrac{8}{15}\right) = -\dfrac{4}{5} + \dfrac{8}{15} = -\dfrac{12}{15} + \dfrac{8}{15} = -\dfrac{\textbf{4}}{\textbf{15}}$

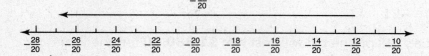

3. $-\dfrac{3}{5}\left(-\dfrac{10}{13}\right) = -\dfrac{3}{1}\left(-\dfrac{2}{13}\right) = \dfrac{\textbf{6}}{\textbf{13}}$

4. $-\dfrac{3}{5} - \dfrac{3}{4} = -\dfrac{3}{5} + \left(-\dfrac{3}{4}\right) = -\dfrac{12}{20} + \left(-\dfrac{15}{20}\right) = -\dfrac{\textbf{27}}{\textbf{20}}$

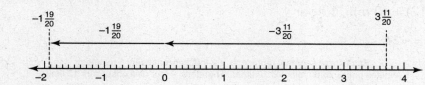

5. $-\dfrac{9}{26} - \left(-\dfrac{2}{13}\right) = -\dfrac{9}{26} + \dfrac{2}{13} = -\dfrac{9}{26} + \dfrac{4}{26} = -\dfrac{\textbf{5}}{\textbf{26}}$

6. $3\dfrac{11}{20} + \left(-\dfrac{11}{2}\right) = 3\dfrac{11}{20} + \left(-\dfrac{11}{2}\right) = 3\dfrac{11}{20} - 5\dfrac{1}{2} = -5\dfrac{10}{20} + 3\dfrac{11}{20} = -4\dfrac{30}{20} + 3\dfrac{11}{20} = -\textbf{1}\dfrac{\textbf{19}}{\textbf{20}}$

7. $-\dfrac{7}{5} - \left(-\dfrac{5}{6}\right) = -\dfrac{42}{30} + \dfrac{25}{30} = -\dfrac{\textbf{17}}{\textbf{30}}$

8. $-\dfrac{3}{5} - \dfrac{6}{15} = -\dfrac{9}{15} + \left(-\dfrac{6}{15}\right) = -\dfrac{15}{15} = \mathbf{-1}$

9. $-\dfrac{4}{5} \div \left(-\dfrac{8}{15}\right) = -\dfrac{4}{5}\left(-\dfrac{15}{8}\right) = -\dfrac{4}{1}\left(-\dfrac{3}{8}\right) = -\dfrac{1}{1}\left(-\dfrac{3}{2}\right) = \dfrac{\mathbf{3}}{\mathbf{2}}$

10. $-\dfrac{3}{5} + \left(-\dfrac{10}{13}\right) = -\dfrac{39}{65} + \left(-\dfrac{50}{65}\right) = -\dfrac{\mathbf{89}}{\mathbf{65}}$

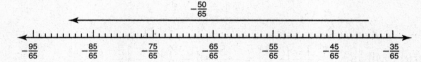

11. $-\dfrac{3}{5} \div \dfrac{3}{4} = -\dfrac{3}{5}\left(\dfrac{4}{3}\right) = -\dfrac{1}{5}\left(\dfrac{4}{1}\right) = -\dfrac{\mathbf{4}}{\mathbf{5}}$.

12. $-\dfrac{9}{26} - \dfrac{2}{13} = -\dfrac{9}{26} + \left(-\dfrac{4}{26}\right) = -\dfrac{13}{26} = -\dfrac{\mathbf{1}}{\mathbf{2}}$

13. $\dfrac{6}{26} \div \left(-\dfrac{12}{2}\right) = \dfrac{6}{26}\left(-\dfrac{2}{12}\right) = \dfrac{1}{26}\left(-\dfrac{2}{2}\right) = \dfrac{1}{13}\left(-\dfrac{1}{2}\right) = -\dfrac{\mathbf{1}}{\mathbf{26}}$

14. $-\dfrac{4}{6} + \dfrac{8}{5} = -\dfrac{20}{30} + \dfrac{48}{30} = \dfrac{28}{30} = \dfrac{\mathbf{14}}{\mathbf{15}}$

15. $-\dfrac{1}{2}\left(-\dfrac{1}{2}\right)\left(-\dfrac{1}{2}\right) = -\dfrac{\mathbf{1}}{\mathbf{8}}$

16. $-\dfrac{1}{2}\left(-\dfrac{1}{2}\right)\left(-\dfrac{1}{2}\right)\left(-\dfrac{1}{2}\right) = \dfrac{\mathbf{1}}{\mathbf{16}}$

17. $-\dfrac{12}{28}\left(-\dfrac{6}{12}\right)\left(-\dfrac{5}{10}\right)\left(\dfrac{3}{4}\right) = -\dfrac{\mathbf{9}}{\mathbf{112}}$

18. $-\dfrac{1}{2} - \dfrac{1}{2} - \dfrac{1}{2} = -\dfrac{1}{2} + \left(-\dfrac{1}{2}\right) + \left(-\dfrac{1}{2}\right) = -\dfrac{\mathbf{3}}{\mathbf{2}}$

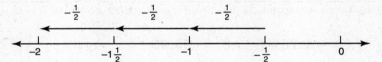

19. $A = \text{length(width)}$

    $A = 4\dfrac{5}{6}\left(3\dfrac{3}{5}\right) = \dfrac{29}{6}\left(\dfrac{18}{5}\right) = \dfrac{87}{5} = \mathbf{17.4}$ units squared

20. Tina can make **five** batches of cookies.

    $$12\dfrac{1}{2} \div 2\dfrac{1}{4} = \dfrac{25}{2} \div \dfrac{9}{4} = \dfrac{25}{2} \times \dfrac{4}{9} = \dfrac{50}{9} = 5\dfrac{5}{9}$$

    She will have $\mathbf{1\dfrac{1}{4}}$ **cups** of sugar left.

    $$12\dfrac{1}{2} - 5\left(2\dfrac{1}{4}\right) = 12\dfrac{2}{4} - \dfrac{5}{1}\left(\dfrac{9}{4}\right) = \dfrac{50}{4} - \dfrac{45}{4} = \dfrac{5}{4}$$

21. Stefani gave away $\frac{7}{8}$ of the bag of red rope candy she had.

    She has $\frac{1}{8}$ of a bag left.

    $$1\left(\frac{1}{2}\right)\left(\frac{1}{4}\right) = \frac{1}{8}$$

    $$1 - \frac{1}{8} = \frac{8}{8} - \frac{1}{8} = \frac{7}{8}$$

22. Scenarios will vary. $-\frac{1}{2} + \left(-\frac{4}{5}\right) = -\frac{5}{10} + \left(-\frac{8}{10}\right) = -\frac{13}{10}$

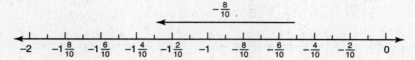

23. Scenarios will vary. $12\left(\frac{3}{8}\right) = \frac{12}{1}\left(\frac{3}{8}\right) = \frac{9}{2}$

Lesson 1.3: Decimal Operations

Practice, page 25

1. $-4.5 + 2.7 = \textbf{-1.8}$

2. $-4.5 - 2.7 = -4.5 + (-2.7) = \textbf{-7.2}$

3. $-4.5 - (-2.7) = -4.5 + 2.7 = \textbf{-1.8}$

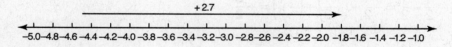

4. $-18.23 - 17.8 = -18.23 + (-17.8) = \textbf{-36.03}$

5. $-18.23 - (-17.8) = -18.23 + 17.8 = \textbf{-0.43}$

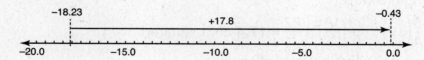

6. $-18.23 + 17.8 = \textbf{-0.43}$

7. $-6.3 - 9.1 - (-2.8) = -6.3 + (-9.1) + 2.8 = -15.4 + 2.8 = \textbf{-12.6}$

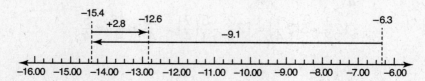

8. $0.21 \div -0.3 = \mathbf{-0.7}$

9. $(-0.11)(0.3) = \mathbf{-0.033}$

10. $-0.2 \div -0.3 = \dfrac{\mathbf{2}}{\mathbf{3}}$

11. $0.3 \div -0.2 = -\dfrac{\mathbf{3}}{\mathbf{2}}$

12. $(-0.1)(-0.1)(-0.1)(-0.1) = \mathbf{0.0001}$

13. $(-0.2)(-0.2)(-0.2)(-0.2)(-0.2) = \mathbf{-0.00032}$

14. Kevin owes the candy store **$11.72**.

    $-3.58 + (-8.14) = -11.72$

15. Apple stock fell **$2.20** in two days.

    $-0.88 + (-1.32) = -2.2$

    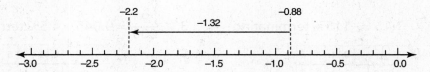

16. The difference between the two is **6.476 km**.

    $6.194 - (-0.282) = 6.194 + 0.282 = 6.476$

    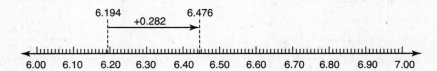

17. No, Tyson is **short 85 cents**.

    $25 - (5.95 + 11.95 + 7.95) = 25 - 5.95 - 11.95 - 7.95 = -0.85.$

    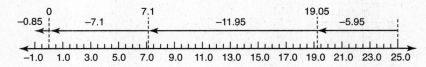

18. The African giant snail is **13.1 times** longer than an average garden snail.

    $39.3 \div 3 = 13.1.$

19. William has **1.95 points**. $12(1.25) + 9(-1.45) = 15 + (-13.05) = \mathbf{1.95 \text{ points}}$

20. Olivia has descended **-62.5 feet**. $-12.5(5) = \mathbf{-62.5 \text{ feet}}$

21. Jake descended **4.5 feet** after one hour.

$$-0.75(6) = -4.5$$

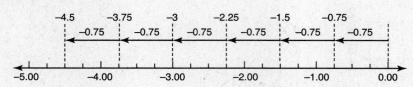

22. Word problems will vary. Possible solution: **−6.6**

23. Word problems will vary. Possible solution: **−9.2**

Lesson 1.4: Fractions, Decimals, and Percents

Practice (used with *CalculatorSoup.com*), pages 28–29

1. $-\dfrac{23}{20} = -1.15 = -115\%$ terminating

			−	0	1.	1	5
−	2	0	+	2	3.	0	0
			−		0		
				2	3		
			−	2	0		
					3	0	
				−	2	0	
					1	0	0
				−	1	0	0
							0

3. $\dfrac{9}{200} = 0.045 = 4.5\%$ terminating

			0.	0	4	5
2	0	0	9.	0	0	0
			−	0		
			9	0		
			−		0	
			9	0	0	
			−	8	0	0
			1	0	0	0
			−	1	0	0	0
						0

2. $8\dfrac{3}{5} = 8.6 = 860\%$ terminating

		0	8.	6
5	4	3.	0	
	−	0		
		4	3	
	−	4	0	
			3	0
		−	3	0
				0

4. $-1\dfrac{1}{8} = -1.125 = -112.5\%$ terminating

5.　$\dfrac{2}{9} = 0.\overline{2}$ repeating

6.　$-\dfrac{56}{99} = -0.\overline{56}$ repeating

7.　$\dfrac{4}{33} = 0.\overline{12} = 12.12\%$ repeating

8.　$-\dfrac{9}{11} = -0.\overline{81}$ repeating

			−	0.	8	1	8	1
−	1	1	+	9.	0	0	0	0
			−		0			
					9	0		
				−	8	8		
						2	0	
					−	1	1	
							9	0
						−	8	8
								2	0
							−	1	1
									9

9.　$\dfrac{3}{125} = 0.024 = 2.4\%$ terminating

			0.	0	2	4
1	2	5	3.	0	0	0
			−	0		
				3	0	
			−		0	
				3	0	0
			−	2	5	0
					5	0	0
				−	5	0	0
							0

10. The correct answers are **D** and **E**. They are **equivalent**.

    D. $-\dfrac{-2}{-3} = -\dfrac{2}{3}$

    E. $-66\dfrac{2}{3}\% = -\dfrac{2}{3}$

11. All are equivalent.

    A. $0.125 = 125 \text{ thousandths} = \dfrac{125}{1000} = \dfrac{1}{8}$

    B. $\dfrac{-1}{-8} = \dfrac{1}{8}$

    C. $12.5\% = \dfrac{12.5}{100} = \dfrac{125}{1000} = \dfrac{1}{8}$

    D. $-\dfrac{1}{-8} = \dfrac{1}{8}$

    E. $\dfrac{2}{16} = \dfrac{1}{8}$

12. The answers are **A**, **C**, **D**, and **E**.

    A. $750\% = \dfrac{750}{100} = \dfrac{75}{10} = \dfrac{15}{2} = \mathbf{7.5}$

    B. $7500\% = \dfrac{7500}{100} = \dfrac{75}{1} = \mathbf{75}$

    C. $7\dfrac{1}{2} = \mathbf{7.5}$

    D. $\dfrac{15}{2} = \mathbf{7.5}$

    E. $\dfrac{-15}{-2} = \dfrac{15}{2} = \mathbf{7.5}$

13. $0.875, 87.5\%, \dfrac{14}{16}, \dfrac{21}{24}, \dfrac{70}{80}$

14. $-1.5, -150\%, \dfrac{-3}{2}, \dfrac{3}{-2}, -1\dfrac{1}{2}$

15. $-0.75, -75\%, \dfrac{-3}{4}, \dfrac{3}{-4}, -\dfrac{-3}{-4}$

Lesson 1.5: Order of Operations

Practice, page 30

1. $-2 \underline{- 2 \div 2} \times 2 + 2 - 2 \div 2$
   $-2 \underline{- 1 \times 2} + 2 - 2 \div 2$
   $-2 - 2 + 2 \underline{- 2 \div 2}$
   $\underline{-2 - 2} + 2 - 1$
   $\underline{-4 + 2} - 1$
   $-2 - 1$
   $-2 + -1$
   $\mathbf{-3}$

2. $\underline{10 \div -10}(-10) - 10 + 10 \div (-10)(-10)$
   $\underline{-1(-10)} - 10 + 10 \div (-10)(-10)$
   $10 - 10 + \underline{10 \div (-10)}(-10)$
   $10 - 10 + \underline{10 \div (-10)}(-10)$
   $10 - 10 + \underline{-1(-10)}$
   $\underline{10 - 10} + 10$
   $0 + 10$
   $\mathbf{10}$

3. $\dfrac{0.25 \div -0.5(0.5) \div (-5)}{}$

$-0.5(0.5) \div (-5)$

$-0.25 \div (-5)$

0.05

4. $\underline{-0.1 \div 0.1}(0.1) - 0.1$

$-1(0.1) - 0.1$

$-0.1 - 0.1$

−0.2

5. $-0.8 - (-0.04) \div 2(20\%) + 1.6 \div \dfrac{2}{5}$

$-0.8 + 0.04 \div 2(0.2) + 1.6 \div 0.4$

Convert to decimal

$-0.8 + \underline{0.04 \div 2}(0.2) + 1.6 \div 0.4$

$-0.8 + \underline{0.02(0.2)} + 1.6 \div 0.4$

$-0.8 + 0.004 + 4$

3.204

6. $\underline{-10(-10)} \div 10(10) \div 10$

$\underline{100 \div 10}(10) \div 10$

$\underline{10(10)} \div 10$

$100 \div 10$

10

7. $\dfrac{1 \div -1 - (-1)(-1)}{}$

$-1 - \underline{(-1)(-1)}$

$-1 - 1$

$-1 + -1$

−2

8. $\dfrac{1}{10} \div 0.1(10\%) - \dfrac{1}{10}$

$0.1 \div 0.1(0.1) - 0.1$

$1(0.1) - 0.1$

$0.1 - 0.1$

0

9. $20\% \div \dfrac{3}{25}(0.4) - \dfrac{10}{20}$

$\dfrac{2}{10} \div \left(\dfrac{3}{25}\right)\left(\dfrac{4}{10}\right) - \dfrac{10}{20}$

$\dfrac{2}{10}\left(\dfrac{3}{25}\right)\left(\dfrac{4}{10}\right) - \dfrac{10}{20}$

$\dfrac{1}{5}\left(\dfrac{25}{3}\right)\left(\dfrac{2}{5}\right) - \dfrac{10}{20}$

$\dfrac{1}{5}\left(\dfrac{5}{3}\right)\left(\dfrac{2}{1}\right) - \dfrac{10}{20}$

$\dfrac{1}{1}\left(\dfrac{1}{3}\right)\left(\dfrac{2}{1}\right) - \dfrac{10}{20}$

$\dfrac{2}{3} - \dfrac{10}{20}$

$\dfrac{40}{60} - \dfrac{30}{60}$

$\dfrac{10}{60} = \dfrac{\mathbf{1}}{\mathbf{6}}$

10. $-\dfrac{7}{20} - 45\% - (-0.95)$

$-0.35 + (-0.45) + 0.95$

0.15

11. $\dfrac{\mathbf{65}}{\mathbf{12}}$ and $\mathbf{5}\dfrac{\mathbf{5}}{\mathbf{12}}$ are halfway between $3\dfrac{1}{2}$ and $7\dfrac{1}{3}$.

METHOD 1 Average $= \dfrac{\text{total}}{\#}$

$$\dfrac{3\dfrac{1}{2} + 7\dfrac{1}{3}}{2} = \dfrac{3\dfrac{3}{6} + 7\dfrac{2}{6}}{2} = 10\dfrac{5}{6}\left(\dfrac{1}{2}\right) = \dfrac{65}{6}\left(\dfrac{1}{2}\right) = \dfrac{65}{12} = 5\dfrac{5}{12}$$

METHOD 2 Half of the distance between the two.

Find the distance between the two points: $7\dfrac{2}{6} - 3\dfrac{3}{6} = 6\dfrac{8}{6} - 3\dfrac{3}{6} = 3\dfrac{5}{6}$

Divide the distance in half: $3\dfrac{5}{6}\left(\dfrac{1}{2}\right) = \dfrac{23}{6}\left(\dfrac{1}{2}\right) = \dfrac{23}{12} = 1\dfrac{11}{12}$

Add it back to the point closest to 0: $3\frac{3}{6} + 1\frac{11}{12} = 3\frac{6}{12} + 1\frac{11}{12} = 4\frac{17}{12} = 5\frac{5}{12}$

Check your answer by subtracting the halfway distance from the point furthest

away from 0: $7\frac{2}{6} - 1\frac{11}{12} = 7\frac{4}{12} - 1\frac{11}{12} = 6\frac{16}{12} - 1\frac{11}{12} = \mathbf{5\frac{5}{12}}$

Double check your answer by graphing all three points on the number line:

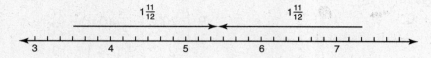

12. $\frac{21}{40}$ is one-quarter of the distance from $\frac{2}{5}$ to $\frac{9}{10}$.

Find the distance between the two points: $\frac{18}{20} - \frac{8}{20} = \frac{10}{20} = \frac{1}{2}$

Divide the distance into four. The length of each distance is: $\frac{1}{2}\left(\frac{1}{4}\right) = \frac{1}{8}$

Add it back to the point closest to 0: $\frac{8}{20} + \frac{1}{8} = \frac{32}{80} + \frac{10}{80} = \frac{42}{80} = \frac{21}{40}$

Check your answer by subtracting the three-quarters of the distance from the

point furthest away from 0: $\frac{18}{20} - 3\left(\frac{1}{8}\right) = \frac{18}{20} - \frac{3}{8} = \frac{36}{40} - \frac{15}{40} = \frac{21}{40}$

Double check your answer by graphing all 3 points on the number line:

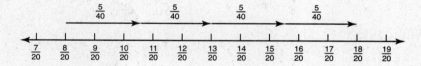

Chapter 2 Algebraic Expressions

Lesson 2.1: Factoring and Expanding Algebraic Terms

Practice, page 37

1. A. $81a + 9 = \mathbf{9(9a + 1)}$

	9a	+1
9	$9(9a) = 81a$	$9(1) = 9$

B. $81 - 9a = \mathbf{9(9 - a)}$

	9	$-a$
9	$9(9) = 81$	$9(-a) = -9a$

C. $-81a - 9 = \mathbf{-9(9a + 1)}$

	$9a$	1
-9	$-9(9a) = -81a$	$-9(1) = -9$

D. $-81a + 9 = \mathbf{9(-9a + 1)}$

	$-9a$	1
9	$(9)(-9a) = -81a$	$9(1) = 9$

E. $-24x + 12y - 6 = \mathbf{-6(4x - 2y + 1)}$

	$4x$	$-2y$	$+1$
-6	$-6(4x) = -24x$	$-6(-2y) = 12y$	$-6(1) = -6$

F. $3a - 12b + 18 = \mathbf{3(a - 4b + 6)}$

	a	$-4b$	$+6$
3	$3(a) = 3a$	$3(-4b) = -12b$	$3(6) = 18$

G. $-x - 2y = \mathbf{-(x + 2y)}$

	x	$+2y$
-1	$-1(x) = -x$	$-1(2y) = -2y$

H. $-10x + 20y = \mathbf{10(-x + 2y)}$

	$-x$	$+2y$
10	$10(-x) = -10x$	$10(2y) = 20y$

I. $-3x - 3y = \mathbf{-3(x + y)}$

	x	y
-3	$-3(x) = -3x$	$-3(y) = -3y$

J. $-5a - 10b =$ **$-5(a + 2b)$**

	a	$2b$
-5	$-5(a) = -5a$	$-5(2b) = -10b$

2. A. $2(3a + 4) =$ **$2(3a) + 2(4) = 6a + 8$**

	$3a$	$+4$
2	$2(3a) = 6a$	$2(4) = 8$

B. $-2(3a + 4) =$ **$-2(3a) + (-2)(4) = -6a + (-8) = -6a - 8$**

	$3a$	$+4$
-2	$-2(3a) = -6a$	$-2(4) = -8$

C. $2(3a - 4) =$ **$2(3a) + 2(-4) = 6a + (-8) = 6a - 8$**

	$3a$	-4
2	$2(3a) = 6a$	$2(-4) = -8$

D. $-2(3a - 4) =$ **$-2(3a) + (-2)(-4) = -6a + 8$**

	$3a$	-4
-2	$-2(3a) = -6a$	$-2(-4) = 8$

E. $-2(-3a - 4) =$ **$-2(-3a) + (-2)(-4) = 6a + 8$**

	$-3a$	-4
-2	$-2(-3a) = 6a$	$-2(-4) = 8$

F. $-(4a + 13) =$ **$(-1)(4a) + (-1)(13) = -4a + (-13) = -4a - 13$**

	$4a$	$+13$
-1	$-1(4a) = -4a$	$-1(13) = -13$

G. $-(4a - 13) =$ **$(-1)(4a) + (-1)(-13) = -4a + 13 = -4a + 13$**

	$4a$	-13
-1	$-1(4a) = -4a$	$-1(-13) = 13$

H. $-(-4a - 13) = \textbf{(–1)(–4a) + (–1)(–13) = 4a + 13}$

	$-4a$	-13
-1	$-1(-4a) = 4a$	$-1(-13) = 13$

I. $-(-a - b) = \textbf{(–1)(–a) + (–1)(–b) = a + b}$

	$-a$	$-b$
-1	$-1(-a) = a$	$-1(-b) = b$

J. $-(-2 + c) = \textbf{(–1)(–2) + (–1)(c) = 2 – c}$

	-2	$+c$
-1	$-1(-2) = 2$	$-1(c) = -c$

K. $\frac{1}{2}(-4x - 10y) = \mathbf{\frac{1}{2}(-4x) + \frac{1}{2}(-10y) = -2x - 5y}$

	$-4x$	$-10y$
$\frac{1}{2}$	$\frac{1}{2}(-4x) = -2x$	$\frac{1}{2}(-10y) = -5y$

L. $\frac{3}{4}(-16x + 12y) = \mathbf{\frac{3}{4}(-16x) + -\frac{3}{4}(12y) = -12x + 9y}$

	$-16x$	$+12y$
$\frac{3}{4}$	$\frac{3}{4}(-16x) = -12x$	$\frac{3}{4}(12y) = 9y$

M. $-\frac{1}{3}(12x - 18y) = \mathbf{-\frac{1}{3}(12x) + -\frac{1}{3}(-18y) = -4x + 6y}$

	$12x$	$-18y$
$-\frac{1}{3}$	$-\frac{1}{3}(12x) = -4x$	$-\frac{1}{3}(-18y) = 6y$

N. $-\frac{2}{3}(-7x - 4y) = \mathbf{-\frac{2}{3}(-7x) \pm \frac{2}{3}(-4y) = \frac{14}{3}x + \frac{8}{3}y}$

	$-7x$	$-4y$
$-\frac{2}{3}$	$-\frac{2}{3}(-7x) = \frac{14}{3}x$	$-\frac{2}{3}(-4y) = \frac{8}{3}y$

O. $-\frac{1}{4}(-10x + 22y) = -\frac{1}{4}(-10x) + \left(-\frac{1}{4}\right)(22y) = \frac{5}{2}x - \frac{11}{2}y$

	$-10x$	$22y$
$-\frac{1}{4}$	$-\frac{1}{4}(-10x) = \frac{5}{2}x$	$-\frac{1}{4}(22y) = -\frac{11}{2}y$

P. $-0.5(6y + 3x) = \mathbf{(-0.5)(6y) + (-0.5)(3x) = -3y - 1.5x}$

	$6y$	$3x$
-0.5	$-0.5(6y) = -3y$	$-0.5(3x) = -1.5x$

Q. $-0.5(-6y - 3x) = \mathbf{(-0.5)(-6y) + (-0.5)(-3x) = 3y + 1.5x}$

	$-6y$	$-3y$
-0.5	$-0.5(-6y) = 3y$	$-0.5(-3y) = 1.5x$

R. $0.3x(10 - x) = \mathbf{(0.3x)(10) + (0.3x)(-x) = 3x - 0.3x^2}$

	10	$-x$
$0.3x$	$0.3x(10) = 3x$	$0.3x(-x) = -0.3x^2$

S. $1.2(12x + 1.2y) = \mathbf{1.2(12x) + (1.2)(1.2y) = 14.4x + 1.44y}$

	$12x$	$1.2y$
1.2	$1.2(12x) = 14.4x$	$1.2(1.2y) = 1.44y$

T. $-(-0.7x - 0.7y) = \mathbf{(-1)(-0.7x) + (-1)(-0.7y) = 0.7x + 0.7y}$

	$-0.7x$	$-0.7y$
-1	$-1(-0.7x) = 0.7x$	$-1(-0.7y) = 0.7y$

3. The correct answers are **C** and **E**.

   C. $\frac{1}{3}(-9x - 15)$ and $-\frac{1}{3}(9x + 15)$

   $\frac{1}{3}\left(-\frac{9x}{1}\right) + \left(\frac{1}{3}\right)\left(-\frac{15}{1}\right)$ and $-\frac{1}{3}\left(\frac{9x}{1}\right) + \left(-\frac{1}{3}\right)\left(\frac{15}{1}\right)$

   $-3x - 5$ and $-3x - 5$ are **equivalent**.

   E. $0.1(82x + 95y)$ and $-0.01(-820x - 950y)$

   $8.2x + 9.5y$ and $8.2x + 9.5y$ are **equivalent**.

Lesson 2.2: Adding and Subtracting Algebraic Terms

Practice, page 39

1. $-(-3x + 5) - 6x$
   $(-1)(-3x) + (-1)(5) - 6x$
   $3x - 5 - 6x$
   $-3x - 5$

2. $-3(-5x + 3) + 15x$
   $15x - 9 + 15x$
   $30x - 9$

3. $-(x - 4) + 8x - 10$
   $(-1)(x) + (-1)(-4) + 8x - 10$
   $-x + 4 + 8x - 10$
   $7x - 6$

4. $-3x - 7(-2 + 3x) - 8$
   $-3x + (-7)(-2) + (-7)(3x) - 8$
   $-3x + 14 + (-21x) - 8$
   $-24x + 6$

5. $-3(x + 5y) - 9x$
   $-3(x) + (-3)(5y) - 9x$
   $-3x - 15y - 9x$
   $-12x - 15y$

6. $-x(4 - y) - 12x - 3xy$
   $-x(4) + (-x)(-y) - 12x - 3xy$
   $-4x + xy + (-12x) + (-3xy)$
   $-16x - 2xy$

7. $-9(9x - 5) - 3(7 - x)$
   $-9(9x) + (-9)(-5) + (-3)(7) + (-3)(-x)$
   $-81x + 45 + (-21) + 3x$
   $-78x + 24$

8. $3(-4y - 2x) - 2(17x - 6y)$
   $3(-4y) + 3(-2x) + (-2)(17x) + (-2)(-6y)$
   $-12y + (-6x) + (-34x) + 12y$
   $-12y + 12y + (-6x) + (-34x)$
   $-40x$

9. $-(11x - 9) - 2x(3 - 6y) - 2(x + 8)$ [Hint: simplify $3 - 6$ before you distribute.]
   $(-1)(11x) + (-1)(-9) + (-2x)(3) + (-2x)(-6y) + (-2)(x) + (-2)(8)$
   $-11x + 9 + (-6x) + 12xy + (-2x) + (-16)$
   $-11x + (-6x) + (-2x) + 12xy + 9 + (-16)$
   $-19x + 12xy - 7$

10. $-\frac{1}{2}x - \frac{3}{5}y + \frac{7}{10}x - \frac{9}{10}y = -\frac{1}{2}x + \frac{7}{10}x + \left(-\frac{3}{5}y\right) + \left(-\frac{9}{10}y\right)$

$= -\frac{5}{10}x + \frac{7}{10}x + \left(-\frac{6}{10}y\right) + \left(-\frac{9}{10}y\right) = \frac{2}{10}x + -\frac{5}{10}x = \frac{1}{5}x - \frac{3}{2}y$

11. $-\frac{1}{4}x + \frac{5}{6}y - \frac{11}{12}x + \frac{2}{3}y = -\frac{1}{4}x + \left(-\frac{11}{12}x\right) + \frac{5}{6}y + \frac{2}{3}y$

$= -\frac{3}{12}x + \left(-\frac{11}{12}x\right) + \frac{5}{6}y + \frac{4}{6}y = -\frac{14}{12}x + \frac{9}{6}y = -\frac{7}{6}x + \frac{3}{2}y$

12. $-\frac{2}{5}x + \frac{1}{4}y + \frac{19}{20}x + \frac{9}{10}y = -\frac{2}{5}x + \frac{19}{20}x + \frac{1}{4}y + \left(-\frac{9}{10}y\right)$

$= -\frac{8}{20}x + \frac{19}{20}x + \frac{5}{20}y + \left(-\frac{18}{20}y\right) = \frac{11}{20}x + \left(-\frac{13}{20}y\right) = \frac{11}{20}x - \frac{13}{20}y$

13. $\frac{1}{5}x - \frac{2}{3}y - \left(\frac{11}{15}y - \frac{7}{15}x\right) = \frac{1}{5}x - \frac{2}{3}y + (-1)\left(\frac{11}{15}y\right) + (-1)\left(-\frac{7}{15}x\right)$

$= \frac{1}{5}x - \frac{2}{3}y + \left(-\frac{11}{15}y\right) + \frac{7}{15}x = \frac{1}{5}x + \frac{7}{15}x - \frac{2}{3}y + \left(-\frac{11}{15}y\right)$

$= \frac{3}{15}x + \frac{7}{15}x - \frac{10}{15}y + \left(-\frac{11}{15}y\right) = \frac{10}{15}x + \left(-\frac{21}{15}y\right) = \frac{2}{3}x + \left(-\frac{7}{5}y\right)$

$= \frac{2}{3}x - \frac{7}{5}y$

14. $-\frac{3}{8}x - \frac{4}{3}y + \frac{2}{3}\left(\frac{5}{16}x - \frac{3}{4}y\right) = -\frac{3}{8}x - \frac{4}{3}y + \frac{2}{3}\left(\frac{5}{16}x\right) + \frac{2}{3}\left(-\frac{3}{4}y\right)$

$= -\frac{3}{8}x - \frac{4}{3}y + \frac{5}{24}x + \left(-\frac{1}{2}y\right) = -\frac{3}{8}x + \frac{5}{24}x + \left(-\frac{4}{3}y\right) + \left(-\frac{1}{2}y\right)$

$= -\frac{9}{24}x + \frac{5}{24}x + \left(-\frac{8}{6}y\right) + \left(-\frac{3}{6}y\right) = -\frac{4}{24}x + \left(-\frac{11}{6}y\right) = -\frac{1}{6}x - \frac{11}{6}y$

15. $4.5x - 0.8y + 1.2x - 3.3y$

$4.5x + 1.2x - 0.8y - 3.3y$

$5.7x - 4.1y$

16. $-0.6x - 0.2y - 0.4y - 0.5x$

$-0.6x + (-0.5x) + (-0.2y) + (-0.4y)$

$-1.1x + (-0.6y)$

$-1.1x - 0.6y$

17. $2 + 2.3x + 2.4 - 6.3x$

$2 + 2.4 + 2.3x - 6.3x$

$4.4 - 4.0x$

18. $-7.3x - 8.1y + 3.7x + 5.9y$

$-7.3x + 3.7x - 8.1y + 5.9y$

$-3.6x - 2.2y$

19. $0.1(-3x + 4y) - 10x$

$0.1(-3x) + (0.1)(4y) - 10x$

$-0.3x + 0.4y - 10x$

$-0.3x - 10x + 0.4y$

$-10.3x + 0.4y$

20. $-0.1(-3x - 4y) - 9x - 6y$

$-0.1(-3x) + (-0.1)(-4y) - 9x - 6y$

$0.3x + 0.4y - 9x - 6y$

$0.3x - 9x + 0.4y - 6y$

$-8.7x - 5.6y$

Lesson 2.3: Writing Algebraic Expressions

Practice, pages 44–46

1. A. Two-thirds x increased by $9 = \dfrac{2}{3}x + 9$.

    B. The sum of one-sixth x and $7 = \dfrac{1}{6}x + 7$.

    C. Three fewer than the product of x and $y = xy - 3$.

    D. The quotient of one and six x reduced by $7 = \dfrac{1}{6}x - 7$.

    E. Twenty percent of the sum of one-half x and
    $$10 = 20\%\left(\dfrac{1}{2}x + 10\right) = \dfrac{1}{5}\left(\dfrac{1}{2}x + 10\right) = \dfrac{1}{10}x + 2$$

    F. The difference between y squared and x cubed $= y^2 - x^3$.

    G. Double the sum of x and $y = 2(x + y) = 2x + 2y$.

    H. The product of negative x and negative x: $(-x)(-x) = (-x)^2 = x^2$.

    I. The product of negative 1 and x squared: $(-1)(x^2) = -x^2$.

    J. The product of negative 1 and double the amount of x: $(-1)(2x) = -2x$.

    K. The product of $6x$ and 7 divided by 2: $\dfrac{(6x)(7)}{2} = \dfrac{42x}{2} = 21x$.

    L. The sum of one-third x, two-thirds x, and three-fourths
    $$y = \dfrac{1}{3}x + \dfrac{2}{3}x + \dfrac{3}{4}y = x + \dfrac{3}{4}y$$

    M. One-half subtracted from the product of $9x$ and
    $$7y = (9x)(7y) - \dfrac{1}{2} = 63xy - \dfrac{1}{2}$$

    N. Four-fifths of the sum of $8x$ and 2 less than
    $$10 = 10 - \dfrac{4}{5}(8x + 2) = 10 + \left(-\dfrac{4}{5}\right)\left(\dfrac{8x}{1}\right) + \left(-\dfrac{4}{5}\right)\left(\dfrac{2}{1}\right) = 10 - \dfrac{8}{5} - \dfrac{32}{5}x = \dfrac{42}{5} - \dfrac{32}{5}x$$

    O. The quotient of 6 and x reduced by $y = \dfrac{6}{x-y}$ or 6 divided by $(x- y)$.

2. A. $3a - 7b = $ **7 times b subtracted from the product of 3 and a. The product of 3 and a decreased by the product of 7 and a.**

    B. $7b - 3a = $ **$3a$ less than $7b$. $3a$ fewer than $7b$.**

    C. $\dfrac{3a}{7b} = $ **the quotient of $3a$ and $7b$. $3a$ divided by $7b$.**

    D. $\dfrac{7b}{3a} = $ **the quotient of $7b$ and $3a$. $7b$ divided by $3a$.**

    E. $(3a)(7b) = $ **the product of $3a$ and $7b$. $3a$ times $7b$.**

F. $5a^2$ = **the product of 5 and _a_ squared. 5 times _a_ squared.**

G. $(5a)^3$ = **the product of 5 and _a_, cubed. The quantity of 5 times _a_, to the third power.**

H. $\dfrac{x+2}{6y}$ = **the quantity of _x_ plus 2 divided by the quantity of 6 times _y_. The quotient of _x_ + 2 and 6_y_.**

I. $(x-9)^2$ = **the quantity of _x_ − 9 squared. The quantity of _x_ less 9, squared.**

J. x^2-9^2 = **_x_ squared minus 9 squared. The difference between _x_ squared and 9 squared.**

K. x^2+y^2 = **_y_ squared added to _x_ squared. _x_ squared increased by _y_ squared.**

L. $\dfrac{1}{4}xy^2$ = **one-fourth of the product of _x_ and _y_ squared. One quarter of _x_ times _y_ to the second power.**

M. $9x^2y^3$ = **the product of 9, _x_ squared, and _y_ cubed.**

N. $8a+\dfrac{2}{b}$ = **the product of 8 and _a_ increased by the quotient of 2 and _b_. 8 times _a_ added to 2 divided by _b_.**

O. $\dfrac{3x-1}{y+2}$ = **the quotient of 3_x_ − 1 and _y_ + 2. The quantity of 3_x_ minus 1 divided by the quantity of _y_ more than 2.**

3. Let _w_ equal the width of one side of the rectangle.
    Length = **3_w_ − 8**
    Area = length(width) = **(3_w_ − 8)_w_ = 3_w_² − 8_w_ units squared.**

4. **METHOD 1** Let _L_ equal the length of one side of the rectangle.
    Length = _L_
    _W_ = 0.2_L_
    Perimeter = add up all sides = **_L_ + _L_ + 0.2_L_ + 0.2_L_ = 2.4_L_ units.**

    METHOD 2 Let _w_ equal the width of one side of the rectangle.
    Width = _w_
    Length = 5_w_
    Perimeter = add up all sides = **_w_ + _w_ + 5_w_ +5_w_ = 12_w_ units.**

5. Let _w_ equal the width of one side of the rectangle.
    Length = 3.5_w_
    Area = length(width) = **3.5_w_(_w_) = 3.5_w_²**

6. Let L equal the length of one side of the rectangle.
   Width $= 0.5L$

   If area = length (width) then length $= \dfrac{\text{area}}{\text{width}} = \dfrac{20L}{0.5L} = \mathbf{40\ units}$.

7. Area of square $= (\text{side})^2 = (7x)^2 = (7x)(7x) = \mathbf{49x^2\ units\ squared}$.

8. **Mark messed up on Step 1.** When he distributed, he should have distributed the -1 to both terms inside both sets of parentheses like this:

   $(-1)(2x) + (-1)(9) + (-1)(-7) + (-1)(-5x)$
   $-2x - 9 + 7 + 5x$
   $-2x + 5x - 9 + 7$
   $3x - 2$

9. The work is correct but Stefani should have factored both terms with $-10x$ instead of $+10x$. Here is the correct work:
   $$\frac{-10x}{-10x} + \frac{-20xy}{-10x} = \mathbf{1 + 2y}$$
   Her factored expression that is equivalent to the original problem should be:
   $-10x(1 + 2y)$

10. **Ellen's mistake started in the first step.** She forgot to distribute -1 to the $-x$ in the second set of parentheses. Here is the work she should have shown:

    $(-3)(x) + (-3)(-1) + (-1)(6) + (-1)(-x)$
    $-3x + 3 - 6 + x$
    $-3x + x + 3 - 6$
    $-2x - 3$

Chapter 3 Algebraic Equations and Inequalities

Lesson 3.1: Solving Algebraic Equations

Practice, page 58

1. $\begin{aligned} 3x - 12 &= 7x + 21 \\ 3x - 12 + 12 &= 7x + 21 + 12 \\ 3x &= 7x + 33 \\ 3x - 7x &= 7x - 7x + 33 \\ -4x &= 33 \\ \frac{-4x}{-4} &= \frac{33}{-4} \\ x &= -\frac{33}{4} \end{aligned}$

2. $\begin{aligned} -5x - 13 &= -x - 11 \\ -5x - 13 + 13 &= -x - 11 + 13 \\ -5x &= -x + 2 \\ -5x + x &= -x + 2 + x \\ -4x &= 2 \\ \frac{-4x}{-4} &= \frac{2}{-4} \\ x &= -\frac{1}{2} \end{aligned}$

3.
$$-0.5x - 0.13 = -0.1x - 0.11$$
$$-0.5x - 0.13 + 0.13 = -0.1x - 0.11 + 0.13$$
$$-0.5x = -0.1x + 0.02$$
$$-0.5x + 0.1x = -0.1x + 0.1x + 0.02$$
$$-0.4x = 0.02$$
$$\frac{-0.4x}{-0.4} = \frac{+0.02}{-0.4}$$
$$\boldsymbol{x = -\,0.05}$$

4.
$$-\frac{3}{4}x + 12 = 28$$
$$-\frac{3}{4}x + 12 - 12 = 28 - 12$$
$$-\frac{3}{4}x = 16$$
$$-\frac{4}{3}\left(-\frac{3}{4}x\right) = (16)\left(-\frac{4}{3}\right)$$
$$\boldsymbol{x = -\frac{64}{3} = -21\frac{1}{3}}$$

5.
$$-17 + 2x = -6x - 33$$
$$-17 + 2x - 2x = -6x - 33 - 2x$$
$$-17 = -8x - 33$$
$$-17 + 33 = -8x - 33 + 33$$
$$16 = -8x$$
$$\frac{16}{-8} = \frac{-8x}{-8}$$
$$\boldsymbol{-2 = x}$$

6.
$$-2x - 12 + 5x = -9x + 21 - 2x$$
$$3x - 12 = -11x + 21$$
$$3x - 12 + 12 = -11x + 21 + 12$$
$$3x = -11x + 33$$
$$3x + 11x = -11x + 33 + 11x$$
$$14x = 33$$
$$\frac{14x}{14} = \frac{33}{14}$$
$$\boldsymbol{x = \frac{33}{14}}$$

7. $\frac{3}{5}\left(\frac{1}{4}x+1\right)=4$

METHOD 1 Distribute.

$$\frac{3}{5}\left(\frac{1}{4}x\right)+\left(\frac{3}{5}\right)(1)=4$$

$$\frac{3}{20}x+\frac{3}{5}=4$$

$$\frac{3}{20}x-\frac{3}{5}+\frac{3}{5}=4-\frac{3}{5}$$

$$\frac{3}{20}x=\frac{17}{5}$$

$$+\frac{20}{3}\left(\frac{3}{20}x\right)=\left(\frac{17}{5}\right)\left(-\frac{20}{3}\right)$$

$$x=-\frac{68}{3}=\mathbf{-22\frac{2}{3}}$$

METHOD 2 Divide $\frac{3}{5}$ or multiply by the reciprocal of $\frac{3}{5}$.

$$\left(-\frac{5}{3}\right)\left(-\frac{3}{5}\right)\left(\frac{1}{4}x+1\right)=4\left(\frac{5}{3}\right)$$

$$\frac{1}{4}x+1=\frac{20}{3}$$

$$\frac{1}{4}x+1-1=\frac{20}{3}-1$$

$$\frac{1}{4}x=\frac{20}{3}-\frac{3}{3}$$

$$\frac{1}{4}x=-\frac{17}{3}$$

$$\frac{4}{1}\left(\frac{1}{4}x\right)=-\frac{17}{3}\left(\frac{4}{1}\right)$$

$$x=-\left(\frac{17}{3}\right)\left(\frac{4}{1}\right)=-\frac{68}{3}=\mathbf{-22\frac{2}{3}}$$

8. $\dfrac{-x-4}{7}=2$

$$7\left(\frac{-x-4}{7}\right)=(2)7$$

$$-x-4=14$$

$$-x-4+4=14+4$$

$$-x=18$$

$$-1(-x)=(18)(-1)$$

$$\mathbf{x=-18}$$

9. $-5-\dfrac{2}{3}x=-9$

$$-5-\frac{2}{3}x+5=-9+5$$

$$-\frac{2}{3}x=-4$$

$$\left(-\frac{3}{2}\right)\left(-\frac{2}{3}x\right)=\left(-\frac{4}{1}\right)\left(-\frac{3}{2}\right)$$

$$\mathbf{x=\frac{12}{2}=6}$$

10. $-\dfrac{2}{9}\left(-\dfrac{1}{6}x - 18\right) = -27$

METHOD 1 Distribute.

$$-\dfrac{2}{9}\left(-\dfrac{1}{6}x\right) + \left(-\dfrac{2}{9}\right)(-18) = -27$$

$$\dfrac{1}{27}x + 4 = -27$$

$$\dfrac{1}{27}x + 4 - 4 = -27 - 4$$

$$\dfrac{1}{27}x = -31$$

$$\dfrac{27}{1}\left(-\dfrac{1}{27}x\right) = (-31)(27)$$

$$x = -837$$

METHOD 2 Multiply by the reciprocal of $-\dfrac{2}{9}$.

$$-\dfrac{9}{2}\left(-\dfrac{2}{9}\right)\left(-\dfrac{1}{6}x - 18\right) = \left(-\dfrac{27}{1}\right)\left(-\dfrac{9}{2}\right)$$

$$-\dfrac{1}{6}x - 18 = \dfrac{243}{2}$$

$$-\dfrac{1}{6}x - 18 + 18 = \dfrac{243}{2} + 18$$

$$-\dfrac{1}{6}x = \dfrac{279}{2}$$

$$\left(-\dfrac{6}{1}\right)\left(-\dfrac{1}{6}x\right) = \left(\dfrac{279}{2}\right)\left(-\dfrac{6}{1}\right)$$

$$x = -837$$

11. $-\dfrac{7}{8}x + 14 = \dfrac{1}{2}x - 2$

METHOD 1 Combine the constants first.

$$-\dfrac{7}{8}x + 14 - 14 = \dfrac{1}{2}x - 2 - 14$$

$$-\dfrac{7}{8}x = \dfrac{1}{2}x - 16$$

$$-\dfrac{7}{8}x - \dfrac{1}{2}x = \dfrac{1}{2}x - 16 - \dfrac{1}{2}x$$

$$-\dfrac{7}{8}x - \dfrac{4}{8}x = -16$$

$$-\dfrac{11}{8}x = -16$$

$$\left(-\dfrac{8}{11}\right)\left(-\dfrac{11}{8}x\right) = (-16)\left(-\dfrac{8}{11}\right)$$

$$x = \dfrac{128}{11}$$

METHOD 2 Combine the algebraic terms first.

$$-\frac{7}{8}x + 14 + \frac{7}{8}x = \frac{1}{2}x - 2 + \frac{7}{8}x$$

$$14 = \frac{4}{8}x - 2 + \frac{7}{8}x$$

$$14 = \frac{11}{8}x - 2$$

$$14 + 2 = \frac{11}{8}x - 2 + 2$$

$$\left(\frac{8}{11}\right)(16) = \left(\frac{11}{8}x\right)\left(\frac{8}{11}\right)$$

$$\mathbf{\frac{128}{11} = x}$$

12. $-\frac{2}{5}x - \frac{1}{6} = -\frac{1}{2}x - 2$

METHOD 1 Combine the constants first.

$$-\frac{2}{5}x - \frac{1}{6} + \frac{1}{6} = -\frac{1}{2}x - 2 + \frac{1}{6}$$

$$-\frac{2}{5}x = -\frac{1}{2}x - \frac{12}{6} + \frac{1}{6}$$

$$-\frac{2}{5}x = -\frac{1}{2}x - \frac{11}{6}$$

$$-\frac{2}{5}x + \frac{1}{2}x = -\frac{1}{2}x - \frac{11}{6} + \frac{1}{2}x$$

$$-\frac{4}{10}x + \frac{5}{10}x = -\frac{11}{6}$$

$$\frac{1}{10}x = -\frac{11}{6}$$

$$\left(\frac{10}{1}\right)\left(\frac{1}{10}x\right) = \left(-\frac{11}{6}\right)\left(\frac{10}{1}\right)$$

$$\mathbf{x = -\frac{55}{3}}$$

METHOD 2 Combine the algebraic terms first.

$$-\frac{2}{5}x - \frac{1}{6} + \frac{2}{5}x = -\frac{1}{2}x - 2 + \frac{2}{5}x$$

$$-\frac{1}{6} = -\frac{5}{10}x - 2 + \frac{4}{10}x$$

$$-\frac{1}{6} = -\frac{1}{10}x - 2$$

$$-\frac{1}{6} + 2 = -\frac{1}{10}x - 2 + 2$$

$$-\frac{1}{6} + \frac{12}{6} = -\frac{1}{10}x$$

$$\frac{11}{6} = -\frac{1}{10}x$$

$$-\frac{10}{1}\left(\frac{11}{6}\right) = \left(-\frac{1}{10}x\right)\left(-\frac{10}{1}\right)$$

$$\mathbf{-\frac{55}{3} = x}$$

13. $0.4(-0.2x - 3) = 0.5$

METHOD 1   Distribute 0.4.

$0.4(-0.2x) + 0.4(-3) = 0.5$

$-0.08x - 1.2 = 0.5$

$-0.08x - 1.2 + 1.2 = 0.5 + 1.2$

$-0.08x = 1.7$

$\dfrac{-0.08x}{-0.08} = \dfrac{1.7}{-0.08}$

$\boldsymbol{x = -21.25}$

METHOD 2   Divide by 0.4.

$\dfrac{0.4(-0.2x - 3)}{0.4} = \dfrac{0.5}{0.4}$

$-0.2x - 3 = 1.25$

$-0.2x - 3 + 3 = 1.25 + 3$

$-0.2x = 4.25$

$\dfrac{-0.2x}{-0.2} = \dfrac{4.25}{-0.2}$

$\boldsymbol{x = -21.25}$

14. $-14 = \dfrac{-90 - 5x}{10}$ also looks like: $-14 = \dfrac{-90}{10} - \dfrac{5x}{10}$ or $-14 = \dfrac{-90 - 5x}{1}\left(\dfrac{1}{10}\right)$

METHOD 1   Multiply by the reciprocal of $\dfrac{1}{10}$.

$10(-14) = \left(\dfrac{-90 - 5x}{10}\right)\left(\dfrac{10}{1}\right)$

$-140 = -90 - 5x$

$-140 + 90 = -90 - 5x + 90$

$-50 = -5x$

$\dfrac{-50}{-5} = \dfrac{-5x}{-5}$

$\boldsymbol{10 = x}$

METHOD 2   Combine the constants.

$-14 = \dfrac{-90}{10} - \dfrac{5x}{10}$

$-14 = -9 - \dfrac{1}{2}x$

$-14 + 9 = -9 - \dfrac{1}{2}x + 9$

$-5 = -\dfrac{1}{2}x$

$(-2)(-5) = \left(-\dfrac{1}{2}x\right)\left(-\dfrac{2}{1}\right)$

$\boldsymbol{10 = x}$

15. $$-(-x-1)+6=-2(-3x+4)-8x$$
$$(-1)(-x)+(-1)(-1)+6=(-2)(-3x)+(-2)(4)-8x$$
$$x+1+6=6x-8-8x$$
$$x+7=-8-2x$$
$$x+7+2x=-8-2x+2x$$
$$7+3x=-8$$
$$7+3x-7=-8-7$$
$$3x=-15$$
$$\frac{3x}{3}=-\frac{15}{3}$$
$$\boldsymbol{x=-5}$$

16. $\dfrac{-6x+24}{-12}=-9$

METHOD 1 Multiply by the reciprocal of $-\dfrac{1}{12}$.

$$-\frac{12}{1}\left(\frac{-6x+24}{-12}\right)=(-9)(-12)$$
$$-6x+24=108$$
$$-6x+24-24=108-24$$
$$-6x=84$$
$$\frac{-6x}{6}=\frac{84}{-6}$$
$$\boldsymbol{x=-14}$$

METHOD 2 Combine the constants.

$$\frac{-6x}{-12}+\frac{24}{-12}=-9$$
$$\frac{1}{2}x-2=-9$$
$$\frac{1}{2}x-2+2=-9+2$$
$$\frac{1}{2}x=-7$$
$$\left(\frac{2}{1}\right)\left(\frac{1}{2}x\right)=(-7)(2)$$
$$\boldsymbol{x=-14}$$

17.
$$-3(0.5x - 4) - 2(-4x - 1) = 1$$
$$-3(0.5x) + (-3)(-4) + (-2)(-4x) + (-2)(-1) = 1$$
$$-1.5x + 12 + 8x + 2 = 1$$
$$6.5x + 14 = 1$$
$$6.5x + 14 - 14 = 1 - 14$$
$$6.5x = -13$$
$$\frac{6.5x}{6.5} = \frac{-13}{6.5}$$
$$\boldsymbol{x = -2}$$

18. $\frac{1}{2}\left(-\frac{1}{2}x + \frac{1}{2}\right) = \frac{1}{2}$

METHOD 1 Distribute $\frac{1}{2}$.

$$\frac{1}{2}\left(-\frac{1}{2}x\right) + \left(\frac{1}{2}\right)\left(\frac{1}{2}\right) = \frac{1}{2}$$
$$-\frac{1}{4}x + \frac{1}{4} = \frac{1}{2}$$
$$-\frac{1}{4}x + \frac{1}{4} - \frac{1}{4} = \frac{1}{2} - \frac{1}{4}$$
$$-\frac{1}{4}x = \frac{2}{4} - \frac{1}{4}$$
$$-\frac{1}{4}x = \frac{1}{4}$$
$$-\frac{4}{1}\left(-\frac{1}{4}x\right) = \left(\frac{1}{4}\right)\left(-\frac{4}{1}\right)$$
$$\boldsymbol{x = -1}$$

METHOD 2 Multiply by the reciprocal of $\frac{1}{2}$.

$$\left(\frac{2}{1}\right)\left(\frac{1}{2}\right)\left(-\frac{1}{2}x + \frac{1}{2}\right) = \frac{1}{2}\left(\frac{2}{1}\right)$$
$$-\frac{1}{2}x + \frac{1}{2} = 1$$
$$-\frac{1}{2}x + \frac{1}{2} - \frac{1}{2} = 1 - \frac{1}{2}$$
$$-\frac{1}{2}x = \frac{2}{2} - \frac{1}{2}$$
$$-\frac{1}{2}x = \frac{1}{2}$$
$$\left(-\frac{2}{1}\right)\left(-\frac{1}{2}x\right) = \left(\frac{1}{2}\right)\left(-\frac{2}{1}\right)$$
$$\boldsymbol{x = -1}$$

19.　$-0.8(2.3x - 0.1) = -0.4(2 - 6x)$

METHOD 1　Distribute.

$$-0.8(2.3x) + (-0.8)(-0.1) = -0.4(2) + (-0.4)(-6x)$$
$$-1.84x + 0.08 = -0.8 + 2.4x$$
$$-1.84x + 0.08 - 0.08 = -0.8 + 2.4x - 0.08$$
$$-1.84x = -0.88 + 2.4x$$
$$-1.84x - 2.4x = -0.88 + 2.4x - 2.4x$$
$$-4.24x = -0.88$$
$$\frac{-4.24x}{-4.24} = \frac{-0.88}{-4.24}$$
$$\mathbf{x \approx 0.2075}$$

METHOD 2　Divide by -0.4 and then divide by 2.

$$\frac{-0.8(2.3x - 0.1)}{-0.4} = \frac{-0.4(2 - 6x)}{-0.4}$$
$$2(2.3x - 0.1) = 2 - 6x$$
$$\frac{2(2.3x - 0.1)}{2} = \frac{2 - 6x}{2}$$
$$\frac{2(2.3x - 0.1)}{2} = \frac{2}{2} - \frac{6x}{2}$$
$$2.3x - 0.1 = 1 - 3x$$
$$2.3x - 0.1 + 0.1 = 1 - 3x + 0.1$$
$$2.3x = 1.1 - 3x$$
$$2.3x + 3x = 1.1 - 3x + 3x$$
$$5.3x = 1.1$$
$$\frac{5.3x}{5.3} = \frac{1.1}{5.3}$$
$$\mathbf{x \approx 0.2075}$$

METHOD 3 Divide by −0.4 and then distribute 2.

$$\frac{-0.8(2.3x - 0.1)}{-0.4} = \frac{-0.4(2 - 6x)}{-0.4}$$

$$2(2.3x - 0.1) = 2 - 6x$$

$$2(2.3x - 0.1) = 2 - 6x$$

$$2(2.3x) + (2)(-0.1) = 2 - 6x$$

$$2(2.3x) + (2)(-0.1) = 2 - 6x$$

$$4.6x - 0.2 = 2 - 6x$$

$$4.6x - 0.2 + 0.2 = 2 - 6x + 0.2$$

$$4.6x = 2.2 - 6x$$

$$4.6x + 6x = 2.2 - 6x + 6x$$

$$10.6x = 2.2$$

$$\frac{10.6x}{10.6} = \frac{2.2}{10.6}$$

$$\boldsymbol{x \approx 0.2075}$$

20.
$$\frac{1}{2}\left(-\frac{2}{3}x + \frac{3}{2}\right) = \frac{1}{3}\left(\frac{5}{2}x - \frac{7}{12}\right)$$

$$\frac{1}{2}\left(-\frac{2}{3}x\right) + \frac{1}{2}\left(\frac{3}{2}\right) = \frac{1}{3}\left(\frac{5}{2}x\right) + \frac{1}{3}\left(-\frac{7}{12}\right)$$

$$-\frac{1}{3}x + \frac{3}{4} = \frac{5}{6}x - \frac{7}{36}$$

$$\frac{36}{1}\left(-\frac{1}{3}x + \frac{3}{4}\right) = \left(\frac{5}{6}x - \frac{7}{36}\right)\left(\frac{36}{1}\right)$$

$$\frac{36}{1}\left(-\frac{1}{3}x\right) + \left(\frac{36}{1}\right)\left(\frac{3}{4}\right) = \frac{36}{1}\left(\frac{5}{6}x\right) + \left(\frac{36}{1}\right)\left(-\frac{7}{36}\right)$$

$$-12x + 27 = 30x - 7$$

$$-12x + 27 + 7 = 30x - 7 + 7$$

$$-12x + 34 = 30x$$

$$-12x + 34 + 12x = 30x + 12x$$

$$34 = 42x$$

$$\frac{34}{42} = \frac{42x}{42}$$

$$\boldsymbol{0.8095 \approx x}$$

Lesson 3.2: Real-World Problems: Algebraic Equations

Practice, page 64

1. $$-2x - 15 = -7x - 35$$
$$-2x - 15 + 7x = -7x - 35 + 7x$$
$$5x - 15 = -35$$
$$5x - 15 + 15 = -35 + 15$$
$$5x = -20$$
$$\frac{5x}{5} = -\frac{20}{5}$$
$$\mathbf{x = -4}$$

2. $$-24 = \frac{-4x + 8}{3}$$
$$3(-24) = \left(\frac{-4x + 8}{3}\right)\left(\frac{3}{1}\right)$$
$$-72 = -4x + 8$$
$$-72 - 8 = -4x + 8 - 8$$
$$-80 = -4x$$
$$\frac{-80}{-4} = \frac{-4x}{-4}$$
$$\mathbf{20 = x}$$

3. $$3 - \frac{1}{2}x = -10$$
$$3 - \frac{1}{2}x - 3 = -10 - 3$$
$$-\frac{1}{2}x = -13$$
$$-\frac{2}{1}\left(-\frac{1}{2}x\right) = (-13)(-2)$$
$$\mathbf{x = 26}$$

4. $$14 = -2(-x + 8)$$

   METHOD 1 Distribute −2.
$$14 = -2(-x) + (-2)(8)$$
$$14 = 2x - 16$$
$$14 + 16 = 2x - 16 + 16$$
$$30 = 2x$$
$$\frac{30}{2} = \frac{2x}{2}$$
$$\mathbf{15 = x}$$

   METHOD 2 Divide by −2.
$$\frac{14}{-2} = \frac{-2(-x + 8)}{-2}$$
$$-7 = -x + 8$$
$$-7 - 8 = -x + 8 - 8$$
$$-15 = -x$$
$$\frac{-15}{-1} = \frac{-x}{-1}$$
$$\mathbf{15 = x}$$

5. $$\frac{45x}{-5} = -3(4x - 1)$$
$$-9x = -3(4x - 1)$$
$$\frac{-9x}{-3} = \frac{-3(4x - 1)}{-3}$$
$$3x = 4x - 1$$
$$3x - 4x = 4x - 4x - 1$$
$$-x = -1$$
$$-x(-1) = -1(-1)$$
$$\mathbf{x = 1}$$

6. Think of the same expressions that work for each set of 2 consecutive numbers:

$3 = x$	$10 = x$	$98 = x$	$200 = x$
$4 = x + 1$	$11 = x + 1$	$99 = x + 1$	$201 = x + 1$

Let x = the first number or the smaller number.

Write your equation in words: first number + second number = total

Use the expressions and plug in what you have: $x + x + 1 = \mathbf{505}$.

Solve for x and find both numbers: $2x + 1 = 505$

$$2x + 1 - 1 = 505 - 1$$
$$2x = 504$$
$$\frac{2x}{2} = \frac{504}{2}$$
$$\mathbf{x = 252}$$

Plug in the solution to find the second number: $x + 1 = 252 + 1 = 253$

Articulate your solution in a sentence: The sum of consecutive numbers 252 and 253 is **505**.

7. Think of the same expressions that work for each set of the four consecutive odd numbers:

$3 = x$	$11 = x$	$57 = x$	$121 = x$
$5 = x + 2$	$13 = x + 2$	$59 = x + 2$	$123 = x + 2$
$7 = x + 4$	$15 = x + 4$	$61 = x + 4$	$125 = x + 4$
$9 = x + 6$	$17 = x + 6$	$63 = x + 6$	$127 = x + 6$

Let x = the first number.

Write your equation in words: First # + second # + third # + fourth # = total.

Use the expressions and plug in what you have: $x + x + 2 + x + 4 + x + 6 = \mathbf{80}$.

Solve for x and find both numbers: $4x + 12 = 80$

$$4x + 12 - 12 = 80 - 12$$
$$4x = 68$$
$$\frac{4x}{4} = \frac{68}{4}$$
$$\mathbf{x = 17}$$

Plug x into the original expressions to find the other three numbers:

First consecutive odd number $\quad = x = 17$

Second consecutive odd number $\quad = x + 2 = 17 + 2 = 19$

Third consecutive odd number $\quad = x + 4 = 17 + 4 = 21$

Fourth consecutive odd number $\quad = x + 6 = 17 + 6 = 23$

Articulate your solution in a sentence: The sum of these four consecutive odd numbers 17, 19, 21, and 23 is **80**.

8. Find a book and open it up so that two book pages appear. Do this three more times and write down the numbers to use them to find your expression. Then think of expressions that work for all four pairs of your book pages.

$3 = x$	$51 = x$	$82 = x$	$326 = x$
$4 = x + 1$	$52 = x + 1$	$83 = x + 1$	$327 = x + 1$

Let x = the first number.

Write your equation in words: first page + second page = total.

Use the expressions and plug in what you have: $x + x + 1 = \textbf{197}$.

Solve for x and find both numbers: $2x + 1 = 197$

$$2x + 1 - 1 = 197 - 1$$
$$2x = 196$$
$$\frac{2x}{2} = \frac{196}{2}$$
$$\textbf{x = 98}$$

Plug x into the original expressions to find the other page.

First page: $x = 98$

Second page: $x + 1 = 98 + 1 = 99$

Articulate your solution in a sentence: The sum of book pages 98 and 99 is **197**.

9. Write the equation using words: adult tickets + children's tickets = total cost.

Let c = the number of children the adults chaperoned.

Plug in what you have: $8.50(3) + 4.25c = 55.25$.

Solve for c:

$$25.50 + 4.25c = 55.25 \qquad \text{Multiply 8.5 and 3.}$$
$$25.50 + 4.25c - 25.5 = 55.25 - 25.50 \qquad \text{Subtract 25.50 to both sides.}$$
$$\frac{4.25c}{4.25} = \frac{29.75}{4.25} \qquad \text{Divide 4.25 to both sides.}$$
$$\textbf{c = 7}$$

Articulate your solution in a sentence: At the movie theater, the **three adults** chaperoned **seven children**.

Check your answer by plugging 7 back into your original equation:

$$8.50(3) + 4.25(7) = 55.25$$
$$25.50 + 29.75 = 55.25$$
$$\textbf{55.25 = 55.25}$$

10. Let x equal the first number, and $y =$ the second number.

    Translate the sentences into expressions:

    $$x - y = 12$$
    $$y = \frac{1}{2}x - 3$$

    Plug in the expression for y in the first equation:

    $$x - \left(\frac{1}{2}x - 3\right) = 12$$

    Solve for the first number x:

    $$x + (-1)\left(\frac{1}{2}x\right) + (-1)(-3) = 12$$
    $$x - \frac{1}{2}x + 3 = 12$$
    $$\frac{1}{2}x + 3 = 12$$
    $$\frac{1}{2}x + 3 - 3 = 12 - 3$$
    $$\frac{1}{2}x = 9$$
    $$\frac{2}{1}\left(\frac{1}{2}x\right) = (9)2$$
    $$\boldsymbol{x = 18}$$
    $$\boldsymbol{y = \frac{1}{2} \cdot 18 - 3 = 6}$$

    Check:

    $$18 - \left(\frac{1}{2} \cdot 18 - 3\right) = 12$$
    $$18 - (9 - 3) = 12$$
    $$18 - 6 = 12$$
    $$\boldsymbol{12 = 12}$$

11. Let $n =$ an unknown number of nickels.

    To create an expression for the value of an unknown number of nickels, plug in a number that makes sense, find the pattern, and then plug in n to write the expression:

Number of Nickels	Value in Dollars
3	3(0.05) = 0.15
4	4(0.05) = 0.20
10	10(0.05) = 0.50
n	n(0.05) = 0.05n

Write your equation to represent the problem and solve for n.

$$0.05n = 1.35$$
$$\frac{0.05n}{0.05} = \frac{1.35}{0.05}$$
$$\boldsymbol{n = 27}$$

Articulate your solution in a sentence: The value of 27 nickels is **$1.35**.

Check your answer by plugging 27 back into your original equation:

$$0.05(27) = 1.35$$
$$\boldsymbol{1.35 = 1.35}$$

12. Let q = an unknown number of quarters.

To create an expression for the value of an unknown number of quarters, plug in a number that makes sense, find the pattern, and then plug in n to write the expression:

Number of Quarters	Value in Dollars
2	2(0.25) = 0.50
3	3(0.25) = 0.75
4	4(0.25) = 1.00
q	**q(0.25) = 0.25q**

Write your equation to represent the problem and solve for n.

$$0.25q = 11.75$$
$$\frac{0.25q}{0.25} = \frac{11.75}{0.25}$$
$$\boldsymbol{q = 47}$$

Articulate your solution in a sentence: The value of 47 quarters is **$11.75**.

Check your answer by plugging 47 back into your original equation:

$$0.25(47) = 11.75$$
$$\boldsymbol{11.75 = 11.75}$$

13. Let s = one side of an equilateral triangle.

Write your equation in words: Perimeter = add up all sides.

Plug in the expressions for your equation and solve for s:

$$21 = s + s + s$$
$$21 = 3s$$
$$\frac{21}{3} = \frac{3s}{3}$$
$$\boldsymbol{7 = s}$$

Articulate your solution in a sentence: Each side of the equilateral triangle is **7 units**.

Check your answer by plugging 7 back into your original equation:

$$3(7) = 21$$
$$\mathbf{21 = 21}$$

14. $6.5x + 25 = 70.5$, 7 hours of babysitting

Let $h =$ the number of hours Chloe babysits each week.

Create a table, plug in numbers, find a pattern, and find your expression from there.

# of Hours Babysitting	Total Amount Earned for One Week
2	25 + 6.50(2)
3	25 + 6.50(3)
4	25 + 6.50(4)
h	**25 + 6.50(h) = 25 + 6.50h**

Write your equation in words:

Weekly allowance + babysitting income = total earned each week

Plug in what you know: $25 + 6.50h = 70.50$

Solve for h: $25 + 6.50h - 25 = 70.50 - 25$

$$6.50h = 45.50$$
$$\frac{6.50h}{6.50} = \frac{45.50}{6.50}$$
$$\mathbf{h = 7}$$

Articulate your solution in a sentence: If Chloe babysits for 7 hours in one week, she will have earned **$70.50 total**, including her weekly allowance of $25.

Check your answer by plugging 7 back into your original equation:

$$25 + 6.50(7) = 70.50$$
$$25 + 45.50 = 70.50$$
$$\mathbf{70.50 = 70.50}$$

15. Let Anna = Anna (instead of plugging A for Anna, use the actual name since all the names start with A)

Abby = 3(Alice) = 3[2(Anna)] = 6(Anna)

Alice = 2(Anna)

Anna = A

Abby's age + Alice's age + Anna's age = 27

$$6A + 2A + A = 27$$
$$9A = 27$$
$$\mathbf{A = 3}$$

Plug in Anna's age to find the other ages:

Abby = 3(Alice) = 3[2(Anna)] = 6(Anna) = 6(3) = 18

Alice = 2(Anna) = 2(3) = 6

Anna = 3

Explain your solution:

Abby is **18** years old, Alice is **6** years old, and Anna is **3** years old.

16.
$$2x + 16 = 52$$
$$2x + 16 - 16 = 52 - 16$$
$$2x = 36$$
$$\frac{2x}{2} = \frac{36}{2}$$
$$\mathbf{x = 18}$$

The sides of the isosceles triangle measure 18 inches, 18 inches, and 16 inches. Plug in the solution to check your work: perimeter = base + 2(sides)

$$52 = 16 + 2(18)$$
$$52 = 16 + 36$$
$$\mathbf{52 = 52}$$

Lesson 3.3: Solving Algebraic Inequalities
Practice, page 77

1. $6 + 3x < 18$

$$6 + 3x - 6 < 18 - 6$$
$$3x < 12$$
$$\frac{3x}{3} < \frac{12}{3}$$
$$\mathbf{x < 4}$$

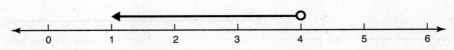

2. $6 - 3x \geq 18$

$$6 - 3x - 6 \geq 18 - 6$$
$$-3x \geq 12$$
$$\frac{-3x}{-3} \geq \frac{12}{-3}$$
$$\mathbf{x \leq -4}$$

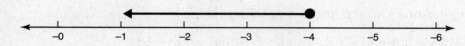

3. $-6 + 3x \leq -18$

$$-6 + 3x + 6 \leq -18 + 6$$
$$3x \leq -12$$
$$\frac{3x}{3} \leq -\frac{12}{3}$$
$$\mathbf{x \leq -4}$$

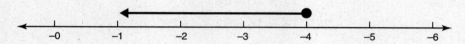

4. $-6 - 3x > -18$

$$-6 - 3x + 6 > -18 + 6$$
$$-3x > -12$$
$$\frac{-3x}{-3} > \frac{-12}{-3}$$
$$\mathbf{x < 4}$$

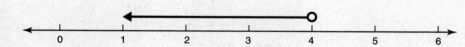

5. $-\frac{1}{3}x < 2$

$$-\frac{3}{1}\left(-\frac{1}{3}x\right) < -3(2)$$
$$\mathbf{x > -6}$$

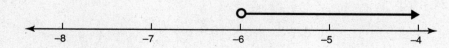

6. $-4x < -13$

$$\frac{-4x}{-4} < \frac{-13}{-4}$$
$$\mathbf{x > 3.25}$$

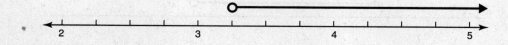

7. $-4x - 1 \geq 12$

$$-4x - 1 + 1 \geq 12 + 1$$

$$\frac{-4x}{-4} \geq \frac{13}{-4}$$

$$\mathbf{x \leq -3.25}$$

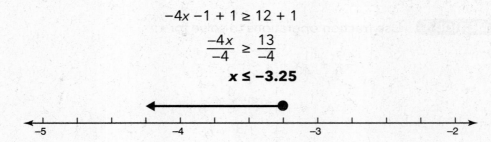

8. $-\dfrac{2}{3}x + \dfrac{5}{6} < \dfrac{11}{18}$

METHOD 1   Use fraction operations to solve for x:

$$-\frac{2}{3}x + \frac{5}{6} < \frac{11}{18}$$

$$-\frac{2}{3}x + \frac{5}{6} - \frac{5}{6} < \frac{11}{18} - \frac{5}{6}$$

$$-\frac{2}{3}x < \frac{11}{18} - \frac{15}{18}$$

$$-\frac{2}{3}x < -\frac{4}{18}$$

$$-\frac{3}{2}\left(-\frac{2}{3}x\right) < -\frac{3}{2}\left(-\frac{4}{18}\right)$$

$$\mathbf{x > \frac{1}{3}}$$

METHOD 2   Multiply by the LCM between 3, 6, and 18.

$$\frac{18}{1}\left(-\frac{2}{3}x + \frac{5}{6}\right) < \frac{18}{1}\left(\frac{11}{18}\right)$$

$$-12x + 15 < 11$$

$$-12x + 15 - 15 < 11 - 15$$

$$-12x < -4$$

$$\frac{-12x}{-12} < \frac{-4}{-12}$$

$$\mathbf{x > \frac{1}{3}}$$

9. $-\dfrac{7}{8} + \dfrac{1}{4}x < -\dfrac{1}{2}$

   METHOD 1 Use fraction operations to solve for x:

   $$-\dfrac{7}{8} + \dfrac{1}{4}x + \dfrac{7}{8} < -\dfrac{1}{2} + \dfrac{7}{8}$$

   $$\dfrac{1}{4}x < -\dfrac{4}{8} + \dfrac{7}{8}$$

   $$\dfrac{1}{4}x < \dfrac{3}{8}$$

   $$\dfrac{4}{1}\left(\dfrac{1}{4}x\right) < \dfrac{4}{1}\left(\dfrac{3}{8}\right)$$

   $$\boldsymbol{x < \dfrac{3}{2}}$$

   METHOD 2 Multiply by the LCM between 2, 4, and 8.

   $$8\left(-\dfrac{7}{8} + \dfrac{1}{4}x\right) < \dfrac{8}{1}\left(-\dfrac{1}{2}\right)$$

   $$-7 + 2x < -4$$

   $$-7 + 2x + 7 < -4 + 7$$

   $$2x < 3$$

   $$\dfrac{2x}{2} < \dfrac{3}{2}$$

   $$\boldsymbol{x < \dfrac{3}{2}}$$

   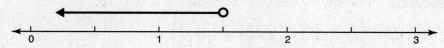

10. $0.4 - 1.2x < -3.2$

    $$0.4 - 1.2x - 0.4 < -3.2 - 0.4$$

    $$-1.2x < -3.6$$

    $$\dfrac{-1.2x}{-1.2} < \dfrac{-3.6}{-1.2}$$

    $$\boldsymbol{x > 3}$$

11. $6x - 8 \geq -2x - 32$

$$6x - 8 + 8 \geq -2x - 32 + 8$$
$$6x \geq -2x - 24$$
$$6x + 2x \geq -2x - 24 + 2x$$
$$8x \geq -24$$
$$\frac{8x}{8} \geq -\frac{24}{8}$$
$$\boldsymbol{x \geq -3}$$

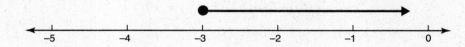

12. $-3x - 1 \leq -16 - x$

$$-3x - 1 + 1 \leq -16 - x + 1$$
$$-3x \leq -15 - x$$
$$-3x + x \leq -15 - x + x$$
$$-2x \leq -15$$
$$\frac{-2x}{-2} \leq \frac{-15}{-2}$$
$$\boldsymbol{x \geq 7.5}$$

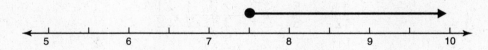

13. $-\frac{2}{5}x + \frac{1}{3} \geq \frac{7}{5} - \frac{14}{15}x$

METHOD 1 Use fraction operations to solve for x:

$$-\frac{2}{5}x + \frac{1}{3} - \frac{1}{3} \geq \frac{7}{5} - \frac{14}{15}x - \frac{1}{3}$$
$$-\frac{2}{5}x \geq -\frac{14}{15}x + \frac{21}{15} - \frac{5}{15}$$
$$-\frac{2}{5}x \geq -\frac{14}{15}x + \frac{16}{15}$$
$$-\frac{2}{5}x + \frac{14}{15}x \geq -\frac{14}{15}x + \frac{16}{15} + \frac{14}{15}x$$
$$-\frac{6}{15}x + \frac{14}{15}x \geq \frac{16}{15}$$
$$\frac{8}{15}x \geq \frac{16}{15}$$
$$\frac{15}{8}\left(\frac{8}{15}x\right) \geq \frac{15}{8}\left(\frac{16}{15}\right)$$
$$\boldsymbol{x \geq 2}$$

METHOD 2 Multiply by the LCM between 3, 5, and 15.

$$15\left(-\frac{2}{5}x + \frac{1}{3}\right) \geq 15\left(\frac{7}{5} - \frac{14}{15}x\right)$$

$$\frac{15}{1}\left(-\frac{2}{5}x\right) + \frac{15}{1}\left(\frac{1}{3}\right) \geq \frac{15}{1}\left(\frac{7}{5}\right) + \frac{15}{1}\left(-\frac{14}{15}x\right)$$

$$-6x + 5 \geq 21 - 14x$$

$$-6x + 5 - 5 \geq 21 - 14x - 5$$

$$-6x \geq 16 - 14x$$

$$-6x + 14x \geq 16 - 14x + 14x$$

$$8x \geq 16$$

$$\frac{8x}{8} \geq \frac{16}{8}$$

$$\mathbf{x \geq 2}$$

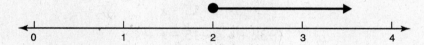

14. $\frac{11}{12}x - \frac{5}{6} \leq -\frac{2}{3}x + \frac{1}{2}$

METHOD 1 Use fraction operations to solve for x:

$$\frac{11}{12}x - \frac{5}{6} - \frac{1}{2} \leq -\frac{2}{3}x + \frac{1}{2} - \frac{1}{2}$$

$$\frac{11}{12}x - \frac{5}{6} - \frac{3}{6} \leq -\frac{2}{3}x$$

$$\frac{11}{12}x - \frac{8}{6} \leq -\frac{2}{3}x$$

$$\frac{11}{12}x - \frac{11}{12}x - \frac{8}{6} \leq -\frac{2}{3}x - \frac{11}{12}x$$

$$-\frac{8}{6} \leq -\frac{8}{12}x - \frac{11}{12}x$$

$$-\frac{8}{6} \leq -\frac{19}{12}x$$

$$-\frac{12}{19}\left(-\frac{8}{6}\right) \leq -\frac{12}{19}\left(-\frac{19}{12}x\right)$$

$$\mathbf{\frac{16}{19} \geq x}$$

METHOD 2 Multiply by the LCM between 2, 3, 6, and 12.

$$12\left(\frac{11}{12}x - \frac{5}{6}\right) \le 12\left(-\frac{2}{3}x + \frac{1}{2}\right)$$

$$\frac{12}{1}\left(\frac{11}{12}x\right) + \frac{12}{1}\left(-\frac{5}{6}\right) \le \frac{12}{1}\left(-\frac{2}{3}x\right) + \frac{12}{1}\left(\frac{1}{2}\right)$$

$$11x - 10 \le -8x + 6$$

$$11x - 10 - 6 \le -8x + 6 - 6$$

$$11x - 16 \le -8x$$

$$11x - 16 - 11x \le -8x - 11x$$

$$-16 \le -19x$$

$$\frac{-16}{-19} \le \frac{-19x}{-19}$$

$$\boldsymbol{\frac{16}{19} \ge x}$$

15. $-0.7x - 3.9 > 1.8 - 0.5x$

$$-0.7x - 3.9 + 3.9 > 1.8 - 0.5x + 3.9$$

$$-0.7x > 5.7 - 0.5x$$

$$-0.7x + 0.5x > 5.7 - 0.5x + 0.5x$$

$$-0.2x > 5.7$$

$$\frac{-0.2x}{-0.2} > \frac{5.7}{-0.2}$$

$$\boldsymbol{x < -28.5}$$

16. $9.2 - x < -1.8 - 0.5x$

$$9.2 - x - 9.2 < -1.8 - 0.5x - 9.2$$

$$-x < -11 - 0.5x$$

$$-x + 0.5x < -11 - 0.5x + 0.5x$$

$$-0.5x < -11$$

$$\frac{-0.5x}{-0.5} < \frac{-11}{-0.5}$$

$$\boldsymbol{x > 22}$$

17. $-2\left(3x+\dfrac{1}{2}\right) \geq -0.2(-8-20x)$

METHOD 1 Distribute.

$$-2(3x) + (-2)\left(\dfrac{1}{2}\right) \geq -0.2(-8) + (-0.2)(-20x)$$

$$-6x - 1 \geq 1.6 + 4x$$

$$-6x - 1 + 1 \geq 1.6 + 4x + 1$$

$$-6x \geq 2.6 + 4x$$

$$-6x - 4x \geq 2.6 + 4x - 4x$$

$$-10x \geq 2.6$$

$$\dfrac{-10x}{-10} \geq \dfrac{2.6}{-10}$$

$$\boldsymbol{x \leq -0.26}$$

METHOD 2 Divide by -0.2.

$$\dfrac{-2\left(3x+\dfrac{1}{2}\right)}{-0.2} \geq \dfrac{-0.2(-8-20x)}{-0.2}$$

$$10\left(3x+\dfrac{1}{2}\right) \leq -8 - 20x$$

$$10(3x) + 10\left(\dfrac{1}{2}\right) \leq -8 - 20x$$

$$30x + 5 \leq -8 - 20x$$

$$30x + 5 - 5 \leq -8 - 20x - 5$$

$$30x \leq -13 - 20x$$

$$30x + 20x \leq -13 - 20x + 20x$$

$$50x \leq -13$$

$$\dfrac{50x}{50} \leq -\dfrac{13}{50}$$

$$x \leq -\dfrac{13}{50}$$

$$\boldsymbol{x \leq -0.26}$$

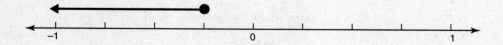

Lesson 3.4: Real-World Problems: Algebraic Inequalities

Practice, pages 82–84

1. The sum of 8 and $2x$ is no less than 12.

$$8 + 2x \geq 12$$
$$8 + 2x - 8 \geq 12 - 8$$
$$2x \geq 4$$
$$\frac{2x}{2} \geq \frac{4}{2}$$
$$\boldsymbol{x \geq 2}$$

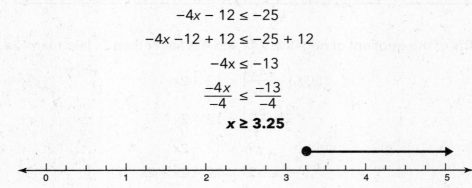

2. The difference between $-4x$ and 12 is at most negative 25.

$$-4x - 12 \leq -25$$
$$-4x - 12 + 12 \leq -25 + 12$$
$$-4x \leq -13$$
$$\frac{-4x}{-4} \leq \frac{-13}{-4}$$
$$\boldsymbol{x \geq 3.25}$$

3. The product of -3 and $x + 2$ is more than its sum.

$$-3(x + 2) > -3 + x + 2$$
$$-3x - 6 > -1 + x$$
$$-3x - 6 + 6 > -1 + x + 6$$
$$-3x > 5 + x$$
$$-3x - x > 5 + x - x$$
$$-4x > 5$$
$$\frac{-4x}{-4} > \frac{5}{-4}$$
$$\boldsymbol{x < -\frac{5}{4}}$$

4. One-quarter of the sum of 8x and 12 is less than three-eighths.

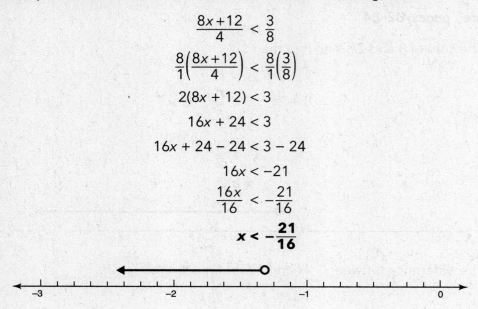

$$\frac{8x+12}{4} < \frac{3}{8}$$

$$\frac{8}{1}\left(\frac{8x+12}{4}\right) < \frac{8}{1}\left(\frac{3}{8}\right)$$

$$2(8x + 12) < 3$$

$$16x + 24 < 3$$

$$16x + 24 - 24 < 3 - 24$$

$$16x < -21$$

$$\frac{16x}{16} < -\frac{21}{16}$$

$$\boldsymbol{x < -\frac{21}{16}}$$

5. 150% of the quotient of negative 24x and 4 is fewer than 2x less than 12.

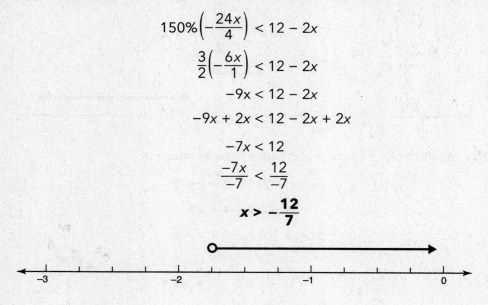

$$150\%\left(-\frac{24x}{4}\right) < 12 - 2x$$

$$\frac{3}{2}\left(-\frac{6x}{1}\right) < 12 - 2x$$

$$-9x < 12 - 2x$$

$$-9x + 2x < 12 - 2x + 2x$$

$$-7x < 12$$

$$\frac{-7x}{-7} < \frac{12}{-7}$$

$$\boldsymbol{x > -\frac{12}{7}}$$

6. Conor needs to score a minimum of **87** on the fourth test in order to keep his scholarship.

   Let x = the score on Conor's fourth test.

   Average ≥ 85

$$\frac{\text{total}}{\#} \geq 85$$

$$\frac{78+92+83+x}{4} \geq 85$$

$$\frac{4}{1}\left(\frac{78+92+83+x}{4}\right) \geq (85)4$$

$$78 + 92 + 83 + x \geq 340$$

$$253 + x \geq 340$$

$$253 + x - 253 \geq 340 - 253$$

$$\mathbf{x \geq 87}$$

7. Julia needs to score at least **87** on the fifth quiz in order to be exempt from the final exam.

   Let x = the score on the fifth quiz.

   Average ≥ 90

$$\frac{\text{total}}{\#} \geq 90$$

$$\frac{95+82+97+89+x}{5} \geq 90$$

$$\frac{363+x}{5} \geq 90$$

$$\frac{5}{1}\left(\frac{363+x}{5}\right) \geq (90)5$$

$$363 + x \geq 450$$

$$363 + x - 363 \geq 450 - 363$$

$$\mathbf{x \geq 87}$$

8. Estella needs no less than a **3.7** on her fifth course in order to apply for the fellowship.

    Let x = the score on her fifth course.

    Average ≥ 3.5

    $$\frac{\text{total}}{\#} \geq 3.5$$

    $$\frac{2.9 + 3.9 + 3.4 + 3.6 + x}{5} \geq 3.5$$

    $$\frac{13.8 + x}{5} \geq 3.5$$

    $$\frac{5}{1}\left(\frac{13.8 + x}{5}\right) \geq (3.5)5$$

    $$13.8 + x \geq 17.5$$

    $$13.8 + x - 13.8 \geq 17.5 - 13.8$$

    $$\boldsymbol{x \geq 3.7}$$

    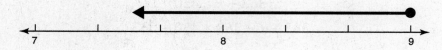

9. Maya can spend **no more than $9** on each centerpiece without going over her $50 budget.

    Let c = the amount Maya can spend on each centerpiece.

    Balloons + wall decorations + centerpieces ≤ total budget

    $$14 + 9 + 3c \leq 50$$

    $$23 + 3c \leq 50$$

    $$23 + 3c - 23 \leq 50 - 23$$

    $$3c \leq 27$$

    $$\frac{3c}{3} \leq \frac{27}{3}$$

    $$\boldsymbol{c \leq 9}$$

Amount Spent on Each Centerpiece	23 + 3c ≤ 50	True/False and Explanation
8	23 + 3(8) ≤ 50 23 + 24 ≤ 50 49 ≤ 50	**True.** If Maya spends $8 on each centerpiece, she will be under budget by $1.
9	23 + 3(9) ≤ 50 23 + 27 ≤ 50 52 ≤ 50	**False.** If Maya spends over $9 on each centerpiece, she will be over budget.

10. Orion must have traveled **more than 16 miles** to incur a bill of over $20.

Let m = the number of miles Orion traveled.

Total charged > 20

Flat rate + charge based on the mileage > 20

$$2.5 + 1.15m > 20$$
$$2.5 + 1.15m - 2.5 > 20 - 2.5$$
$$1.15m > 17.5$$
$$\frac{1.15m}{1.15} > \frac{17.5}{1.15}$$
$$\mathbf{m > 15.217}$$

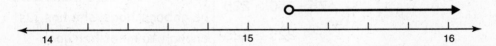

# of Miles Traveled	2.5 + 1.15m > 20	True/False and Explanation
15	2.5 + 1.15(15) > 20 2.5 + 17.25 > 20 19.75 > 20	**False.** If Orion traveled 15 miles, his bill would not be over $20.
16	2.5 + 1.15(16) > 20 2.5 + 18.4 > 20 20.9 > 20	**True.** If Orion traveled 16 miles, his bill would be over $20.

11. Isabella needs to walk her neighbors' dogs for a **minimum of ten hours** total in order to afford the necklace for her mother.

Let h = the number of hours Isabella walks her neighbors' dogs.

Already saved + amount earned from walking the dogs: ≥225

$$75 + 15h \geq 225$$
$$75 + 15h - 75 \geq 225 - 75$$
$$15h \geq 150$$
$$\frac{15h}{15} \geq \frac{150}{15}$$
$$\mathbf{h \geq 10}$$

# of Hours Isabella Walked Her Neighbors' Dogs	Goal ≥225 75 + 15h ≥ 225	True/False and Explanation
9	75 + 15(9) ≥ 225 75 + 135 ≥ 225 210 ≥ 225	**False.** If Isabella spent a total of nine hours walking her neighbors' dogs, she would be $15 shy of her goal.
10	75 + 15(10) ≥ 225 75 + 150 ≥ 225 225 ≥ 225	**True.** If Isabella spent a total of ten hours walking her neighbors' dogs, she has just enough to meet her goal.
11	75 + 15(11) ≥ 225 75 + 165 ≥ 225 240 ≥ 225	**True.** If Isabella spent a total of eleven hours walking her neighbors' dogs, she would have exceeded her goal by $15.

12. Kaitlyn can sign up for **up to nine months** of Netflix and still have **$50 left over** to buy new clothes for school.

Let m = the number of months of Netflix Kaitlyn can afford.

Total amount in her piggy bank ≥ cost of Netflix + money saved for clothes

$$125 \geq 8m + 50$$
$$125 - 50 \geq 8m + 50 - 50$$
$$75 \geq 8m$$
$$\frac{75}{8} \geq \frac{8m}{8}$$
$$\mathbf{9.375 \geq m}$$

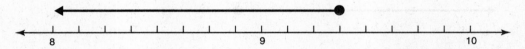

# of Months of Netflix	125 ≥ 8m + 50	True/False and Explanation
8	125 ≥ 8(8) + 50 125 ≥ 64 + 50 125 ≥ 114	**True.** Kaitlyn can afford eight months of Netflix. Since 125 − 114 = 11, she can afford one more month.
9	125 ≥ 8(9) + 50 125 ≥ 72 + 50 125 ≥ 122	**True.** Kaitlyn can afford nine months of Netflix. Since 125 − 122 = 3, she cannot afford another month of Netflix.
10	125 ≥ 8(10) + 50 125 ≥ 130	**False.** Kaitlyn cannot afford ten months because she would then be over her budget by $5.

13. Medina can watch **up to 3 movies** without exceeding the 20 GB data plan on her cell phone.

Let m = the number of movies Medina can watch on her phone.

Amount already used + amount used to watch movies ≤ data limit

$$9.25 + 3.5m \leq 20$$

$$9.25 + 3.5m - 9.25 \leq 20 - 9.25$$

$$3.5m \leq 10.75$$

$$\frac{3.5m}{3.5} \leq \frac{10.75}{3.5}$$

$$\boldsymbol{m \leq 3.0714}$$

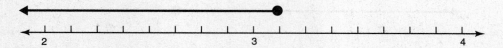

# of Movies Medina Can Watch	$9.25 + 3.5m \leq 20$	True/False and Explanation
2	$9.25 + 3.5(2) \leq 20$ $9.25 + 7 \leq 20$ $16.25 \leq 20$	**True.** If Medina watches 2 movies, she will not exceed her 20 GB limit. Since 20 − 16.25 = 3.75, she has enough to watch one more movie.
3	$9.25 + 3.5(3) \leq 20$ $9.25 + 10.5 \leq 20$ $19.75 \leq 20$	**True.** If Medina watches 3 movies, she will not exceed her 20 GB limit. Since 20 − 19.75 = 0.25, she does not have enough to watch one more movie.
4	$9.25 + 3.5(4) \leq 20$ $9.25 + 14 \leq 20$ $23.25 \leq 20$	**False.** If she watches 4 movies, she will exceed her data plan.

14. Katie will need to sell **more than 30 drinks** in order to start making a profit at the holiday fair.

Let d = the number of drinks Katie sells.

Profit > cost of supplies

$$2.75d > 85$$

$$\frac{2.75d}{2.75} > \frac{85}{2.75}$$

$$\boldsymbol{d > 30.909}$$

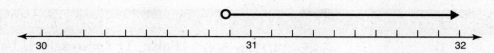

# of Drinks Katie Sells	2.75d > 85	True/False and Explanation
30	2.75(30) > 85 82.5 > 85	**False.** If Katie sells 30 drinks, she will not have enough to break even on her supplies. Since 85 − 82.5 = 2.5, she will be $2.5 short.
31	2.75(31) > 85 85.25 > 85	**True.** If Katie sells 31 drinks, she will have met her break even point by 25 cents.

15. If Karen sells the same number of boxes each day, she will need to sell **more than 11 boxes** a day for the next two weeks to meet her goal. If she sells 12 boxes a day for the next two weeks, she will have exceeded her goal by 13 boxes.

Let b = the boxes of Girl Scout cookies Karen sells.

There are 14 days in two weeks. The equation below is how many boxes Karen needs to sell each day.

Boxes already sold + boxes Karen needs to sell ≥ 500

$$345 + 14b \geq 500$$
$$345 + 14b - 345 \geq 500 - 345$$
$$14b \geq 155$$
$$\frac{14b}{14} \geq \frac{155}{14}$$
$$\boldsymbol{b \geq 11.0714}$$

# of Boxes Karen Sells	$345 + 14x \geq 500$	True/False and Explanation
11	$345 + 14(11) \geq 500$ $345 + 154 \geq 500$ $499 \geq 500$	**False.** If Karen sells 11 boxes a day for the next two weeks, she will be one box shy of her goal.
12	$345 + 14(12) \geq 500$ $513 \geq 500$	**True.** If Karen sells 12 boxes a day for the next two weeks, she will have met her goal.

16. Jackie would need to take **more than seven classes** for the unlimited yoga class pass to be worthwhile. Another way to say this: Jackie would need to take eight or more yoga classes for the unlimited monthly pass to be worthwhile.

Let c = the number of yoga classes Jackie attends.

Pay as you go > unlimited.

$$15 + 22c > 185$$
$$15 + 22c - 15 > 185 - 15$$
$$22c > 170$$
$$\frac{22c}{22} > \frac{170}{22}$$
$$\mathbf{c > 7.73}$$

# of Yoga Classes Jackie Attends	$15 + 22c > 185$	True/False and Explanation
7	$15 + 22(7) > 185$ $15 + 154 > 185$ $169 > 185$	**False.** If Jackie only takes seven yoga classes, she pays $169 total. Therefore, it would not be worth it to pay for unlimited yoga classes for the month.
8	$15 + 22(8) > 185$ $15 + 176 > 185$ $191 > 185$	**True.** If Jackie takes eight yoga classes, her total is $191.

17. The electric car will be cheaper **after 679 miles**.

Let m = number of miles both cars will drive.

Electric car < Gas car

$$190(12) + 1m < 100(12) + 2.59m$$
$$2{,}280 + 1m < 1{,}200 + 2.59m$$
$$2{,}280 + 1m - 1{,}200 < 1{,}200 - 1{,}200 + 2.59m$$
$$1{,}080 + 1m < 2.59m$$
$$1{,}080 + 1m - 1m < 2.59m - 1m$$
$$1{,}080 < 1.59m$$
$$\frac{1{,}080}{1.59} < \frac{1.59m}{1.59}$$
$$\mathbf{679.245 < m}$$

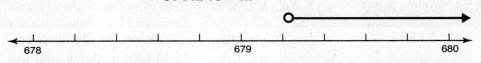

# of Miles (m)	Electric Car < Gas Car $2{,}280 + 1m < 1{,}200 + 2.59m$	True/False and Explanation
678	$2{,}280 + 1(678) < 1{,}200 + 2.59(678)$ $2{,}280 + 678 < 1{,}200 + 1{,}756.02$ $2{,}958 < 2{,}956.02$	**False.** If the electric car was driven 678 miles, the total cost would be \$2,958, which is more than what it would cost the gas car if it had driven the same number of miles.
679	$2{,}280 + 1(679) < 1{,}200 + 2.59(679)$ $2{,}280 + 679 < 1{,}200 + 1{,}758.61$ $2{,}959 < 2{,}958.61$	**False.** If the electric car was driven 679 miles, the total cost would be \$2,959, which is more than what it would cost the gas car if it had driven the same number of miles.
680	$2{,}280 + 1(680) < 1{,}200 + 2.59(680)$ $2{,}280 + 680 < 1{,}200 + 1{,}761.2$ $2{,}960 < 2{,}961.2$	**True.** If the electric car was driven 680 miles, the total cost would be \$2,960, which is less than what it would cost the gas car if it had driven the same number of miles.

18. Quinn needs to sell **more than 1,684** gift baskets in order to no longer pay the investor's royalty fee.

    Let b = the number of gift baskets Quinn sells.

    Investment < total profit

    $$8,000 < 4.75b$$

    $$\frac{8,000}{4.75} < \frac{4.75b}{4.75}$$

    $$\textbf{1,684.2105} < \textbf{\textit{b}}$$

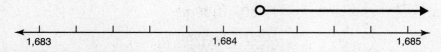

# of Gift Baskets Quinn Sells	8,000 < 4.75b	True/False and Explanation
1,684	8,000 < 4.75b 8,000 < 4.75(1,684) 8,000 < 7,999	**False.** If Quinn sells 1,684 baskets, she will be $1 short from paying the investor's $8,000 investment back.
1,685	8,000 < 4.75b 8,000 < 4.75(1,685) 8,000 < 8,003.75	**True.** If Quinn sells 1,685 baskets, she will have paid the investor back in full.

19. Bryan can play **three more games** if he plays the $1.25 games and not the $1.50 games.

    Let g = number of games Bryan plays at the arcade.

$2.75 + 1.25g < 25$	$2.75 + 1.5g < 25$
$2.75 + 1.25g - 2.75 < 25 - 2.75$	$2.75 + 1.5g - 2.75 < 25 - 2.75$
$1.25g < 22.25$	$1.5g < 22.25$
$\dfrac{1.25g}{1.25} < \dfrac{22.25}{1.25}$	$\dfrac{1.5g}{1.5} < \dfrac{22.25}{1.5}$
$g < 17.8$	$g < 14.833$
At $1.25 per game, Bryan can play up to 17 games.	At $1.50 per game, Bryan can play up to 14 games.

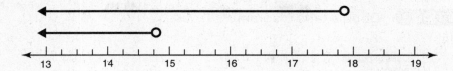

20. She needs to sell **25 less cupcakes** to recoup her costs if she sells them at $3.00 instead of $2.50.

    Let c = the number of cupcakes Jessica sells.

$0.75c > 46$	$1.25c > 46$
$\dfrac{0.75c}{0.75} > \dfrac{46}{0.75}$	$\dfrac{1.25c}{1.25} > \dfrac{46}{1.25}$
$c > 61.333$	$c > 36.8$
If she sells the cupcakes at $2.50 each, she will need to sell more than 61 cupcakes in order to break even on the cost of her supplies.	If she sells the cupcakes at $3.00 each, she will need to sell more than 36 cupcakes in order to break even on the cost of her supplies.

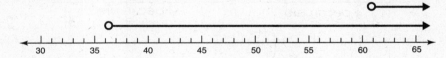

Chapter 4 Ratios and Proportional Relationships

Lesson 4.1: Unit Rates

Practice, pages 92–94

1. It will take 2 cups of peanut butter.

   METHOD 1 Equivalent fractions

   $$\frac{\frac{1}{8} \text{ peanut butter}}{\frac{1}{16} \text{ pan}} \cdot \frac{16}{16} = \frac{2 \text{ cups}}{1 \text{ pan}}$$

   METHOD 2 Cross-multiply.

   $$\frac{\frac{1}{8} \text{ peanut butter}}{\frac{1}{16} \text{ pan}} = \frac{x}{1 \text{ pan}}$$

   $$\left(\frac{1}{8}\right)(1) = \frac{1}{16}x$$

   $$\frac{1}{8} = \frac{1}{16}x$$

   $$\frac{16}{1}\left(\frac{1}{8}\right) = \left(\frac{1}{16}x\right)\left(\frac{16}{1}\right)$$

   $$\mathbf{2 = x}$$

METHOD 3   Double tape diagram

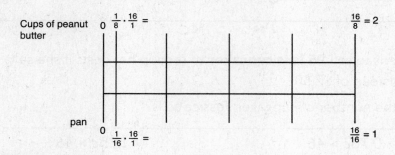

Cups of peanut butter 0 $\frac{1}{8} \cdot \frac{16}{1} =$ $\frac{16}{8} = 2$

pan 0 $\frac{1}{16} \cdot \frac{16}{1} =$ $\frac{16}{16} = 1$

2.   **METHOD 1**   Equivalent fractions

$$\frac{\frac{1}{4} \text{ stick of unsalted butter}}{\frac{1}{8} \text{ pecan pie}} \cdot \frac{8}{8} = \frac{2 \text{ sticks of unsalted butter}}{1 \text{ pecan pie}}$$

METHOD 2   Proportion

$$\frac{\frac{1}{4} \text{ stick of unsalted butter}}{\frac{1}{8} \text{ pecan pie}} = \frac{x \text{ sticks of unsalted butter}}{1 \text{ pecan pie}}$$

$$\left(\frac{1}{4}\right)(1) = \frac{1}{8}x$$

$$\frac{1}{4} = \frac{1}{8}x$$

$$\frac{8}{1}\left(\frac{1}{4}\right) = \left(\frac{1}{8}x\right)\left(\frac{8}{1}\right)$$

$$\mathbf{2 = x}$$

3.   **METHOD 1**   Equivalent fractions

$$\frac{\frac{3}{7} \text{ gallons of paint}}{\frac{3}{10} \text{ painted baby room}} \div \frac{\frac{3}{10}}{\frac{3}{10}} = \frac{\frac{10}{7} \text{ gallons of paint}}{1 \text{ painted baby room}}$$

METHOD 2   Proportion

$$\frac{\frac{3}{7} \text{ gallons of paint}}{\frac{3}{10} \text{ painted baby room}} = \frac{x \text{ gallons of paint}}{1 \text{ painted baby room}}$$

$$\left(\frac{3}{7}\right)(1) = \frac{3}{10}x$$

$$\left(\frac{3}{7}\right)\left(\frac{10}{3}\right) = \left(\frac{3}{10}x\right)\left(\frac{10}{3}\right)$$

$$\mathbf{\frac{10}{7} = x}$$

METHOD 3 Tape diagram

$$\frac{3}{10} \div 3 = \frac{3}{10} \cdot \frac{1}{3} = \frac{1}{10}$$

$$\frac{3}{7} \div 3 = \frac{3}{7} \cdot \frac{1}{3} = \frac{1}{7}$$

$$\frac{1}{10} \cdot 10 = \frac{10}{10} = 1$$

$$\mathbf{\frac{1}{7} \cdot 10 = \frac{10}{7}}$$

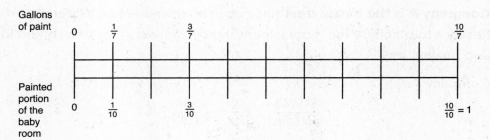

4. Massage place B is a better deal by **$3.33**. Other factors to consider: (*answers may vary*) quality of massage, customer service, and distance from home.

    Massage location A:

    $$\frac{\$55}{0.5 \text{ hr}} \cdot \frac{2}{2} = \frac{\$110}{1 \text{ hr}}$$

    Massage location B:

    $$\frac{\$80}{\frac{3}{4} \text{ hr}} \div \frac{\frac{3}{4}}{\frac{3}{4}} = \frac{\$106.67}{1 \text{ hr}}$$

5. Peter can blow up the mattress faster.

    METHOD 1 The one unit of measure is in minutes.

    Peter:

    $$\frac{\frac{3}{10} \text{ mattress}}{2 \text{ min}} \div \frac{2}{2} = \frac{0.15 \text{ mattress}}{1 \text{ min}}$$

    Irene:

    $$\frac{\frac{2}{9} \text{ mattress}}{2.5 \text{ min}} \div \frac{2.5}{2.5} = \frac{0.09 \text{ mattress}}{1 \text{ min}}$$

> **METHOD 2** The one unit of measure is the mattress.

Peter:

$$\frac{2 \text{ min}}{\frac{3}{10} \text{ mattress}} \cdot \frac{\frac{10}{3}}{\frac{10}{3}} = \frac{\frac{20}{3} \text{ min}}{1 \text{ mattress}} = \frac{6.67 \text{ min}}{1 \text{ mattress}}$$

Irene:

$$\frac{2.5 \text{ min}}{\frac{2}{9} \text{ mattress}} \cdot \frac{\frac{9}{2}}{\frac{9}{2}} = \frac{\frac{45}{4} \text{ min}}{1 \text{ mattress}} = \frac{11.25 \text{ min}}{1 \text{ mattress}}$$

6. **Company A is the better deal** since one can save three cents per roll. Reasons to purchase the more expensive roll: (*answers may vary*) brand loyalty and quality.

    Company A:

    $$\frac{\$19.47}{36 \text{ rolls}} \div \frac{36}{36} = \frac{\$0.54}{1 \text{ roll}}$$

    Company B:

    $$\frac{\$27.40}{48 \text{ rolls}} \div \frac{48}{48} = \frac{\$0.57}{1 \text{ roll}}$$

7. Two dozen bananas for **$7 is the best deal** because the bananas end up costing 29 cents each. (*Answers may vary*.) You could purchase the extra bananas and freeze them later.

    Deal #1:

    $$\frac{\$0.50}{1 \text{ banana}}$$

    Deal #2:

    $$\frac{\$4}{12 \text{ bananas}} \div \frac{12}{12} = \frac{\$0.33}{1 \text{ banana}}$$

    Deal #3:

    $$\frac{\$7}{24 \text{ bananas}} \div \frac{24}{24} = \frac{\$0.29}{1 \text{ banana}}$$

8. **Purchasing the chips at the local grocery store is a better deal** because you can get 33 cents per bag of chips vs. 50 cents per bag. Convenience stores typically charge more for items because small convenience stores may not have the luxury of purchasing in bulk to offer better prices. In

addition, convenience stores capitalize on consumers that pay more for the convenience of picking something up on the go.

Local grocery store:

$$\frac{\$7}{12 \text{ bags}} \div \frac{12}{12} = \frac{\$0.33}{1 \text{ bag}}$$

Convenience store:

$$\frac{\$1}{2 \text{ bags}} \div \frac{2}{2} = \frac{\$0.50}{1 \text{ bag}}$$

9. Answers may vary.

10. Answers may vary.

11. His average speed is **72.5 miles per hour**. At this rate, Cary has approximately 5 hours left on his journey.

Solution: total miles = 68(1.5) + 74(4.5) = 102 + 333 = 673

$$\text{Average} = \frac{\text{total miles}}{\text{total hours}} = \frac{435 \text{ miles}}{1.5 + 4.5} = \frac{435}{6} = 72.5 \frac{\text{miles}}{\text{hour}} = 72.5 \text{ mph}$$

$$795 - 435 = 360 \text{ miles left}$$

$$\frac{360}{72.5} \approx \textbf{4.97 hours}$$

12. It will take Kevin approximately **66 minutes** or **1 hr and 6 minutes** to watch the garden snail crawl across the sidewalk.

$$\frac{0.55 \text{ inches}}{1 \text{ minute}} = \frac{36 \text{ inches}}{x \text{ minutes}}$$

$$0.55x = 36(1)$$

$$\frac{0.55x}{0.55} = \frac{36}{0.55}$$

$$x \approx \textbf{65.45}$$

13. Francesco's average speed:

$$\frac{\text{total miles}}{\text{\# of miles}} = \frac{14(6) + 18(4)}{6 + 4} = \frac{84 + 72}{10} = \frac{156}{10} = \textbf{15.6 miles per minute}$$

Francesco has already biked: 14(0.1 min) + 18(0.067 min) = 1.4 + 1.2 = 2.6 miles. Miles he has left to bike: 5.4 − 2.6 = 2.8 miles

$$\frac{16 \text{ miles}}{60 \text{ minutes}} = \frac{2.8 \text{ miles}}{x \text{ minutes}}$$

$$16x = 60(2.8)$$

$$\frac{16x}{16} = \frac{60(2.8)}{16}$$

$$x = \mathbf{10.5}$$

He has approximately **2.8 miles** left to bike, and this length will take him about 10.5 minutes if he does not run into traffic lights or stops along the way.

14. Toby will have caught up to the squirrel after about **2 seconds**.

1 mile = 5,280 feet

Squirrel speed:

$$\frac{19 \cdot 5,280 \text{ feet}}{1 \text{ hr}} = \frac{100,320 \text{ feet}}{60 \text{ min}} \div \frac{60}{60} = \frac{1,672 \text{ feet}}{1 \text{ min}}$$

Toby's speed:

$$\frac{20 \cdot 5,280 \text{ feet}}{1 \text{ hr}} = \frac{105,600 \text{ feet}}{60 \text{ min}} \div \frac{60}{60} = \frac{1,760 \text{ feet}}{1 \text{ min}}$$

$$\frac{60 \text{ feet}}{x \text{ seconds}} = \frac{1,760 \text{ feet}}{60 \text{ seconds}}$$

$$1,760x = 60(60)$$

$$\frac{1,760x}{1,760} = \frac{60(60)}{1,760}$$

$$x \approx \mathbf{2.05}$$

15. The average speed of the commercial airplane is **500 mph**.

$$\frac{9,500 \text{ miles}}{19 \text{ hr}} = \frac{x \text{ miles}}{1 \text{ hr}}$$

METHOD 1 Equivalent fractions

$$\frac{9,500 \text{ miles}}{19 \text{ hr}} \div \frac{19}{19} = \frac{x \text{ miles}}{1 \text{ hr}}$$

$$x = \mathbf{9,500 \div 19 = 500}$$

METHOD 2 Cross-multiply or cross-product.

$$\frac{9,500 \text{ miles}}{19 \text{ hr}} = \frac{x \text{ miles}}{1 \text{ hr}}$$

$$19x = 9,500(1)$$

$$\frac{19x}{19} = \frac{9,500(1)}{19}$$

$$\boldsymbol{x = 500}$$

16. Mac pays **$57.50** to park from 9 A.M. to 4 P.M.

Times	Charges	Total Hours	Total Charges
First two hours	$25	2	$25
After the second hour	$6.50 per hour	5	6.5(5) = $32.50
Total		7	25 + 32.50 = $57.50

17. He rented the car for **35 hours** total in one year.

$$35 + 9h = 349$$

$$35 + 9h - 35 = 349 - 35$$

$$9h = 314$$

$$\frac{9h}{9} = \frac{314}{9}$$

$$\boldsymbol{h = 34.9 \approx 35}$$

18. It would cost **$8.98** to travel 0.9 miles in a New York taxi.

Charges	Total Miles	Total Cost
Initial charge = $2.50	0.2	$2.50
$1.85 for every additional 0.2 miles	0.7	$6.48
Total	0.9	$8.98

$$\frac{\$1.85}{0.2 \text{ miles}} = \frac{x}{0.7 \text{ miles}}$$

$$0.2x = 1.85(0.7)$$

$$\frac{0.2x}{0.2} = \frac{1.85(0.7)}{0.2}$$

$$\boldsymbol{x = 6.475}$$

19. It costs **$12.03** to travel 3.3 miles in a San Francisco taxi.

Charges	Total Miles	Total Cost
$3.50 for the first 0.2 miles	0.2	$3.50
$0.55 for every additional 0.2 miles	3.1	$8.525
Total	3.3	$12.03

$$\frac{\$0.55}{0.2 \text{ miles}} = \frac{x}{3.1 \text{ miles}}$$

$$0.2x = 0.55(3.1)$$

$$\frac{0.2x}{0.2} = \frac{0.55(3.1)}{0.2}$$

$$x = 8.525$$

20. If Annalise invites just one friend, then each person can choose up to 24 toppings apiece.

$$2.99(2) + 0.29t = 20$$

$$5.98 + 0.29t = 20$$

$$5.98 + 0.29t - 5.98 = 20 - 5.98$$

$$0.29t = 14.02$$

$$\frac{0.29t}{0.29} = \frac{14.02}{0.29}$$

$$t = 48$$

48 toppings/2 for each person = 24 toppings for each person.

If Annalise invites two friends, then each person can choose up to 12 toppings apiece.

$$2.99(3) + 0.29t = 20$$

$$8.97 + 0.29t = 20$$

$$8.97 + 0.29t - 8.97 = 20 - 8.97$$

$$0.29t = 11.03$$

$$\frac{0.29t}{0.29} = \frac{11.03}{0.29}$$

$$t = 38$$

38 toppings/3 for each person = 12 toppings for each person.

If Annalise invites four friends, then each person can choose up to 6 toppings apiece.

$$2.99(4) + 0.29t = 20$$
$$11.96 + 0.29t = 20$$
$$11.96 + 0.29t - 11.96 = 20 - 11.96$$
$$0.29t = 8.04$$
$$\frac{0.29t}{0.29} = \frac{8.04}{0.29}$$
$$t = 27$$

27 toppings/4 for each person = 6 toppings for each person.

If Annalise invites five friends, then each person can choose up to 3 toppings apiece.

$$2.99(5) + 0.29t = 20$$
$$14.95 + 0.29t = 20$$
$$14.95 + 0.29t - 14.95 = 20 - 14.95$$
$$0.29t = 5.05$$
$$\frac{0.29t}{0.29} = \frac{5.05}{0.29}$$
$$t = 17$$

17 toppings/5 for each person = 3 toppings for each person.

Lesson 4.2: Constant of Proportionality
Practice, pages 100–103

1. A. $\frac{38}{2} = 19$; $\frac{57}{3} = 19$; $\frac{76}{4} = 19$; $\frac{133}{7} = 19$; $k = 19$

   $k =$ **\$19 for every DVD**.

   B. $xk = y$

   $19x = y$

   C. Coordinate (10, 190) means ten DVDs cost **\$190**.

   $19(10) = 190$

2. $\frac{20}{2} = 10$; $\frac{27.50}{3} = 9.167$; $\frac{35}{4} = 8.75$

There is **no constant** because the value of k for each coordinate is different.

3. $\frac{29}{1} = 29$; $\frac{145}{5} = 29$; $\frac{175}{7} = 25$; $\frac{250}{10} = $ **25**

There is **no constant** because the value of k for each coordinate is different.

4. A. $\frac{31.416}{10} = 3.1416$; $\frac{6.283}{2} = 3.1415$; $\frac{21.991}{7} = 3.1415$; $\frac{40.841}{13} = $ **3.1416**

$k = $ **3.14**

The constant represents the quotient of the circumference divided by the diameter.

B. $$xk = \textbf{y}$$
$$3.14x = \textbf{y}$$

C. Coordinate **(25, 78.5)** means a circle with a diameter of 25 cm has a circumference of 78.5 cm or $3.14(25) = 78.5$.

5. A. $\frac{250}{2} = 125$; $\frac{500}{4} = 125$; $\frac{625}{5} = 125$; $\frac{875}{7} = 125$; **k = 125**

The constant means the electric gets **125 miles** for every charge.

B. $$xk = y$$
$$125x = y$$

C. Coordinate **(6, 750)** means if the car has been charged six times, assuming it started at 0 miles, there will have been a total of **750 miles** charged on the electric car.

6. $$k = \frac{8.5 \text{ minutes}}{2 \text{ white boards}} = 4.25$$

$$k = \frac{17 \text{ minutes}}{4 \text{ white boards}} = 4.25$$

This means it takes **4.25 minutes** for Arya to clean one white board.

Equation: **4.25x = y**

7. $$k = \frac{50 \text{ hot dogs}}{12 \text{ minutes}} = 4.167$$

This means one of the competitors can eat **4.167** hot dogs in 1 minute.

Equation: **4.167x = y**

8.
$$k = \frac{122 \text{ miles}}{2 \text{ hours}} = 61$$

The constant means the cheetah was running at **61 mph**.

Equation: **61x = y**

9.
$$k = \frac{\$810}{18 \text{ clients}} = 45$$

The constant means Jeff charges **$45** per client.

Equation: **45x = y**

10.
$$k = \frac{\$22.50}{5 \text{ mochi balls}} = 4.5$$

The constant means each mochi ball costs **$4.50**.

Equation: **4.5x = y**

11.

Coordinate (x, y)	$k = \frac{y}{x}$
(3, 1.1811)	$\frac{1.1811}{3} \approx 0.39$
(4, 1.5758)	$\frac{1.5758}{4} \approx 0.39$
(6, 2.3622)	$\frac{2.3622}{6} \approx 0.39$

The constant means that **0.39 inches** is approximately equal to 1 centimeter.

Equation: **0.39x = y**

To find the number of inches in 30 cm, plug 30 in for y and solve for x.

$$0.39x = 30$$

$$\frac{0.39x}{0.39} = \frac{30}{0.39}$$

$$x \approx 76.92$$

There is approximately **76.92 cm** in 30 inches.

12.

Coordinate (x, y)	$k = \dfrac{y}{x}$
(5, 4)	$\dfrac{4}{5} = 0.8$
(10, 8)	$\dfrac{8}{10} = 0.8$
(15, 12)	$\dfrac{12}{15} = 0.8$

The constant means **0.8** British pounds is equal to 1 U.S. dollar.

The equation is **0.8x = y**

To find how much 30 British pounds would cost in U.S. dollars, plug 30 in for y and solve for x.

$$0.8x = 30$$
$$\frac{0.8x}{0.8} = \frac{30}{0.8}$$
$$x = 37.50$$

30 pounds is equal to **$37.50**.

13.

Coordinate (x, y)	$k = \dfrac{y}{x}$
(2, 500)	$\dfrac{500}{2} = 250$
(4, 1,000)	$\dfrac{1,000}{4} = 250$

The constant means each night costs **$250** at the local hotel.

The equation is **250x = y**

The coordinate (4, 1,000) means 4 nights cost **$1,000**.

14. For the graph to start at (0, 50) means there is a registration fee to sign up for the classes.

15. The coordinate (5, 2,875) means that in five hours the commercial aircraft carrier will travel 2,875 miles.

    How far will the commercial aircraft travel in 12 hours?

    The answer is **12 · 575 = 6,900 miles**.

    How long would it take the commercial aircraft carrier to travel 71,875 miles?

Time (x)	Distance (y)	$k = \dfrac{y}{x}$
4	2,300	$\dfrac{2,300}{4} = 575$
8	4,600	$\dfrac{4,600}{8} = 575$
12	6,900	$\dfrac{6,900}{12} = 575$

$$k = 575$$
$$575x = y$$
$$575x = 71,875$$
$$\frac{575x}{575} = \frac{71,875}{575}$$
$$x = 125$$

It would take the aircraft carrier **125 hours** to travel 71,875 miles.

Lesson 4.3: Percent Decrease: Discounts and Markdowns
Practice, pages 106–107

1. The decreased percent is **3.3%**.

   METHOD 1 Start with the decrease amount.

   Amount decrease = 60 − 58 = 2

   $$\frac{\text{decrease}}{\text{original}} = \frac{2}{60} = \frac{\text{decrease percent}}{100\%}$$
   $$2(100\%) = 60(\text{decrease percent})$$
   $$\frac{2(100\%)}{60} = \frac{60(\text{decrease percent})}{60}$$
   $$3.33\% \approx \text{decrease percent}$$

METHOD 2   Start with the percent paid.

$$\text{Original(\% paid)} = \text{sales price}$$

$$\text{Original}(100\% - \text{decrease \%}) = \text{sales price}$$

$$60(100\% - \text{decrease \%}) = 58$$

$$60(1 - \text{decrease}) = 58$$

$$60(1) - 60(\text{decrease}) = 58$$

$$60(1) - 60(\text{decrease}) - 60 = 58 - 60$$

$$-60(\text{decrease}) = -2$$

$$\frac{-60(\text{decrease})}{-60} = \frac{-2}{-60}$$

$$\text{decrease} = \frac{2}{60} = \frac{1}{30} \approx 0.0333 = 3.33\%$$

2.   The percent decrease = **60%**.

METHOD 1   Start with the decrease amount.

$$\text{Amount decrease} = 25 - 10 = 15$$

$$\frac{\text{decrease}}{\text{original}} = \frac{15}{25} = \frac{\text{decrease percent}}{100\%}$$

$$\frac{15}{25} \cdot \frac{4}{4} = \frac{\text{decrease percent}}{100\%}$$

$$\frac{15}{25} \cdot \frac{4}{4} = \frac{60\%}{100\%}$$

METHOD 2   Start with the percent paid.

$$\text{Original(\% paid)} = \text{sales price}$$

$$\text{Original}(100\% - \text{decrease \%}) = \text{sales price}$$

$$25(100\% - \text{decrease \%}) = 10$$

$$25(1 - \text{decrease}) = 10$$

$$25(1) - 25(\text{decrease}) = 10$$

$$25(1) - 25(\text{decrease}) - 25 = 10 - 25$$

$$-25(\text{decrease}) = -15$$

$$\frac{-25(\text{decrease})}{-25} = \frac{-15}{-25}$$

$$\text{decrease} = \frac{15}{25} = \frac{3}{5} = 60\%$$

$$\text{decrease} = \frac{2}{60} = \frac{1}{30} \approx 0.0333 = 3.33\%$$

3. The sales price of the tablet = **$125.80**

    METHOD 1   Start with the discount amount.

    Discount amount = original price(percent discount)

    $$148(15\%) = 148(0.15) = 22.2$$

    Original cost − discount amount = sales price

    $$148 - 22.2 = \textbf{125.8}$$

    METHOD 2   Start with the percent paid.

    Original(% paid) = sales price

    Original(100% − decrease %) = sales price

    $$148(100\% - 15\%) = 148(85\%) = 148(0.85) = \textbf{125.8}$$

4. The original price of the video game = **$50**

    Original(% paid) = sales price

    Original(100% − decrease %) = sales price

    Original(100% − 10%) = 45

    Original(90%) = 45

    $$\frac{\text{Original}(90\%)}{90\%} = \frac{45}{90\%}$$

    $$\text{Original} = \frac{45}{0.9} = \textbf{50}$$

5. The original price of the basketball shoes = **$171.43**

    Percent discount = 30%

    Percent paid = 70%

    Original percent = 100%

    METHOD 1   Start with the amount and percent paid and then set up a proportion.

    $$\frac{\text{paid}}{\text{original}} = \frac{70\%}{100\%} = \frac{120}{\text{original price}}$$

    $$70\%(\text{original price}) = 100\%(120)$$

    $$\frac{70\%(\text{original price})}{70\%} = \frac{120(100\%)}{70\%}$$

    $$\text{Original price} = \frac{120(1)}{0.7} = \textbf{171.43}$$

METHOD 2 Start with the percent paid and set up an equation.

$$\text{Original}(\% \text{ paid}) = \text{sales price}$$

$$\text{Original}(70\%) = 120$$

$$\frac{(\text{Original price})70\%}{70\%} = \frac{120}{70\%}$$

$$\text{Original price} = \frac{120(1)}{0.7} = 171.43$$

6. Eric would have saved **$14.00**. Some stores allow customers to receive the difference within one month of the purchase.

$$\text{Discount amount} = \text{original price}(\text{percent discount})$$

$$\text{Discount amount} = 56(25\%) = 56(0.25) = 14$$

7. Amount decrease = **6 − 2 = 4**

$$\frac{\text{decrease}}{\text{original}} = \frac{4}{6} = \frac{\text{decrease percent}}{100\%}$$

$$4(100\%) = 6(\text{decrease percent})$$

$$4(1) = 6(\text{decrease})$$

$$\frac{4}{6} = \frac{6(\text{decrease})}{6}$$

$$\text{Decrease} \approx 0.6667 \approx 66.67\%$$

The population decrease is approximately **66.67%**.

8. There was a **5.6% decrease** in AQI.

AQI in August = 54

AQI in September = 51

Change = decrease, 3 units on the AQI index.

$$\frac{\text{decrease}}{\text{original}} = \frac{3}{54} = \frac{\text{decrease percent}}{100\%}$$

$$3(100\%) = 54(\text{decrease percent})$$

$$\frac{3(100\%)}{54} = \frac{54(\text{decrease percent})}{54}$$

$$\text{Decrease percent} = \frac{3}{54} \approx 0.0556 \approx 5.56\%$$

9. You save **$5** on the **first deal**, **$11.25** on the **second deal**, and **$20** on the **third deal**. The best deal depends on how much you are willing to spend. You save $20 on the last deal, but are spending $50 more than the first deal.

10. The answer is **38.1% decrease**.
    2015 gas price = $3.80
    2016 gas price = $2.45
    Decrease amount = 3.80 − 2.45 = $1.35

    METHOD 1 Start with the decrease amount and set up a proportion.

    $$\frac{\text{decrease}}{\text{original}} = \frac{1.35}{3.8} = \frac{\text{decrease percent}}{100\%}$$

    $$\frac{1.35}{3.8} = \frac{\text{decrease}}{1}$$

    $$\frac{1.35}{3.8} \div \frac{3.8}{3.8} = \frac{\text{decrease}}{1}$$

    Decrease ≈ 0.355 ≈ 35.5%

    METHOD 2 Start with the decrease amount and set up an equation.

    Original(% of original after decrease has been applied) = gas price after discount

    Original(100% − decrease %) = gas price after discount

    3.8(100% − decrease %) = 2.45

    $$\frac{3.8(100\% - \text{decrease }\%)}{3.8} = \frac{2.45}{3.8}$$

    1 − decrease ≈ 0.644

    1 − decrease −1 ≈ 0.644 − 1

    −decrease ≈ −0.356

    −1(−decrease) ≈ −1(−0.356)

    −Decrease ≈ 0.356 ≈ 35.6%

11. The percent decrease is **88%**. They are worth less now because it is more common to have music options included in the phone than separately.

    Original(% paid) = sales price

    250(100% − decrease %) = 30

    250(1 − decrease) = 30

    250(1) + 250(−decrease) = 30

    250(1) + 250(−decrease) − 250 = 30 − 250

    −250(decrease) = −220

    $$\frac{-250(\text{decrease})}{-250} = \frac{-220}{-250}$$

    Decrease = 0.88 = **88%**

12. Megan could have saved **$65.33** if she waited two months.

    Sales price = original(percent paid)

    Sales price after the first month: 278(90%) = 278(0.9) = 250.20

    Sales price after the second month: 250.2(85%) = 250.2(0.85) = 212.67

    Savings = 278 − 212.67 = **65.33**

13. **It is not the same** because the 15% off is applied to the sale price of the 10% discount, not the original price at $278.

    Sale price = original(percent paid)

    $$278(75\%) = 278(0.75) = 208.50$$

14. Completed table and explanation of the patterns and relationships between each column.

#	Item	Original Price	Sale Price	Amount Saved	Percent Saved	Percent Paid	Percent of the Original
1	Jeans	$98	$78.4	$19.6	20%	80%	100%
2	Tickets for a concert	$150	$135	$15	10%	90%	100%
3	Cell phone	$650	$487.50	$162.50	25%	75%	100%
4	Pet food	$50	$32.50	$17.50	35%	65%	100%
5	Laptop	$1,400	$1,190	$210	15%	85%	100%

Patterns and Relationships:

- Amount saved + sale price = original price
- Percent saved + percent paid = percent of original
- Original price(percent saved) = amount saved
- Original price(percent paid) = sale price
- The quotient of sale price and original price = percent paid
- The quotient of amount saved and original price = percent saved

Lesson 4.4: Percent Increase

Practice, pages 109–110

1. The answer is **100% increase**.

   Original number: 12

   New number after increase: 24

   Increase amount: 24

   METHOD 1   Start with amount increase and set up a proportion.

   $$\frac{\text{increase}}{\text{original}} = \frac{12}{12} = \frac{\text{increase percent}}{100\%}$$

   METHOD 2   Start with the percent of the original after increase and set up an equation.

   Original(% of original after increase has been applied) = amount after increase

   $$12(100\% + \text{increase percent}) = 24$$

   $$\frac{12(100\% + \text{increase percent})}{12} = \frac{24}{12}$$

   $$100\% + \text{increase percent} = 2$$

   $$1 + \text{increase} = 2$$

   $$1 + \text{increase} - 1 = 2 - 1$$

   $$\text{Increase} = 1$$

   $$\text{Increase} = 1 = \textbf{100\%}$$

2. The answer is **0% increase** (no change in the number).

   Original number: 12

   New number after increase: 12

   Increase amount: 0

3. The answer is $33\frac{1}{3}\%$.

   Original number: 12

   New number after increase: 16

   Increase amount: 4

   METHOD 1   Start with amount increase and set up a proportion.

   $$\frac{\text{increase}}{\text{original}} = \frac{4}{12} = \frac{\text{increase percent}}{100\%}$$

   $$4(100\%) = 12(\text{increase percent})$$

   $$\frac{4(100\%)}{12} = \frac{12(\text{increase percent})}{12}$$

   $$\mathbf{33\frac{1}{3}\%} = \text{increase percent}$$

METHOD 2 Start with the percent of the original after increase and set up an equation.

Original(% of original after increase has been applied) = amount after increase

$$12(100\% + \text{increase percent}) = 16$$

$$\frac{12(100\% + \text{increase percent})}{12} = \frac{16}{12}$$

$$100\% + \text{increase percent} = \frac{4}{3}$$

$$1 + \text{increase} = \frac{4}{3}$$

$$1 + \text{increase} - 1 = \frac{4}{3} - 1$$

$$\text{Increase} = \frac{4}{3} - \frac{3}{3} = \frac{1}{3} = \mathbf{33\frac{1}{3}\%}$$

4. The answer is **$106.33 including tax**.

METHOD 1 Start with the amount increase.

Sales amount = original(sales tax percent)

$$98(8.5\%) = 98(0.085) = 8.33$$

Total including tax = original + tax amount

$$98 + 8.33 = \mathbf{106.33}$$

METHOD 2 Start with the percent paid.

Total including tax = original(percent paid)

$$98(100\% + 8.5\%) = 98(108.5\%) = 98(1.085) = \mathbf{106.33}$$

5. The answer is **$30** was the original price.

Total including increase = original(percent paid)

Retail price = wholesale price(100% + markup percent)

$$78 = \text{wholesale price}(100\% + 160\%)$$

$$78 = \text{wholesale price}(260\%)$$

$$\frac{78}{260\%} = \frac{\text{wholesale price}(260\%)}{260\%}$$

$$\text{wholesale price} = \frac{78}{2.6} = \mathbf{30}$$

6.   The answer is **$1.13**.

Interest = PRT = (50)(2.25%)(1) = (50)(0.0225)(1) = 1.125

7.   The answer is **$93.6**.

METHOD 1   Start with tip amount using a calculator.

Tip amount = original(percent tip) = (78)(20%) = 15.6

Dinner + tip amount = total including tip

$$78 + 15.6 = \mathbf{93.6}$$

METHOD 2   Start with tip amount without using a calculator.

10% of 78 = 0.1(78) = 7.8

20% of 78 would be double 7.8 which equals 15.6

Total amount for dinner including tip = 78 + 15.6 = **93.6**

METHOD 3   Think about what percent you pay of the original.

Total including increase = original(percent paid)

Total including tip = original(100% + percent increase)

$$78(100\% + 20\%) = 78(120\%) = 78(1.2) = \mathbf{93.6}$$

8.   The answer is **$197.23**.

Total including increase = original(percent paid)

$$214 = \text{original}(100\% + 8.5\%)$$
$$214 = \text{original}(108.5\%)$$
$$214 = \text{original}(1.085)$$
$$\frac{214}{1.085} = \frac{\text{original}(1.085)}{1.085}$$

197.24 = original

9.   The entrepreneur makes $15.65 from each blanket sale after his operational costs and royalty fees have been taken out.

Royalty amount = cost of product(royalty percent)

$$20(3\%) = 20(0.03) = 0.6$$

Net profit = sale price − cost to make the product − royalty payment

$$20 - 3.75 - 0.6 = \mathbf{15.65}$$

10. The answer is **$720**.

    Commission amount = 600(10%)(12) = **720**

11. The answer is **60%**.

    Original cost of the game: $34

    Current cost of the game: $56

    Increase in cost: 22

    METHOD 1 Use the increase amount and set up a proportion.

    $$\frac{\text{increase}}{\text{original}} = \frac{22}{34} = \frac{\text{increase percent}}{100\%}$$

    $$\frac{\text{increase}}{\text{original}} = \frac{22}{34} = \frac{\text{increase (decimal form)}}{1}$$

    $$\frac{\text{increase}}{\text{original}} = \frac{22}{34} \div \frac{34}{34} = \frac{\text{increase (decimal form)}}{1}$$

    $$\text{increase} = \frac{22}{34} = 0.647 = \mathbf{64.7\%}$$

    METHOD 2 Use the original and current cost and set up an equation.

    Original(% of original after increase has been applied) = amount after increase

    $$34(100\% + \text{increase percent}) = 56$$

    $$\frac{34(1 + \text{increase})}{34} = \frac{56}{34}$$

    $$1 + \text{increase} = 1.647$$

    $$1 + \text{increase} - 1 = 1.647 - 1$$

    $$\text{increase} = 0.647 = \mathbf{64.7\%}$$

12. Dinner cost **$198.38** before tax and tip were included.

    $$(\text{total cost before tax and tip})(100\% + 8.5\% + 15\%) = 245$$

    $$(\text{total cost before tax and tip})(123.5\%) = 245$$

    $$(\text{total cost before tax and tip})(123.5) = 245$$

    $$\text{total cost before tax and tip} = 198.38$$

13. The answer is **$36.98**.

    METHOD 1 Find the tax and tip amount separately.

    Tax amount = original bill(tax percent) = 29(7.5%) = 29(0.075) = 2.175

    Tip amount = original bill(tip percent) = 29(20%) = 29(0.2) = 5.8

    Total amount including tax and tip: 29 + 2.175 + 5.8 = **36.975**

METHOD 2 Percent paid

Original(100% + tip percent+ tax percent) = total including tax and tip

$$29(100\% + 7.5\% + 20\%) = 29(127.5\%) = 29(1.275) = 36.975$$

14. The answer is **54 years**.

    Interest = PRT

    $$60 = (50)(2.25\%)(T)$$
    $$60 = (50)(0.0225)(T)$$
    $$60 = 1.125T$$
    $$\frac{60}{1.125} = \frac{1.125T}{1.125}$$

    $$\mathbf{53.33 \approx T}$$

15. The answer is **$346.64**.

    METHOD 1 Start with the discount amount.

    Discount amount = sales price(percent discount)

    $$375(15\%) = 375(0.15) = 56.25$$

    Sales price = original price − discount amount

    $$375 - 56.25 = 318.75$$

    Tax amount = sales price(tax percent)

    $$318.75(8.5\%) = 318.75(0.085) = \mathbf{345.85}$$

    METHOD 2 Think in terms of percent paid.

    Total including tax = original(percent paid after discount)(percent paid after tax)

    $$375(100\% - 15\%)(100\% + 8.5\%)$$
    $$375(85\%)(108.5\%)$$
    $$375(0.85)(1.085)$$
    $$\mathbf{345.84}$$

16. Completed table and explanations of the patterns and relationships between each column.

#	Item	Original Number	Amount Increase	Total After Increase	Percent of Original	Percent Increase	Percent of Total After Increase
1	60 minute massage	$125	$25	$150	100%	20% tip	120%
2	Total bill from dinner	$80	$6.8	$86.8	100%	8.5% tax	108.5%
3	Wholesale price of a basketball	$20	$14	$34	100%	70% markup	170%
4	Score on a math test	80	8	88	100%	10%	110%
5	Weight of cereal in a box	18 oz.	4.5 oz.	22.5 oz.	100%	25%	125%

Patterns and relationships:

- Original number + amount increase = total after increase
- Percent of original + percent increase = percent of total after increase
- Original number(percent increase) = amount increase
- Original number(percent of total after increase) = total after increase
- The quotient of the amount of the increase and the original number = percent increase
- The quotient of the total after the increase and the original number = percent of total after increase

Chapter 5 Geometry

Lesson 5.1: Scale Drawings
Practice, pages 118–120

1.

Original	Scaled	Is the Scaled Larger or Smaller?	Scale Factor	Percent Reduction or Enlargement?
A	F	Larger, SF > 1	$\frac{1.4}{0.5} = 2.8$	$\frac{1.4 - 0.5}{0.5} = \frac{0.9}{0.5} = 1.8 = 180\%$ increase
F	A	Smaller, SF < 1	$\frac{0.5}{1.4} \approx 0.36$	$\frac{1.4 - 0.5}{1.4} = \frac{0.9}{1.4} \approx 0.64 \approx 64\%$ decrease
B	C	Same, SF = 1	$\frac{0.6}{0.6} = 1$	$\frac{0.6 - 0.6}{0.6} = \frac{0}{0.6} = 0 = 0\%$ increase or decrease
E	B	Smaller, SF < 1	$\frac{0.6}{1} = 0.6$	$\frac{1 - 0.6}{1} = \frac{0.4}{1} = 0.4 = 40\%$ decrease
D	F	Larger, SF > 1	$\frac{1.4}{0.75} \approx 1.87$	$\frac{1.4 - 0.75}{0.75} = \frac{0.65}{0.75} \approx 0.87 \approx 87\%$ increase
F	B	Smaller, SF < 1	$\frac{0.6}{1.4} \approx 0.43$	$\frac{1.4 - 0.6}{1.4} = \frac{0.8}{1.4} \approx 0.57 \approx 57\%$ decrease
E	A	Smaller, SF < 1	$\frac{0.5}{1} = 0.5$	$\frac{1 - 0.5}{1} = \frac{0.5}{1} = 0.5 = 50\%$ decrease

2. Noirin's daughter's knit hat will have a circumference of **46.96** centimeters.

$$0.8 = \frac{\text{scaled}}{58.7}$$

$$58.7(0.8) = \left(\frac{\text{scaled}}{58.7}\right)58.7$$

$$\textbf{46.96 = scaled}$$

3. Find the scaled length and width using the scale factor of 0.7:

Length = 17(0.7) = **11.9**

Width = 14(0.7) = **9.5**

The scaled image with a scale factor of 0.7 or reduction of 30% will have new dimensions of 11.9 inches by 9.5 inches. **This image will not fit on an 8.5 inch by 11 inch piece of paper.**

To find a scale that will work, work backward to find the scale factor for each dimension:

Length	Width
Scale Factor = $\dfrac{\text{scaled}}{\text{original}} = \dfrac{11}{17} \approx 0.647$	Scale Factor = $\dfrac{\text{scaled}}{\text{original}} = \dfrac{8.5}{14} \approx 0.607$

For the image to be proportional, the same scale factor will need to be applied. Therefore, both images will need to be scaled by a scale factor of 0.6 in order to fit on an 8.5 inch by 11 inch piece of paper.

Check your work by applying the new scale factor to make sure the dimensions fit.

Length = 17(0.6) = 10.2 inches

Width = 14(0.6) = 8.4 inches

4. Find the scaled length and width using the scale factor of 1.4:

Length = 2.5(1.4) = **3.5**

Width = 4.75(1.4) = **6.65**

The scaled image with a scale factor of 1.4 or enlargement of 40% will have new dimensions of 3.5 inches by 6.65 inches. **This image will fit on an 8.5 inch by 11 inch piece of paper.**

To find the largest scale factor to maximize all the space on an 8.5 inch by 11 inch piece of paper, work backward to find the scale factor for each dimension:

Length	Width
Scale Factor = $\dfrac{\text{scaled}}{\text{original}} = \dfrac{8.5}{2.5} = 3.4$	Scale Factor = $\dfrac{\text{scaled}}{\text{original}} = \dfrac{11}{4.75} \approx 2.316$

For the image to be proportional, the same scale factor will need to be applied. Therefore, both images will need to be scaled by a scale factor of 2.3 in order to fit on an 8.5 inch by 11 inch piece of paper.

Check your work by applying the new scale factor to make sure the dimensions fit.

Length = 2.5(2.3) = 5.75

Width = 4.75(2.3) = 10.925

If you chose the other scale factor, check your work to find the new dimensions. You will see that part of the image will fit and part of it will not.

Length = 2.5(3.4) = 8.5

Width = 4.75(3.4) = 16.15

5.

Length	Width
Scale Factor = $\dfrac{\text{scaled}}{\text{original}}$	Scale Factor = $\dfrac{\text{scaled}}{\text{original}}$
$= \dfrac{11}{1{,}680} = \dfrac{1}{152.72}$	$= \dfrac{17}{2{,}220} = \dfrac{1}{130.58}$

Nico can use a scale factor of **1:153** or **0.0065**.

6. Joanne's backyard dimensions:

Dimensions	Right Part of Yard
Scale Factor = $\dfrac{\text{scaled}}{\text{original}}$	$0.125 = \dfrac{5.5}{\text{original}}$
Left Part of Yard $0.125 = \dfrac{2.75}{\text{original}}$ $\text{original}(0.125) = \left(\dfrac{2.75}{\text{original}}\right)\text{original}$ $\text{original}(0.125) = 2.75$ $\dfrac{\text{original}(0.125)}{0.125} = \dfrac{2.75}{0.125}$ $\text{original} = \dfrac{2.75}{0.125} = 22\text{ feet}$	$\text{original}(0.125) = \left(\dfrac{5.5}{\text{original}}\right)\text{original}$ $\text{original}(0.125) = 5.5$ $\dfrac{\text{original}(0.125)}{0.125} = \dfrac{5.5}{0.125}$ $\text{original} = \dfrac{5.5}{0.125} = 44\text{ feet}$
Top Part of Yard $0.125 = \dfrac{2.75}{\text{original}}$ $\text{original}(0.125) = \left(\dfrac{3.9}{\text{original}}\right)\text{original}$ $\text{original}(0.125) = 3.9$ $\dfrac{\text{original}(0.125)}{0.125} = \dfrac{3.9}{31.2}$ $\text{original} = \dfrac{2.75}{0.125} = 31.2\text{ feet}$	**Bottom Part of Yard** $0.125 = \dfrac{6.5}{\text{original}}$ $\text{original}(0.125) = \left(\dfrac{6.5}{\text{original}}\right)\text{original}$ $\text{original}(0.125) = 6.5$ $\dfrac{\text{original}(0.125)}{0.125} = \dfrac{6.5}{0.125}$ $\text{original} = \dfrac{6.5}{0.125} = 52\text{ feet}$

7. $\dfrac{1\text{ inch}}{250\text{ km}} = \dfrac{\text{scaled}}{1{,}100\text{ km}}$

$\dfrac{1\text{ inch}}{250\text{ km}} \cdot \dfrac{4.4}{4.4} = \dfrac{\text{scaled}}{1{,}100\text{ km}}$

Scaled = 4.4 inches

The two towns are **4.4 inches** apart on the map.

8. $\dfrac{1\text{ inch}}{41\text{ feet}} = \dfrac{\text{scaled}}{984\text{ feet}}$

$\dfrac{1\text{ inch}}{41\text{ feet}} \cdot \dfrac{24}{24} = \dfrac{\text{scaled}}{984\text{ feet}}$

Scaled = 24 inches

The model of the Eiffel Tower is **24 inches** or 2 feet tall.

9. $\dfrac{0.25\text{ inches}}{10\text{ miles}} = \dfrac{6\text{ inches}}{\text{distance}}$

$\dfrac{0.25\text{ inches}}{10\text{ miles}} \cdot \dfrac{24}{24} = \dfrac{6\text{ inches}}{\text{distance}}$

Distance = 240 miles

Dallas and Houston are **240 miles** apart.

10. $\dfrac{1\text{ inch}}{16\text{ miles}} = \dfrac{1.625}{\text{original}}$

$\dfrac{1\text{ inch}}{16\text{ miles}} \cdot \dfrac{1.625}{1.625} = \dfrac{1.625}{\text{original}}$

Original = 26 miles

The two towns are **26 miles** apart.

11.

Label the Scaled Diagram	Scale Factor	Is the Scaled Getting Larger or Smaller?	What is the Percent Increase or Reduction?	Length	Width
A (original)	NA	NA	NA	6	4
B	0.5	Smaller	100% – 50% = 50% reduction	3	2
C	0.25	Smaller	100% – 25% = 75% reduction	1.5	1
D	0.75	Smaller	100% – 75% = 25% reduction	4.5	3
E	1	Same	100% – 100% = 0%	6	4
F	1.25	Larger	125% – 100% = 25% enlargement	7.5	5
G	1.5	Larger	150% – 100% = 50% enlargement	9	6
H	2	Larger	200% – 100% = 100% enlargement	12	8
I	3	Larger	300% – 100% = 200% enlargement	18	12
J	2.5	Larger	250% – 100% = 150% enlargement	15	10

Lesson 5.2: Geometric Constructions

Practice, page 128

1. A.

    B.

    C.

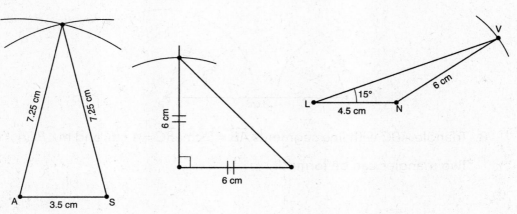

2. A. Triangle *XYZ*, where $\overline{XY}$ = 3 cm,
       $\overline{ZY}$ = 5 cm, and m∠*ZXY* = 120°.

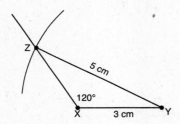

    B. Equilateral triangle *PQR*.

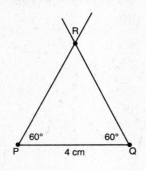

    C. Right triangle *MDL* where
       m∠*MDL* = 90° and
       m∠*DML* = 25°.

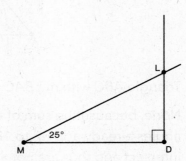

    D. Triangle *TJW* where $\overline{TJ}$ = 5.5 cm,
       $\overline{TW}$ = 7 cm, and $\overline{JW}$ = 3.5 cm.

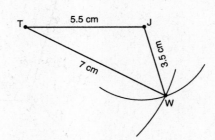

3. A. Triangle *ABC* with line segments $\overline{AB}$ = 8 cm, $\overline{AC}$ = 3 cm, and $\overline{BC}$ = 4 cm.

    None, because the two other line segments are too short and they do not intersect to create the third point.

    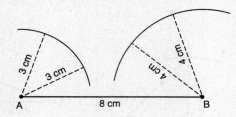

    B. Triangle *ABC* with line segments $\overline{AB}$ = 5 cm, $\overline{BC}$ = 4 cm, and m∠*BCA* = 50°.

    Two triangles can be formed.

    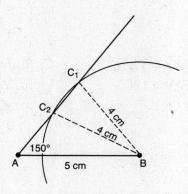

    C. Triangle *ABC* with m∠*BAC* = 105° and m∠*ABC* = 75°.

    None, because the sum of the angles in a triangle is 180°, and these two angles already add up to 180°. Also, the rays from the two triangles never intersect and thus are not able to form a triangle.

    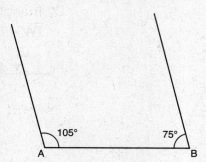

Lesson 5.3: Slicing

Practice, page 130

	A	B	C
D			
E			
F			
G			

Lesson 5.4: Angles

Practice, pages 139–142

1. Angles *A* and *B* are complementary angles. Angles *A* and *C* are supplementary angles. The m∠*B* and m∠*C*:

m∠A	m∠B	m∠C
36°	90° − 36° = 54°	180° − 36° = 144°
89°	90° − 89° = 1°	180° − 89° = 91°
95°	NA	180° − 95° = 85°
12°	90° − 12° = 78°	180° − 12° = 168°

2. Values of x in each diagram.

Letter	Solution	Check Your Solution
A.	$3x + 2x = 90$ $5x = 90$ $\dfrac{5x}{5} = \dfrac{90}{5}$ $x = 18$	 $54° + 36° = 90°$
B.	$3x + 27 = 90$ $3x + 27 - 27 = 90 - 27$ $3x = 63$ $\dfrac{3x}{3} = \dfrac{63}{3}$ $x = 21$	 $63° + 27° = 90°$
C.	$4x + 48 + 2x = 90$ $48 + 6x = 90$ $48 + 6x - 48 = 90 - 48$ $6x = 42$ $\dfrac{6x}{6} = \dfrac{42}{6}$ $x = 7$	 $28° + 48° + 14° = 90°$
D.	$2x + 105 + 3x = 180$ $105 + 5x = 180$ $105 + 5x - 105 = 180 - 105$ $5x = 75$ $\dfrac{5x}{5} = \dfrac{75}{5}$ $x = 15$	 $30° + 105° + 45° = 180°$

Letter	Solution	Check Your Solution
E.	$5x + 4x = 180$ $9x = 180$ $\dfrac{9x}{9} = \dfrac{180}{9}$ $x = 20$	 $100° + 80° = 180°$
F.	$26 + 2.5x + 1.5x = 180$ $26 + 4x = 180$ $26 + 4x - 26 = 180 - 26$ $4x = 154$ $\dfrac{4x}{4} = \dfrac{154}{4}$ $x = 38.5$	 $26° + 96.25° + 57.75° = 180°$
G.	Vertical angles are ≅, therefore, $140 = 7x$ $\dfrac{140}{7} = \dfrac{7x}{7}$ $20 = x$ $140 + z = 180$ $140 + z - 140 = 180 - 140$ $z = 40$ $y = 40$ because vertical angles are ≅.	 $40° + 140° = 180°$
H.	$86 + 4x = 180$ $86 + 4x - 86 = 180 - 86$ $4x = 94$ $\dfrac{4x}{4} = \dfrac{94}{4}$ $x = 23.5$ $y = 4(23.5) = 94$ because vertical angles are ≅. $z = 86$ since vertical angles are ≅.	 $86° + 94° = 180°$

Letter	Solution	Check Your Solution
I.	$40 + x + 3x = 180$ $40 + 4x = 180$ $40 + 4x - 40 = 180 - 40$ $4x = 140$ $\dfrac{4x}{4} = \dfrac{140}{4}$ $x = 35$ $Z = 35$ because vertical angles are $\cong$. $Y = 40$ because vertical angles are $\cong$. $W = 3(35) = 105$ because vertical angles are $\cong$.	 $35° + 40° + 105° = 180°$
J.	$7x + x + 88 = 360$ $8x + 88 = 360$ $8x + 88 - 88 = 360 - 88$ $8x = 272$ $\dfrac{8x}{8} = \dfrac{272}{8}$ $x = 34$	 $238° + 34° + 88° = 360°$
K.	$155 + 3x + 2x = 360$ $155 + 5x = 360$ $155 + 5x - 155 = 360 - 155$ $5x = 205$ $\dfrac{5x}{5} = \dfrac{205}{5}$ $x = 41$	 $123° + 155° + 82° = 360°$
L.	$5x + 2.5x + 2x + 16.5x = 360$ $36x = 360$ $\dfrac{36x}{36} = \dfrac{360}{36}$ $x = 10$	 $150° + 25° + 20° + 165° = 360°$

3. A. Relationship of the angles.

Pairs of Opposite Angles, Vertical Angles ≅.	∠1 and ∠2		m∠1 = 78°
	∠3 and ∠4		m∠2 = 78°
	∠5 and ∠7		m∠3 = 102°
	∠6 and ∠8		m∠4 = 102°
Pairs of Alternate Interior Angles that are ≅.	∠8 and ∠1		m∠5 = 102°
	∠7 and ∠4		m∠6 = 78°
Pairs of Alternate Exterior Angles that are ≅.	∠6 and ∠2		m∠7 = 102°
	∠5 and ∠3		m∠8 = 78°
Pairs of Corresponding Angles that are ≅.	∠1 and ∠6		
	∠4 and ∠5		
	∠3 and ∠7		
	∠2 and ∠8		

In the diagram: 78°, 102°, 102°, 78°, 78°, 102°, 102°, 78°

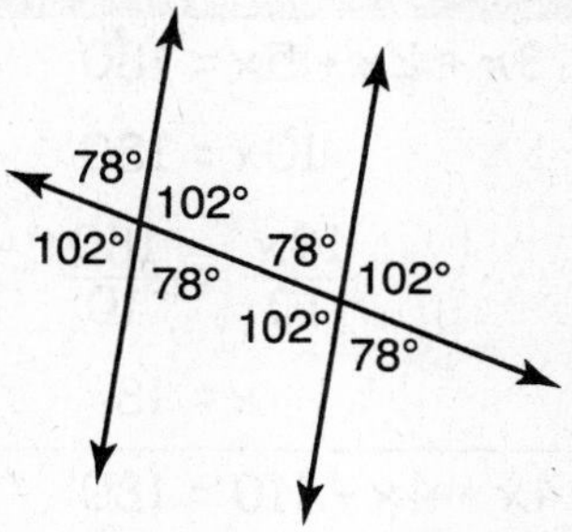

B. Relationship of the angles.

Pairs of Opposite Angles, Vertical Angles ≅.	∠1 and ∠3		m∠1 = 136°
	∠2 and ∠4		m∠2 = 44°
	∠5 and ∠8		m∠3 = 136°
	∠6 and ∠7		m∠4 = 44°
Pairs of Alternate Interior Angles that are ≅.	∠8 and ∠4		m∠5 = 44°
	∠1 and ∠7		m∠6 = 136°
Pairs of Alternate Exterior Angles that are ≅.	∠6 and ∠3		m∠7 = 136°
	∠5 and ∠2		m∠8 = 44°
Pairs of Corresponding Angles that are ≅.	∠1 and ∠6		
	∠4 and ∠5		
	∠3 and ∠7		
	∠2 and ∠8		

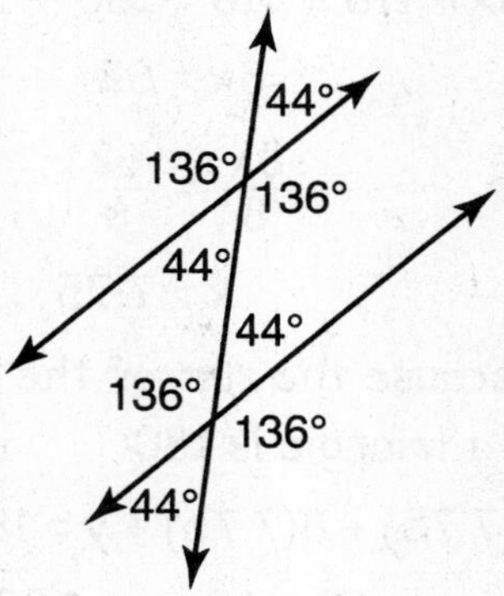

In the diagram: 44°, 136°, 136°, 44°, 44°, 136°, 44°, 136°

4. Value of each unknown variable and the measure of each angle.

Problem #	Solution	Check Your Work
A.	$3x + 2x + 5x = 180$ $10x = 180$ $\dfrac{10x}{10} = \dfrac{180}{10}$ $x = 18$	3(18)=54° 5(18)=90° 2(18)=36° $54° + 90° + 36° = 180°$
B.	$4x + 4x + 110 = 180$ $8x + 110 = 180$ $8x + 110 - 110 = 180 - 110$ $8x = 70$ $\dfrac{8x}{8} = \dfrac{70}{8}$ $x = 8.75$	110° 4(8.75)=35° $2(35)° + 110° = 180°$ $70° + 110° = 180°$
C.	Because they are supplementary angles: $8x + 118 = 180$ $8x + 118 - 118 = 180 - 118$ $8x = 62$ $\dfrac{8x}{8} = \dfrac{62}{8}$ $x = 7.75$ Because the sum of the angles in a triangle is 180: $8(7.75) + 8(7.75) + y = 180$ $62 + 62 + y = 180$ $124 + y = 180$ $124 + y - 124 = 180 - 124$ $y = 56$	56° 8(7.75)=62° 118° $2(62)° + 56° = 180°$ $124° + 56° = 180°$ $62° + 118° = 180°$

Problem #	Solution	Check Your Work
D.	Because of the sum of angles in a triangle is 180: $11x + 65 + 60 = 180$ $11x + 125 = 180$ $11x + 125 - 125 = 180 - 125$ $11x = 55$ $\dfrac{11x}{11} = \dfrac{55}{11}$ $x = 5$ Because opposite angles are ≅: $y = 11x = 11(5) = 55$	 $65° + 60° + 55° = 180°$
E.	$3x = 90$ $\dfrac{3x}{3} = \dfrac{90}{3}$ $x = 30$	 $4(90)° = 360°$
F.	Because they are supplementary angles: $2x + 122 = 180$ $2x + 122 - 122 = 180 - 122$ $2x = 58$ $\dfrac{2x}{2} = \dfrac{58}{2}$ $x = 29$	 $2(58°) + 64° = 180°$ $116° + 64° = 180°$

Problem #	Solution	Check Your Work
F. (cont'd.)	Because they are supplementary angles: $$2x + w = 180$$ $$2(29) + w = 180$$ $$58 + w = 180$$ $$58 + w - 58 = 180 - 58$$ $$w = 122$$ Because in an isosceles triangle, the angles opposite of the congruent sides are congruent: $$y = 2x = 2(29) = 58$$ Because the sum of the angles in a triangle is 180: $$z + y + 2x = 180$$ $$z + 58 + 2(29) = 180$$ $$z + 58 + 58 = 180$$ $$z + 116 = 180$$ $$z + 116 - 116 = 180 - 116$$ $$z = 64$$	
G.	Because the sum of supplementary angles is 180: $$4x + 67 = 180$$ $$4x + 67 - 67 = 180 - 67$$ $$4x = 113$$ $$\frac{4x}{4} = \frac{113}{4}$$ $$x = 28.25$$ Because opposite angles in a parallelogram are congruent: $$4x = 4(28.25) = 113$$	 $$2(113°) + 2(67°) = 360°$$ $$226° + 134° = 360°$$

Problem #	Solution	Check Your Work
G. (cont'd.)	Because the sum of the angles in a quadrilateral is 360: $2(113) + 2y = 360$ $226 + 2y = 360$ $226 + 2y - 226 = 360 - 226$ $2y = 134$ $\dfrac{2y}{2} = \dfrac{134}{2}$ $y = 67$	
H.	Because supplementary angles add up to 180: $131 + y = 180$ $131 + y - 131 = 180 - 131$ $y = 49$ $28 + w = 180$ $28 + w - 28 = 180 - 28$ $w = 152$ Because opposite angles are $\cong$: $x = 87$ Because the sum of angles in a quadrilateral is 360: $w + x + y + z = 360$ $152 + 87 + 49 + z = 360$ $288 + z = 360$ $288 + z - 288 = 360 - 288$ $z = 72$	 $49° + 152° + 72° + 87° = 360°$

5.

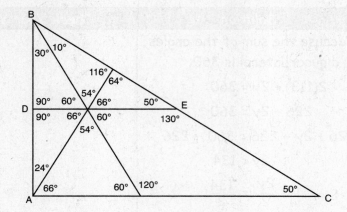

6. In parallelogram *ABCD*, the measure of the angles are in the figure below.

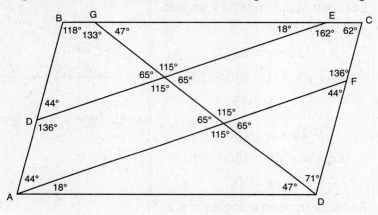

Lesson 5.5: Circles: Circumference and Area
Practice, pages 145–147

1. Completed table.

Radius (*r*)	1 cm	12 m	50 inches
Diameter (*d*)	2 cm	24 m	100 inches
Circumference = 2π*r*			
Use 3.14 for π	2(3.14)(1) = 6.28	2(3.14)(12) = 75.36	2(3.14)(50) = 314
Use 3 for π	2(3)(1) = 6	2(3)(12) = 72	2(3)(50) = 300
Use π	2π(1) = 2π	2π(12) = 24π	2π(50) = 100π
Area = π*r*²			
Use 3.14 for π	3.14(1)² = 3.14	3.14(12)² = 452.16	3.14(50)² = 7,850
Use 3 for π	3(1)² = 3.14	3(12)² = 432	3(50)² = 7,500
Use π	π(1)² = π	π(12)² = 144π	π(50)² = 2,500π

2. Filled in table for the circumference.

Radius (r)	4 cm	0.25 m	25 inches
Diameter (d)	8 km	0.5 m	50 inches
Circumference = $2\pi r$			
Use 3.14 for π	2(3.14)(4) = 25.12	2(3.14)(0.25) = 75.36	2(3.14)(25) = 157
Use 3 for π	2(3)(4) = 24	2(3)(0.25) = 1.5	2(3)(25) = 150
Use π	$2\pi(4) = 8\pi$	$2\pi(0.25) = 0.5\pi$	$2\pi(25) = 25\pi$
Area = πr^2			
Use 3.14 for π	$3.14(4)^2 = 50.24$	$3.14(0.25)^2 = 0.19625$	$3.14(25)^2 = 1{,}962.5$
Use 3 for π	$3(4)^2 = 48$	$3(0.25)^2 = 0.1875$	$3(25)^2 = 1{,}875$
Use π	$\pi(4)^2 = 16\pi$	$\pi(0.25)^2 = 0.0625\pi$	$\pi(25)^2 = 625\pi$

3. Filled in table for the area of the circle.

Radius (r)	0.5 cm	3 m	1.1 inches
Diameter (d)	1 cm	6 m	2.2 inches
Circumference = $2\pi r$			
Use 3.14 for π	2(3.14)(0.5) = 3.14	2(3.14)(3) = 75.36	2(3.14)(1.1) = 6.908
Use 3 for π	2(3)(0.5) = 3	2(3)(3) = 72	2(3)(1.1) = 6.6
Use π	$2\pi(0.5) = \pi$	$2\pi(3) = 24\pi$	$2\pi(1.1) = 2.2\pi$
Area = πr^2			
Use 3.14 for π	$3.14(0.5)^2 = 0.785$	$3.14(3)^2 = 28.26$	$3.14(1.1)^2 = 3.7994$
Use 3 for π	$3(0.5)^2 = 0.75$	$3(3)^2 = 27$	$3(1.1)^2 = 3.63$
Use π	$\pi(0.5)^2 = 0.25\pi$	$\pi(3)^2 = 9\pi$	$\pi(1.1)^2 = 1.21\pi$

4. Rohan cycled for approximately **57 feet** on the unicycle without falling.

$$r = \frac{36}{2} = 18$$

Circumference = one revolution = $2\pi r$ = 2(3.14)(18) = 113.04 inches

6(113.04) = 678.24 inches

678.24 inches/12 inches = 56.52 feet

5. Letitia will need **26.69** inches of lace.

   $R = \dfrac{8.5}{2} = 4.25$

   Circumference $= 2\pi r = 2(3.14)(4.25) = 26.69$ inches

6. It takes approximately **847.8 ft** to reach the top of the Ferris wheel.

   $R = 270$ ft

   Circumference $= 2\pi r = 2(3.14)(270) = 1{,}695.6$ ft

   To get to the top of the Ferris wheel is half the circumference. Therefore, **1,695.6/2 = 847.8 ft**.

7. The ball rolled approximately **13 times**.

   $R = 0.375$ ft

   Circumference $=$ one roll $= 2\pi r = 2(3.14)(0.375) = 2.355$

   Total distance $\div$ circumference $=$ number of rolls

   $30 \div 2.355 = 12.73$ rolls.

8. The diameter of the Colosseum is approximately **181.67 meters**.

   Circumference $= d\pi$

   $$545 = 3d$$
   $$181.67 = d$$

9. The diameter of the pancake is **20 inches**.

   Area $= \pi r^2$

   $314 = 3.14 r^2$

   $$\dfrac{314}{3.14} = r^2$$
   $$100 = r^2$$
   $$\sqrt{100} = \sqrt{r^2}$$
   $$10 = r$$

   Diameter $= 2r = 2(10) = 20$

10. Julia will need **147 square feet** of soil.

    $r = \dfrac{14}{2} = 7$

    Area $= \pi r^2 = 3(7)^2 = 3(49) = 147$ square feet

11. There are approximately **16,818 square feet** of ants in this particular ant mill.

Circumference = $2\pi r$

$650 = 2(3.14)r$

$650 = 6.28r$

$$\frac{650}{6.28} = \frac{6.28r}{6.28}$$

$$103.5 = r$$

Area = $\pi r^2 = 3.14(103.5)^2 = 3.14(10{,}712.25) = 33{,}636.465$ square feet

Half of the area = $0.5(33{,}636.465) = 16{,}818.2325$

12. The **large pizza is the best deal** by approximately half a cent compared to the medium, and a little more than half a cent compared to the small.

Pizza Size	Radius (inches)	Area = πr^2 (square inches)	Unit Rate
Large 14 inch	7	$(3.14)(7)^2 = 153.86$	$\frac{\$9.99}{153.86 \text{ in.}^2} = \frac{\$0.0649}{1 \text{ in.}^2}$
Medium 12 inch	6	$(3.14)(6)^2 = 113.04$	$\frac{\$7.99}{113.04 \text{ in.}^2} = \frac{\$0.0707}{1 \text{ in.}^2}$
Small 10 inch	5	$(3.14)(5)^2 = 78.5$	$\frac{\$5.99}{78.5 \text{ in.}^2} = \frac{\$0.0763}{1 \text{ in.}^2}$

Lesson 5.6: Area of Composite Figures

Practice, pages 150–152

1. A. Total area = circle + square

   Area of circle = $\pi r^2 = (3.14)(5^2) = 3.14(25) = 78.5$

   Area of square = $lw = 5(5) = 25$

   Total area = $0.75(78.5) + 25 = 58.875 + 25 = $ **83.875 in.^{2}**

   B. Total area = left rectangle + right rectangle + bottom rectangle

   Area of left rectangle = $3(4) = 12$

   Area of right rectangle = $3(4) = 12$

   Area of bottom rectangle = $9(3) = 27$

   Total area = $12 + 12 + 27 = $ **51 in.^{2}**

C. Total area = rectangle + semicircle
Area of rectangle = 18(6) =108
Area of circle = πr^2 = (3.14)(9^2) = (3.14)(81) = 254.34
Total area = 108 + 0.5(254.34) = 108 + 127.17 = **235.17 in.^{2}**

D. Total area = circle + square
Area of circle = πr^2 = (3.14)(12^2) = 3.14(144) = 452.16
Area of square = 24(24) = 576
Total area = 452.12 + 576 = **1,028.16 cm^2**

E. Total area = top semicircle + bottom semicircle
Top circle = πr^2 = (3.14)(5^2) = 3.14(25) = 78.5
Bottom circle = πr^2 = (3.14)(4^2) = 3.14(16) = 50.24
Total area = 0.5(78.5) + 0.5(50.24) = 39.25 + 25.12 = **64.37cm^2**

F. Total area = square − circle
Area of square = 10(10) = 100
Area of circle = πr^2 = (3.14)(5^2) = 3.14(25) = 78.5
Total area = 100 − 78.5 = **21.5 cm^2**

G. Total area = rectangle − 1.5(circles)
Area of rectangle = 11(36) = 396
Area of circle = πr^2 = (3.14)(6^2) = 3.14(36) = 113.04
Total area = 396 − 1.5(113.04) = 396 − 169.56 = **226.44 in.^{2}**

H. Total area = square + trapezoid + rectangle
Area of square = 4^2 = 4(4) = 16
Area of trapezoid = 0.5(b_1+b_2)h = 0.5(8 + 12)(4) = 0.5(20)(4) = 40
Area of rectangle = 13(4) = 52
Total area = 16 + 40 + 52 = **108 cm^2**

I. Total area = parallelogram + 1(triangle)
Area of triangle = 0.5bh = 0.5(6)(6) = 0.5(36) = 18
Area of parallelogram = bh = 14(6) = 84
Total area = 18 + 84 = **102 cm^2**

J. Total area = parallelogram − triangle
Area of parallelogram = bh = 22(7) = 154
Area of triangle = 0.5bh = 0.5(22)(2) = 0.5(44) = 22
Total area = 154 + 22 = **176 cm^2**

K. Total area = bottom triangle + top triangle + circle
Area of bottom triangle = 0.5bh = 0.5(14)(7) = 49
Area of top triangle = 0.5bh = 0.5(14)(2) = 14
Area of circle = πr^2 = (3.14)(3^2) = 3.14(9) = 28.26
Total area = 49 + 14 + 28.26 = **91.26 cm^2**

L. Total area = triangle + square
    Area of triangle = $0.5bh = 0.5(1.5 + 1.5 + 4)(5) = 0.5(7)(5) = 17.5$
    Area of Square = $4^2 = 4(4) = 16$
    Total area = $17.5 + 16 =$ **33.5 cm²**

2. A. Area of shaded region = big circle − little circle
        Area of big circle = $\pi r^2 = (3.14)(6^2) = 3.14(36) = 113.04$
        Area of little circle = $\pi r^2 = (3.14)(4^2) = 3.14(16) = 50.24$
        Area of shaded region = $113.04 - 50.24 = 62.8$ in.²

    B. Area of shaded region = square − circle
        Area of square = $12^2 = 12(12) = 144$
        Area of circle = $\pi r^2 = (3.14)(6^2) = 3.14(36) = 113.04$ cm²
        Area of shaded region = $144 - 113.04 = 30.96$ cm²

    C. Area of shaded region = big circle − little circle
        Area of big circle = $\pi r^2 = (3.14)(1^2) = 3.14(1) = 3.14$
        Area of little circle = $\pi r^2 = (3.14)(0.5^2) = 3.14(0.25) = 0.785$
        Area of shaded region = $3.14 - 0.785 = 2.355$ in.²

    D. Area of shaded region = big circle − top circle − bottom circle
        Area of big circle = $\pi r^2 = (3.14)(3^2) = 3.14(9) = 28.26$
        Area of top circle = $\pi r^2 = (3.14)(2^2) = 3.14(4) = 12.56$
        Area of bottom circle = $\pi r^2 = (3.14)(1^2) = 3.14(1) = 3.14$
        Area of shaded region = $28.26 - 12.56 - 3.14 = 12.56$ in.²

    E. Area of shaded region = square − 4(circles)
        Area of square = $10^2 = 10(10) = 100$
        Area of circle = $\pi r^2 = (3.14)(2.5^2) = 3.14(6.25) = 19.625$
        Area of shaded region = $100 - 4(19.625) = 100 - 78.5 = 21.5$ cm²

    F. Area of shaded region = rectangle − 6(circles)
        Area of rectangle = $6(9) = 54$
        Area of circle = $\pi r^2 = (3.14)(1.5^2) = 3.14(2.25) = 7.065$
        Area of shaded region = $54 - 6(7.065) = 54 - 42.39 = 11.61$ cm²

    G. Area of shaded region = big square − 2(triangles)
        Area of big square = $12^2 = 12(12) = 144$
        Area of triangles = $(4)(0.5)(6)(6) = 72$
        Area of shaded region = $144 - 72 = 72$ in.²

    H. Area of shaded region = trapezoid − circle
        Area of trapezoid = $0.5h(b_1 + b_2) = 0.5(12)(24 + 26) = 6(50) = 300$
        Area of circle = $\pi r^2 = (3.14)(6^2) = 3.14(36) = 113.04$
        Area of shaded region = $300 - 113.04 = 186.96$ in.²

I. Area of shaded region = circle − 2(triangles) = circle − square
Area of circle = πr^2 = (3.14)(3^2) = 3.14(9) = 28.26
Area of triangles = 0.5bh = 0.5(6)(3) = 9
Area of shaded region = 28.26 − 2(9) = 28.26 − 18 = 10.26 in.^{2}

3. Area of bigger triangle = $\dfrac{bh}{2} = \dfrac{4(5)}{2} = 10$ ft.^{2}

Area of bigger triangle = $\dfrac{bh}{2} = \dfrac{4(6)}{2} = 12$ ft.^{2}

Total area of the garden = **10 + 12 = 22 ft^2**

4. Circumference = $2\pi r$

2(116) = 2(3.14)r

116 = 3.14r

$$\frac{116}{3.14} = \frac{3.14r}{3.14}$$

$$36.9 = r$$

Area of the track = area of rectangle = area of circle
Area of rectangle = 84(2)(36.9) = 6199.2
Area of circle = πr^2 = (3.14)(36.9^2) = 3.14(1361.61) = 4275.4554
Area of track = **6,199.2 + 4,275.4554 = 10,474.6554 m^2**
Cost to fill in the track is (10,474.65)($2.75) = $28,805.29

5. Area of leftover paper = area of rectangle − area of circle
Area of rectangle = lw = 8.5(11) = 93.5 square inches
Area of circle = πr^2 = 3.14(4.25)^2 = 3.14(18.0625) = 56.71625 square inches
Leftover paper = 93.5 − 56.71625 = 36.78375 square inches
There is approximately **36.78 square inches** of paper left.

6. Answers may vary.

Lesson 5.7: Surface Area and Volume of Prisms and Pyramids
Practice, pages 162–165

1. Surface area = 2(side views) + 4(top views) = 2(6) + 4(15) = 12 + 60 = **72 cm²**

Views		Area of Each Side
Side Views		Count the area: 6 cm^2
Top, Bottom, Left, and Right Views Are All the Same		Rectangle = bh = 5(3) = 15 cm^2

2. Picture the prism as a net.

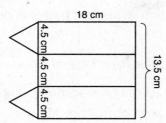

Lateral Area	**Method 1:** Area of rectangle = 18(13.5) = 243 cm² **Method 2:** Find the area of each rectangle: 4.5(18) = 81. Then multiply this number by three since there are three identical rectangles: 81(3) = 243 cm².
Base Area	Since there are two identical bases, find the surface area by working backward algebraically: $$SA = 2(\text{area of triangle}) + LA$$ $$260.6 = 2(\text{area of triangle}) + 243$$ $$260.6 - 243 = 2(\text{area of triangle}) + 243 - 243$$ $$17.6 = 2(\text{area of triangle})$$ $$17.6(0.5) = 2(\text{area of triangle})(0.5)$$ $$8.8 = \text{area of triangle}$$ Each base has an area of 8.8 cm².
Height of Triangular Base	Area of triangle = $\dfrac{bh}{2}$ $$8.8 = \frac{4.5\,h}{2}$$ $$2(8.8) = \left(\frac{4.5\,h}{2}\right)2$$ $$17.6 = 4.5h$$ $$\frac{17.6}{4.5} = \frac{4.5\,h}{4.5}$$ $$3.9 = h$$ The triangular base has a height of approximately 3.9 cm.
Area of Each Rectangular Face	**Method 1:** Since each rectangular face is congruent: $$\frac{\text{lateral area}}{3} = \frac{243}{3} = 81$$ Each rectangular face has an area of 81 cm². **Method 2:** Use the net above. Each rectangle has dimensions of 4.5 cm by 18 cm. Therefore, the area is 4.5(18) = 81 cm².

3. The surface area of the triangular prism is **528.1 square centimeters**. Therefore, at least that much wrapping paper is needed to cover the entire prism (gift box).

$$\text{Surface area} = 2(\text{base}) + \text{Lateral Area}$$

$$= 2(\text{area of triangle}) + 2(\text{area of bottom rectangle}) + \text{area of front rectangle}$$

$$= 2\left(\frac{8 \cdot 8}{2}\right) + 2(8 \cdot 17) + 17(11.3)$$

$$= 64 + 2(136) + 17(11.3)$$

$$= 64 + 272 + 192.1 = \textbf{528.1}$$

4. The height of the triangular base is **3 cm**.

$$SA = 2(\text{area of triangle}) + LA$$

$$204 = 2\left(\frac{8h}{2}\right) + (3 + 4 + 8)12$$

$$204 = 8h + (15)(12)$$

$$24 = 8h$$

$$\textbf{3} = \textbf{\textit{h}}$$

5. Nicole's aquarium was made with **8,263 square inches** of glass.

   METHOD 1   Think of the Lateral Area as one big rectangle.

   $$14(10 + 15 + 10 + 24) = 14(59) = \textbf{826}$$

   METHOD 2   Think of the Lateral Area as four rectangles.

   $$2(14 \cdot 10) + 14(15) + 14(24) = 280 + 210 + 336 = \textbf{826}$$

6. The Lateral Area is **810 square feet** and the total Surface Area is **949.36 square feet**.

   METHOD 1   Lateral Area: $18(9 \cdot 5) = 810$

   METHOD 2 $5(18 \cdot 9) = 810$

   $$\text{Surface Area} = \text{base} + \text{Lateral Area} = 139.36 + 810 = \textbf{949.36}$$

7. You will need enough yellow paint to cover **89.964 square inches** in a box of 24 pencils.

    Lateral Area is the yellow painted part of the pencil.

    METHOD 1 $6(7.5 \cdot 0.0833) = 6(0.62475) = 3.7485$

    METHOD 2 $7.5(0.0833 \cdot 6) = 7.5(0.4998) = 3.7485$

    Total $= 24(3.7485) = 89.964$.

8. The baker will need enough frosting to cover 1,200 square inches of cake. The bottom base of the cake was not included since it would be sitting on the table and not seen.

    Surface Area of larger cake = base + Lateral Area =

    $$(18 \cdot 24) + 4(18 + 18 + 24 + 24) = 432 + 336 = 768$$

    Dimensions of the smaller cake:

    Length $= 0.75(18) = 13.5$

    Width $= 0.75(24) = 18$

    Height $= 0.75(4) = 3$

    Surface Area of smaller cake = base + Lateral Area =

    $$(13.5 \cdot 18) + 3(18 + 18 + 13.5 + 13.5) = 243 + 3(63) = 243 + 189 = 432$$

    Total Surface Area of the bigger and smaller cakes $= 768 + 432 = $ **1,200**.

9. It will cost Thomas and Tony **$32.50** to cover their teepee with the fabric.

    Lateral Area $= 5(\text{area of triangle}) = 5\left(\dfrac{9 \cdot 4}{2}\right) = 5(18) = 90$ square feet

    Let $x =$ the total cost

    $$\frac{\$6.50}{18 \text{ square feet}} = \frac{x}{90 \text{ square feet}}$$

    $$6.5(90) = 18x$$

    $$\frac{6.5(90)}{18} = \frac{18x}{18}$$

    $$\mathbf{32.5 = x}$$

10. The length of the square base is **7 feet**.

$$\text{Volume} = \frac{Bh}{3} = \frac{(\text{area of square})(\text{height of pyramid})}{3}$$

$$147 = \frac{9B}{3}$$

$$3(147) = \left(\frac{9B}{3}\right)\left(\frac{3}{1}\right)$$

$$441 = 9B$$

$$\frac{441}{9} = \frac{9B}{9}$$

$$49 = B = \text{area of square} = s^2$$

$$\sqrt{49} = \sqrt{s^2}$$

$$\mathbf{7 = s}$$

11.

$$\text{Volume} = \frac{Bh}{3} = \frac{(\text{area of rectangle})(\text{height of prism})}{3}$$

$$220 = \frac{11B}{3}$$

$$3(220) = \left(\frac{11B}{3}\right)\left(\frac{3}{1}\right)$$

$$660 = 11B$$

$$\frac{660}{11} = \frac{11B}{11}$$

$$\mathbf{60 = B = \text{area of rectangular base}}$$

Possible dimensions include:

Length (Inches)	Width (Inches)
1	60
2	30
3	20
4	15
5	12
6	10
6.25	9.6
2.5	24

12. The volume of the square pyramid is **256 cubic feet**.

    Surface Area = base + Lateral Area = area of square + 4(area of triangle)

    $$176 = base + 4(28)$$

    $$176 = base + 112$$

    $$176 - 112 = base + 112 - 112$$

    $$64 = base = area\ of\ square = s^2$$

    $$Volume = \frac{Bh}{3} = \frac{64(12)}{3} = 64(4) = 256$$

13. There is **not enough information** to find the Surface Area of the rectangular pyramid. You would need the slant height and dimensions of the rectangle.

    $$Volume = \frac{Bh}{3} = \frac{(area\ of\ rectangle)(height\ of\ prism)}{3}$$

    $$372 = \frac{18B}{3}$$

    $$3(372) = \left(\frac{18B}{3}\right)\left(\frac{3}{1}\right)$$

    $$1{,}116 = 18B$$

    $$\frac{1{,}116}{18} = \frac{18B}{18}$$

    $$62 = B = area\ of\ rectangle$$

14.

3-D Solid	Formula for Volume	Volume (cm³)	Base (cm²)	Height (cm)
Triangular Prism	$V = Bh$ = (area of triangle)(height)	48	12	4
Triangular Prism	$V = Bh$ = (area of triangle)(height)	208	16	13
Rectangular Prism	$V = Bh$ = (area of rectangle)(height)	96	8	12
Rectangular Prism	$V = Bh$ = (area of rectangle)(height)	114	15	7.6
Trapezoidal Prism	$V = Bh$ = (area of trapezoid)(height)	256	16	16
Pentagonal Prism	$V = Bh$ = (area of pentagon)(height)	375	25	15
Pentagonal Prism	$V = Bh$ = (area of pentagon)(height)	247	13	19
Hexagonal Prism	$V = Bh$ = (area of hexagon)(height)	486	27	18
Hexagonal Prism	$V = Bh$ = (area of hexagon)(height)	558	62	9
Cylinder	$V = Bh$ = (area of circle)(height)	600	20	30
Cylinder	$V = Bh$ = (area of circle)(height)	108	12	9

15. **6 inches by 6 inches** is a valid dimension for this rectangular prism because a rectangle can be a square but a square cannot be a rectangle.

$$\text{Volume} = Bh = (\text{area of rectangle})(\text{height of prism})$$
$$288 = 8B$$
$$\frac{288}{8} = \frac{8B}{8}$$
$$\mathbf{36 = B}$$

Possible dimensions of the rectangle:

Length (inches)	Width (inches)
1	36
2	18
3	12
4	9
6	6
4.5	8

16. The maximum number of bracelets that can fit in the larger rectangular box is **4,915**.

$$\text{Volume of hexagonal prism} = Bh = (\text{area of hexagon})(\text{height of prism})$$
$$= 1.875(1.5) = 2.8125 \text{ cubic inches}$$

$$\text{Volume of rectangular box} = lwh = (48)(24)(12) = 13,824 \text{ cubic inches}$$

Maximum number of hexagonal prisms that can fit in the larger rectangular box:

$$\frac{13,824}{2.8125} = \mathbf{4,915.2}$$

17. The height of the base area, which is in the shape of a trapezoid, is **3.2 cm**.

$$48 = 8(6)$$

$$\text{Area of trapezoid} = \frac{(b_1 + b_2)h}{2}$$

$$8 = \frac{5h}{2}$$
$$16 = 5h$$
$$\frac{16}{5} = \frac{5h}{5}$$
$$\mathbf{3.2 = h}$$

18.

Area of Hexagonal Base (cm²)	Height of Prism (cm)
138	2
92	3
69	4
55.2	5
46	6
34.5	8
27.6	10
12	23

19. **STEP 1** Total sq. ft. of barn (not including roof) =
(15)(40)(2) + (60)(15)(2) + (40)(60) = 5,400 sq. ft.

STEP 2 Paint costs: $\frac{\$91.50}{267}$ sq. ft. = $0.34 per sq. ft.

STEP 3 Total cost to paint the barn =
($0.34 per sq. ft.)(5,400 sq. ft.) = $1,836.00

20. The composite solid has a volume of **84 cubic inches**.

Total volume = volume of top pyramid + volume of bottom pyramid

$$= \frac{Bh}{3} + \frac{Bh}{3}$$

$$= \frac{(6 \cdot 6)5}{3} + \frac{(6 \cdot 6)2}{3}$$

$$= \frac{(36)5}{3} + \frac{(36)2}{3}$$

$$= (12)5 + (12)2$$

$$= 60 + 24$$

$$= \mathbf{84}$$

The total Surface Area is **117 square inches**.

Total Surface Area = surface area of top pyramid + surface area of bottom pyramid

$$= LA \text{ of top pyramid} + LA \text{ of bottom pyramid}$$

$$= \frac{4(6 \cdot 6.5)}{2} + \frac{4(6 \cdot 3.25)}{2}$$

$$= 2(39) + 2(19.5)$$

$$= 78 + 39$$

$$= \mathbf{117}$$

21. The volume of Lana's wood now is **513 cubic inches**.

Volume = volume of rectangular prism − volume of triangular prism

$$= lwh - Bh = lwh - (\text{area of triangle})(\text{height of prism})$$
$$= (8 \cdot 12 \cdot 6) - (10.5 \cdot 6)$$
$$= 576 - 63$$
$$= \mathbf{513}$$

Chapter 6 Statistics and Probability

Lesson 6.1: Random Sampling Methods
Practice, page 172

1. This is **convenience sampling** because the data would be received from the students in line already. This data is biased and convenient for the researcher. This would not be a good sample because it would not represent the population. What about students that only purchased snacks on Fridays or other days of the week? What about students that would like to purchase snacks but do not normally go into the lunch line because the options that are currently available are not what they are interested in?

    Systematic sampling is one way to obtain a random sample that represents the population. Students are assigned a number, and every 20th student is surveyed.

2. This is **cluster sampling** because the population is divided into groups based on their geography. Georgia can also use simple random sampling by putting all the addresses into a database, where each address is assigned to a number. She then uses a random number generator to determine which houses she surveys.

3. This is **convenience sampling** since this method is convenient for the researcher. What about the other grocery stores and other people that stop during various days of the week? Nora should get a list of all the addresses in her neighborhood and conduct stratified random sampling by grouping the homes into various home valuation. For each group, she can randomly select ten houses to survey.

4. Laila used **systematic random sampling**. She could have also used cluster sampling where she puts all the buttons she produces every 30 minutes in a separate bucket. She then randomly chooses a button from each bucket.

5. This is **stratified sampling** because the population is divided into two or more groups called strata, according to some criterion. Kevin could have also used simple random sampling by randomly selecting students at the school cafeteria since all students eat at the same time.

Lesson 6.2: Making Inferences from Random Samples
Practice, pages 173–174

1. Based on the sample, you can predict that 4,320 people will vote *yes* for building the new community park.

   Let x = # that will vote yes in the population.

   METHOD 1

   $$\frac{\text{\# voted yes in sample}}{\text{size of sample}} = \frac{\text{\# that will vote yes in population}}{\text{size of population}}$$

   $$\frac{27}{50} = \frac{x}{8,000}$$

   $$\frac{27}{50} \cdot \frac{160}{160} = \frac{x}{8,000}$$

   $$x \approx \mathbf{4,320}$$

   METHOD 2

   Percent of people that voted yes in the sample: $\frac{27}{50} = 0.54 = 54\%$

   Number of people that will likely vote yes in the population:

   $$(54\%)(8,000) = 0.54(8,000) = \mathbf{4,320}.$$

2. Based on the sample, you can predict that 1,633 people will purchase size 8 shoes should the local shoe store place an order of 3,000 women's shoes.

   Let x = # of size 8 shoes that will sell from the population.

   METHOD 1

   $$\frac{\text{\# of size 8 shoes sold in sample}}{\text{size of sample}} = \frac{\text{\# of size 8 shoes that will sell from population}}{\text{size of population}}$$

   $$\frac{245}{450} = \frac{x}{3,000}$$

   $$450x = 245(3,000)$$

   $$\frac{450x}{450} = \frac{245(3,000)}{450}$$

   $$x \approx \mathbf{1,633.33}$$

METHOD 2

Percent of people that purchased size 8 shoes: $\frac{245}{450} \approx 0.544 = 54.4\%$

Number of people that will likely purchase women's size 8 shoes out of 3,000 customers:

$$(54.4\%)(3{,}000) = 0.544(3{,}000) = \textbf{1,632}$$

3. Based on the sample, you can predict that the number of feral cats grew from **40 to 150 in one year**.

   Let x = size of the population.

   METHOD 1

   $$\frac{\text{\# of tagged cats in sample}}{\text{size of sample}} = \frac{\text{\# of tagged cats in population}}{\text{size of population}}$$

   $$\frac{8}{40} = \frac{30}{x}$$

   $$40(30) = 8x$$

   $$\frac{40(30)}{8} = \frac{8x}{8}$$

   $$\boldsymbol{x = 150}$$

   METHOD 2

   Percent of tagged cats in sample size: $\frac{8}{40} = 0.2 = 20\%$

   Number of total cats in the population:

   $$(20\%)x = 30$$

   $$\frac{(20\%)x}{0.2} = \frac{30}{0.2}$$

   $$\boldsymbol{x = 150}$$

4. Based on the sample size, you can predict that Ben will sell about **174 hot dogs** to **745 students** at this school.

   Let x = # of hot dogs he plans to sell from the population.

METHOD 1

$$\frac{\text{# of hot dogs he sells in sample}}{\text{size of sample}} = \frac{\text{# of hot dogs he sells in population}}{\text{size of population}}$$

$$\frac{7}{30} = \frac{x}{745}$$

$$30x = 7(745)$$

$$\frac{30x}{30} = \frac{7(745)}{30}$$

$$\mathbf{x \approx 173.8}$$

METHOD 2

Percent of hot dogs sold in sample: $\frac{7}{30} \approx 0.233 \approx 23.3\%$

Number of hot dogs he plans to sell in the population:

$$(23.3\%)745 = 0.233(745) = \mathbf{173.585}$$

5.

Type of Cupcake	Frequency	Relative Frequency	Number of Cupcakes She Is Expecting to Sell
Chocolate	8	$\frac{8}{31} \approx 0.258$	0.258(500) = 129
Vanilla	9	$\frac{9}{31} \approx 0.290$	0.290(500) = 145
Red Velvet	6	$\frac{6}{31} \approx 0.194$	0.194(500) = 97
Carrot Cake	3	$\frac{3}{31} \approx 0.097$	0.097(500) = 48.5
Peanut Butter	3	$\frac{3}{31} \approx 0.097$	0.097(500) = 48.5
Lemon	2	$\frac{2}{31} \approx 0.065$	0.065(500) = 32.5
Total	31	$\frac{31}{31} = 1.00$	500.5

6. Based on the sample size, you can predict that **88 Ramen Noodle cups** will be sold if about **200 students** visit the snack shop every day.

Let x = # of Ramen Noodle cups sold in the population.

METHOD 1

$$\frac{\text{\# of Ramen Noodle cups sold in sample}}{\text{size of sample}} = \frac{\text{\# of Ramen Noodle cups sold in population}}{\text{size of population}}$$

$$\frac{11}{25} = \frac{x}{200}$$

$$11(200) = 25x$$

$$\frac{11(200)}{25} = \frac{25x}{25}$$

$$\boldsymbol{x = 88}$$

METHOD 2

Percent of Ramen Noodle cups sold in sample: $\frac{11}{25} = 0.44 = 44\%$

Number of Ramen Noodle cups that will likely sell in the population:

$$(44\%)(200) = 0.44(200) = \boldsymbol{88}$$

Lesson 6.3: Measures of Central Tendency and Variability
Practice, pages 179–183

1.

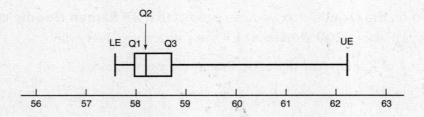

Lower Half	57.565 ——— LE = 57.565
	57.965
	57.965 ——— Q1 = 57.965
	58.032
	58.032
	——— Q2 = (58.298 + 58.032)/2 = 58.165
Upper Half	58.298
	58.549
	58.665 ——— Q3 = 58.665
	60.098
	62.198 ——— UE = 62.198

Range = 62.198 – 57.565 = 4.633

IQR = 58.665 – 57.965 = 0.7

#	Data Value	Mean	Absolute Deviation		
1	62.198	58.6968	| 62.198 − 58.6968 |	| 3.5012 |	3.5012
2	60.098	58.6968	| 60.098 − 58.6968 |	| 1.4012 |	1.4012
3	58.665	58.6968	| 58.665 − 58.6968 |	| −0.0318 |	0.0318
4	58.549	58.6968	| 58.549 − 58.6968 |	| −0.1478 |	0.1478
5	58.298	58.6968	| 58.298 − 58.6968 |	| −0.3988 |	0.3988
6	58.032	58.6968	| 58.032 − 58.6968 |	| −0.6648 |	0.6648
7	58.032	58.6968	| 58.032 − 58.6968 |	| −0.6648 |	0.6648
8	57.965	58.6968	| 57.965 − 58.6968 |	| −0.7318 |	0.7318
9	57.965	58.6968	| 57.965 − 58.6968 |	| −0.7318 |	0.7318
10	57.565	58.6968	| 57.565 − 58.6968 |	| −1.1318 |	1.1318
Total	586.968	NA			9.4058
MAD					$\dfrac{9.4058}{10}$ = 0.94058

Analysis:

25% of the data fall between 57.965 and 57.565.

50% of the scores fall between 58.665 and 57.965.

50% of the scores fall between 58.165 and 57.565.

75% of the scores fall between 58.665 and 57.565.

100% of the data fall between 57.565 and 62.198.

The box plot is relatively short, which suggests that the gymnasts' scores were closer together and that competition was tight. The data is skewed to the right, which means that most of the scores are clustered to the right. Each section of the box plot, which represents 25% of the data, is a different size. The largest section means there is the most variability in the data. This suggests that the gymnast with the highest score was much better than the other gymnasts. The MAD means on average, the score for each gymnast is 0.94058 points away from the mean of 58.6968.

2.

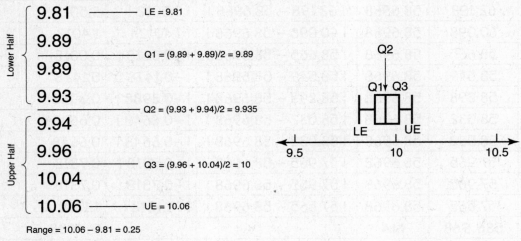

Lower Half {
9.81 ———— LE = 9.81
9.89
———————— Q1 = (9.89 + 9.89)/2 = 9.89
9.89
9.93
}
———————— Q2 = (9.93 + 9.94)/2 = 9.935
Upper Half {
9.94
9.96
———————— Q3 = (9.96 + 10.04)/2 = 10
10.04
10.06 ———— UE = 10.06
}

Range = 10.06 − 9.81 = 0.25

IQR = 10 − 9.89 = 0.11

#	Data Value	Mean	Absolute Deviation		
1	9.81	9.94	❘ 9.81 − 9.94 ❘	❘ −0.13 ❘	0.13
2	9.89	9.94	❘ 9.89 − 9.94 ❘	❘ −0.05 ❘	0.05
3	9.91	9.94	❘ 9.91 − 9.94 ❘	❘ −0.03 ❘	0.03
4	9.93	9.94	❘ 9.93 − 9.94 ❘	❘ −0.01 ❘	0.01
5	9.94	9.94	❘ 9.94 − 9.94 ❘	❘ 0 ❘	0
6	9.96	9.94	❘ 9.96 − 9.94 ❘	❘ 0.02 ❘	0.02
7	10.04	9.94	❘ 10.04 − 9.94 ❘	❘ 0.1 ❘	0.1
8	10.06	9.94	❘ 10.06 − 9.94 ❘	❘ 0.12 ❘	0.12
Total	79.52	NA			0.46
MAD					$\frac{0.46}{8} = 0.0575$

Analysis:

25% of the data fall between 9.81 and 9.89.

50% of the scores fall between 9.99 and 10.

50% of the scores fall between 9.81 and 9.935.

75% of the scores fall between 9.81 and 10.

100% of the data fall between 9.81 and 10.06.

Each section of the box plot, which represents 25% of the data, is about the same size. This means that the competition between the sprinters was fairly equal and there is less variability of data. The MAD means on average, each sprinter's time was 0.06 seconds away from the mean of 9.94.

3.

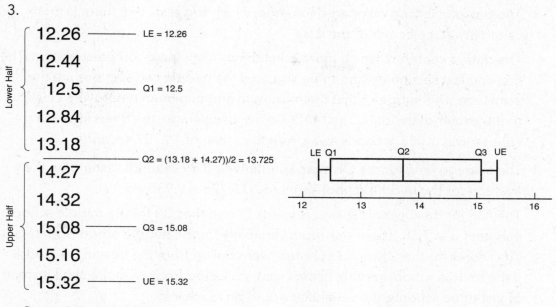

Range = 15.32 − 12.26 = 3.06

IQR = 15.08 − 12.5 = 2.58

#	Data Value	Mean	Absolute Deviation		
1	12.44	13.737	I 12.44 − 13.737 I	I −1.297 I	1.297
2	12.5	13.737	I 12.5 − 13.737 I	I −1.237 I	1.237
3	12.84	13.737	I 12.84 − 13.737 I	I −0.897 I	0.897
4	13.18	13.737	I 13.18 − 13.737 I	I −0.557 I	0.557
5	12.26	13.737	I 12.26 − 13.737 I	I −1.477 I	1.477
6	14.27	13.737	I 14.27 − 13.737 I	I 0.533 I	0.533
7	14.32	13.737	I 14.32 − 13.737 I	I 0.583 I	0.583
8	15.08	13.737	I 15.08 − 13.737 I	I 1.343 I	1.343
9	15.16	13.737	I 15.16 − 13.737 I	I 1.423 I	1.423
10	15.32	13.737	I 15.32 − 13.737 I	I 1.583 I	1.583
Total	137.37				10.93
MAD					$\frac{10.93}{10}$ = 1.093

Analysis:

25% of the data fall between 13.725 and 15.08.

50% of the scores fall between 12.5 and 15.08.

50% of the scores fall between 12.26 and 13.725.

75% of the scores fall between 12.5 and 15.32.

100% of the data fall between 12.26 and 15.32.

The box plot is long compared to range, which suggests that there is more variability in the center of the data.

The data is centered, which means that the median is a good presentation. The first and last section are the same size, and the middle two sections are the same size. This suggests that the maximum and minimum times were closer to the center of the data. The MAD means, on average, the times for each sprinter was 1.093 seconds away from the mean of 13.737 seconds.

The average time for the Olympic sprinter was 3.79 seconds faster than the average for the middle school sprinters. (13.725 − 9.935 = 3.79)

The IQR for the Olympic sprinters was 0.11 and the IQR for the middle school sprinters was 2.58. There was more variability for the middle school sprinters. The scores for the Olympics sprinters were pulled from the best in the world. If the middle school sprinter scores were collected from an entire state instead of just three schools, the variability would be much less.

If the top runner's scores were placed in the top scores from the Olympics, the middle school runner's score would be the entire state and the Q1, Q2, Q3, mean, and median scores would decrease.

If Usain Bolt's scores were mixed in with the middle school scores, the mean, median, Q1, Q2, and Q3 would increase. Usain Bolt's score would be considered an outlier.

4.

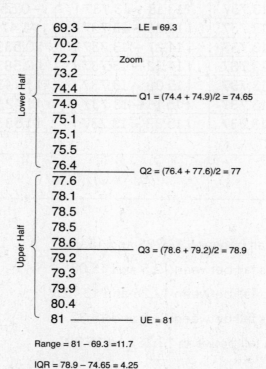

Range = 81 − 69.3 = 11.7

IQR = 78.9 − 74.65 = 4.25

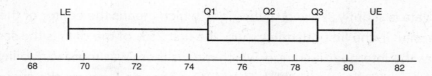

#	Data Value	Mean	Absolute Deviation		
1	69.3	76.395	| 69.3 − 76.395 |	| −7.095 |	7.095
2	70.2	76.395	| 70.2 − 76.395 |	| −6.195 |	6.195
3	72.7	76.395	| 72.7 − 76.395 |	| −3.695 |	3.695
4	73.2	76.395	| 73.2 − 76.395 |	| −3.195 |	3.195
5	74.4	76.395	| 74.4 − 76.395 |	| −1.995 |	1.995
6	74.9	76.395	| 74.9 − 76.395 |	| −1.495 |	1.495
7	75.1	76.395	| 75.1 − 76.395 |	| −1.295 |	1.295
8	75.1	76.395	| 75.1 − 76.395 |	| −1.295 |	1.295
9	75.5	76.395	| 75.5 − 76.395 |	| −0.895 |	0.895
10	76.4	76.395	| 76.4 − 76.395 |	| 0.005 |	0.005
11	77.6	76.395	| 77.6 − 76.395 |	| 1.205 |	1.205
12	78.1	76.395	| 78.1 − 76.395 |	| 1.705 |	1.705
13	78.5	76.395	| 78.5 − 76.395 |	| 2.105 |	2.105
14	78.5	76.395	| 78.5 − 76.395 |	| 2.105 |	2.105
15	78.6	76.395	| 78.6 − 76.395 |	| 2.205 |	2.205
16	79.2	76.395	| 79.2 − 76.395 |	| 2.805 |	2.805
17	79.3	76.395	| 79.3 − 76.395 |	| 2.905 |	2.905
18	79.9	76.395	| 79.9 − 76.395 |	| 3.505 |	3.505
19	80.4	76.395	| 80.4 − 76.395 |	| 4.005 |	4.005
20	81	76.395	| 81 − 76.395 |	| 4.605 |	4.605
Total	1,527.9				54.31
MAD					$\frac{54.31}{20} = 2.7155$

Analysis:

25% of the data fall between 77 and 78.9 degrees.

50% of the scores fall between 74.65 and 78.9 degrees.

50% of the scores fall between 77 and 81 degrees.

75% of the scores fall between 74.65 and 81 degrees.

100% of the data fall between 69.3 and 81 degrees.

The box plot is a little less than half of the range compared, which suggests there is less variability in the center of the data.

The data is slightly skewed to the right, which means the center of the data is warmer. In the first quartile group, the first 25% of the data is the same size as the interquartile range, which means there was more variability in the temperatures during this time. The MAD means on average, the average temperature in 2.7155 degrees away from the mean of 76.395 degrees.

5.

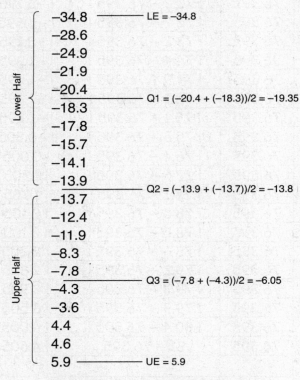

Lower Half
- −34.8 ——— LE = −34.8
- −28.6
- −24.9
- −21.9
- −20.4 ——— Q1 = (−20.4 + (−18.3))/2 = −19.35
- −18.3
- −17.8
- −15.7
- −14.1
- −13.9 ——— Q2 = (−13.9 + (−13.7))/2 = −13.8

Upper Half
- −13.7
- −12.4
- −11.9
- −8.3
- −7.8 ——— Q3 = (−7.8 + (−4.3))/2 = −6.05
- −4.3
- −3.6
- 4.4
- 4.6
- 5.9 ——— UE = 5.9

Range: 5.9 − (−34.8) = 5.9 + 34.8 = 40.7

IQR: −6.05 − (−19.35) = −6.05 + 19.35 = 13.3

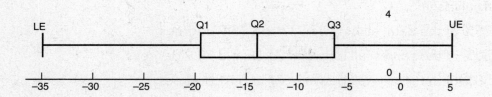

#	Data Value	Mean	Absolute Deviation		
1	−34.8	−12.88	| −34.8 − (−12.88) |	| −21.92 |	21.92
2	−28.6	−12.88	| −28.6 − (−12.88) |	| −15.72 |	15.72
3	−24.9	−12.88	| −24.9 − (−12.88) |	| −12.02 |	12.02
4	−21.9	−12.88	| −21.9 − (−12.88) |	| −9.02 |	9.02
5	−20.4	−12.88	| −20.4 − (−12.88) |	| −7.52 |	7.52
6	−18.3	−12.88	| −18.3 − (−12.88) |	| −5.42 |	5.42
7	−17.8	−12.88	| −17.8 − (−12.88) |	| −4.92 |	4.92
8	−15.7	−12.88	| −15.7 − (−12.88) |	| −2.82 |	2.82
9	−14.1	−12.88	| −14.1 − (−12.88) |	| −1.22 |	1.22
10	−13.9	−12.88	| −13.9 − (−12.88) |	| −1.02 |	1.02
11	−13.7	−12.88	| −13.7 − (−12.88) |	| −0.82 |	0.82
12	−12.5	−12.88	| −12.5 − (−12.88) |	| 0.38 |	0.38
13	−11.9	−12.88	| −11.9 − (−12.88) |	| 0.98 |	0.98
14	−8.3	−12.88	| −8.3 − (−12.88) |	| 4.58 |	4.58
15	−7.8	−12.88	| −7.8 − (−12.88) |	| 5.08 |	5.08
16	−4.3	−12.88	| −4.3 − (−12.88) |	| 8.58 |	8.58
17	−3.6	−12.88	| −3.6 − (−12.88) |	| 9.28 |	9.28
18	4.4	−12.88	| 4.4 − (−12.88) |	| 17.28 |	17.28
19	4.6	−12.88	| 4.6 − (−12.88) |	| 17.48 |	17.48
20	5.9	−12.88	| 5.9 − (−12.88) |	| 18.78 |	18.78
Total	−257.6	NA			164.84
MAD					$\frac{164.84}{20} = 8.242$

Analysis:

25% of the data fall between −19.35 and −13.8 degrees.

50% of the scores fall between −19.35 and −6.05 degrees.

50% of the scores fall between −13.8 and 5.9 degrees.

75% of the scores fall between −19.35 and −6.05 degrees.

100% of the data fall between −34.8 and 5.9 degrees.

The box plot is approximately one-third of the range, which suggests there is a lot of variability in the data. The first quartile group is about the same size as the box plot, the center of the data. This suggests that temperatures in the North Pole are generally much warmer than they had been. The MAD means on average, the average temperature is 8.242 degrees away from the mean of −12.88 degrees.

6.

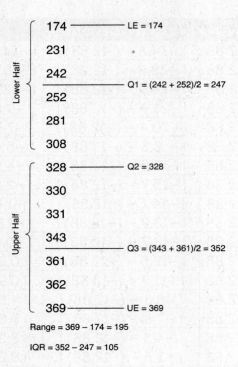

174 ——————— LE = 174

231

Lower Half

242

——————————— Q1 = (242 + 252)/2 = 247

252

281

308

328 ——————— Q2 = 328

330

331

Upper Half

343

——————————— Q3 = (343 + 361)/2 = 352

361

362

369 ——————— UE = 369

Range = 369 − 174 = 195

IQR = 352 − 247 = 105

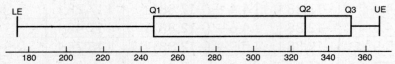

#	Data Value	Mean	Absolute Deviation		
			From 1998-2001		
1	174	300.92	| 174 − 300.92 |	| −126.92 |	126.92
2	231	300.92	| 231 − 300.92 |	| −69.92 |	69.92
3	242	300.92	| 242 − 300.92 |	| −58.92 |	58.92
4	252	300.92	| 252 − 300.92 |	| −48.92 |	48.92
5	281	300.92	| 281 − 300.92 |	| −19.92 |	19.92
6	308	300.92	| 308 − 300.92 |	| 7.08 |	7.08
7	328	300.92	| 328 − 300.92 |	| 27.08 |	27.08
8	330	300.92	| 330 − 300.92 |	| 29.08 |	29.08
9	331	300.92	| 331 − 300.92 |	| 30.08 |	30.08
10	343	300.92	| 343 − 300.92 |	| 42.08 |	42.08
11	361	300.92	| 361 − 300.92 |	| 60.08 |	60.08
12	362	300.92	| 362 − 300.92 |	| 61.08 |	61.08
13	369	300.92	| 369 − 300.92 |	| 68.08 |	68.08
Sum	3,912				649.27
MAD					$\frac{649.27}{13} \approx 49.9$

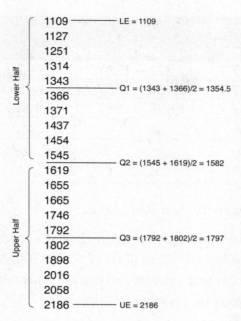

Range = 2186 − 1109 = 1077
IQR = 1797 − 1354.5 = 442.5

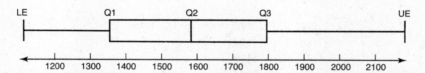

#	Data Value	Mean	Absolute Deviation		
			2016		
1	2,058	1,587.7	| 2,058 − 1,587.7 |	| 470.29 |	470.29
2	1,343	1,587.7	| 1,343 − 1,587.7 |	| −244.7 |	244.7
3	1,314	1,587.7	| 1,314 − 1,587.7 |	| −273.7 |	273.7
4	1,366	1,587.7	| 1,366 − 1,587.7 |	| −221.7 |	221.7
5	1,746	1,587.7	| 1,746 − 1,587.7 |	| 158.3 |	158.3
6	1,665	1,587.7	| 1,665 − 1,587.7 |	| 77.3 |	77.3
7	2,186	1,587.7	| 2,186 − 1,587.7 |	| 598.3 |	598.3
8	1,437	1,587.7	| 1,437 − 1,587.7 |	| −150.7 |	150.7
9	1,792	1,587.7	| 1,792 − 1,587.7 |	| 204.3 |	204.3
10	1,545	1,587.7	| 1,545 − 1,587.7 |	| −42.7 |	42.7
11	1,655	1,587.7	| 1,655 − 1,587.7 |	| 67.3 |	67.3
12	1,127	1,587.7	| 1,127 − 1,587.7 |	| −460.7 |	460.7
13	1,109	1,587.7	| 1,109 − 1,587.7 |	| −478.7 |	478.7
14	2,016	1,587.7	| 2,016 − 1,587.7 |	| 428.3 |	428.3
15	1,619	1,587.7	| 1,619 − 1,587.7 |	| 31.3 |	31.3
16	1,251	1,587.7	| 1,251 − 1,587.7 |	| −336.7 |	336.7
17	1,802	1,587.7	| 1,802 − 1,587.7 |	| 214.3 |	214.3

#	Data Value	Mean	Absolute Deviation		
		2016			
18	1,371	1,587.7	| 1,371 − 1587.7 |	| −216.7 |	216.7
19	1,454	1,587.7	| 1,454 − 1587.7 |	| −133.7 |	133.7
20	1,898	1,587.7	| 1,898 − 1587.7 |	| 310.3 |	310.3
Sum	**31,754**	**NA**			**5,119.99**
MAD					$\dfrac{5{,}119.99}{20} \approx 256$

Comparisons between the two sets of data:

The mean of the price per square foot in 2016 is approximately 5 times more than the mean price from 1998 to 2001 (1,587.7/300.92 ≈ 5.276). Factors could include inflation and a better job market. This means more people move out to Palo Alto to look for housing.

The IQR in 2016 was 442.5 and the IQR from 1998 to 2001 was 105, which means there was more variability in the prices in 2016.

7.

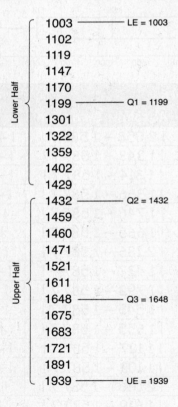

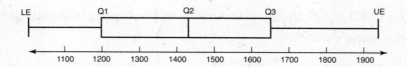

Range = 1939 − 1003 = 936

IQR = 1648 − 1199 = 449

#	Data Value	Mean	Absolute Deviation		
1	1,939	1,437.57	| 1,939 − 1,437.57 |	| 501.43 |	501.43
2	1,891	1,437.57	| 1,891 − 1,437.57 |	| 453.43 |	453.43
3	1,721	1,437.57	| 1,721 − 1,437.57 |	| 283.43 |	283.43
4	1,683	1,437.57	| 1,683 − 1,437.57 |	| 245.43 |	245.43
5	1,675	1,437.57	| 1,675 − 1,437.57 |	| 237.43 |	237.43
6	1,648	1,437.57	| 1,648 − 1,437.57 |	| 210.43 |	210.43
7	1,611	1,437.57	| 1,611 − 1,437.57 |	| 173.43 |	173.43
8	1,521	1,437.57	| 1,521 − 1,437.57 |	| 1,377.43 |	1,377.43
9	1,471	1,437.57	| 1,471 − 1,437.57 |	| 33.43 |	33.43
10	1,460	1,437.57	| 1,460 − 1,437.57 |	| 22.43 |	22.43
11	1,459	1,437.57	| 1,459 − 1,437.57 |	| 21.43 |	21.43
12	1,432	1,437.57	| 1,432 − 1,437.57 |	| −5.57 |	5.57
13	1,429	1,437.57	| 1,429 − 1,437.57 |	| −8.57 |	8.57
14	1,402	1,437.57	| 1,402 − 1,437.57 |	| −35.57 |	35.57
15	1,359	1,437.57	| 1,359 − 1,437.57 |	| −78.57 |	78.57
16	1,322	1,437.57	| 1,322 − 1,437.57 |	| −115.57 |	115.57
17	1,301	1,437.57	| 1,301 − 1,437.57 |	| −136.57 |	136.57
18	1,199	1,437.57	| 1,199 − 1,437.57 |	| −238.57 |	238.57
19	1,170	1,437.57	| 1,170 − 1,437.57 |	| −267.57 |	267.57
20	1,147	1,437.57	| 1,147 − 1,437.57 |	| −290.57 |	290.57
21	1,119	1,437.57	| 1,119 − 1,437.57 |	| −318.57 |	318.57
22	1,102	1,437.57	| 1,102 − 1,437.57 |	| −335.57 |	335.57
23	1,003	1,437.57	| 1,003 − 1,437.57 |	| −434.57 |	434.57
Total	33,064				5,825.57
MAD					$\frac{5,825.57}{23} \approx 253.29$

Since the MAD are both about the same, this suggests that both sets have about the same variability.

The price per square foot sold is more in Palo Alto compared to Atherton, which means that it is more expensive to live in Palo Alto compared to Atherton. (1,587.7 − 1,437.57 = 150.13.)

IQR in Palo Alto is 442.5 and in Atherton it is 449, which suggests that both sets of data have fairly comparable, normal distributions.

Lesson 6.4: Understanding Probability

Practice, pages 185–187

1. Since the dotted, striped, and white spaces occupy the entire spinner, it is certain that the spinner will land on one of those 3 spaces.

$$P(\text{dotted, striped, or white space}) = \frac{\text{dotted, striped, or white space}}{\text{total number of spaces}}$$
$$= \frac{4+1+3}{8} = \frac{8}{8} = 1 = \textbf{100\%}$$

2. There is a 50–50 chance, or even chance that the spinner will land on the striped space since the striped spaces take up one-half of the spinner board.

$$P(\text{striped space}) = \frac{\text{striped space}}{\text{total number of spaces}} = \frac{4}{8} = \frac{1}{2} = 0.5 = \textbf{50\%}$$

3. $P(\text{dotted or white space}) = \frac{\text{striped space}}{\text{total number of spaces}} = \frac{1+3}{8} = \frac{4}{8} = 0.5 = \textbf{50\%}$

    There is a 50–50 chance, or an even chance that the spinner will land on the dotted or white space since they take up one-half of the spinner board.

4. It is unlikely the spinner will land on a solid space since the solid spaces take up less than one-half of the spinner board.

$$P(\text{solid space}) = \frac{\text{solid space}}{\text{total number of spaces}} = \frac{3}{8} = 0.375 = \textbf{37.5\%}$$

5. It is very likely that the spinner will land on a striped or white space since these spaces take up most of the spinner board.

$$P(\text{striped or white space}) = \frac{\text{striped or white space}}{\text{total number of spaces}} = \frac{7}{8} = 0.875 = \textbf{87.5\%}$$

6. It is very unlikely that the spinner will land on a dotted space since the dotted space takes up less than one-quarter of the spinner board.

$$P(\text{dotted space}) = \frac{\text{dotted space}}{\text{total number of spaces}} = \frac{1}{8} = 0.125 = \mathbf{12.5\%}$$

7. The probability of choosing a red card at random is 50%.

$$P(\text{red}) = \frac{\text{red}}{\text{total cards}} = \frac{26}{52} = 0.5 = \mathbf{50\%}$$

8. The probability of choosing a spade at random is 25%.

$$P(\text{spade}) = \frac{\text{spade}}{\text{total cards}} = \frac{13}{52} = 0.25 = \mathbf{25\%}$$

9. The probability of choosing one of the four aces at random is approximately 7.69%. Chances are slim.

$$P(\text{ace}) = \frac{\text{ace}}{\text{total cards}} = \frac{4}{52} \approx 0.0769 = \mathbf{7.69\%}$$

10. $$P(\text{jack, queen, or king}) = \frac{\text{jack, queen, or king}}{\text{total cards}} = \frac{12}{52} \approx 0.231 = \mathbf{23.1\%}$$

11. There are no zero cards to choose from in the deck so there is no chance of choosing a zero from the deck.

$$P(\text{zero}) = \frac{\text{zero}}{\text{total cards}} = \frac{0}{52} = 0 = \mathbf{0\%}$$

12.

Prize	Amount	Probability of Each Event
Stickers	25	$\frac{25}{100} = 0.25 = 25\%$
Gumballs	50	$\frac{50}{100} = 0.5 = 50\%$
Watches	2	$\frac{2}{100} = 0.02 = 2\%$
Bouncy Balls	23	$\frac{23}{100} = 0.23 = 23\%$
Total	100	$\frac{100}{100} = 1.00 = 100\%$

$$P(\text{watch}) = \frac{\text{watch}}{\text{total prizes}} = \frac{2}{100} = 0.02 = \mathbf{2\%}$$

13. **METHOD 1**

    Use the table from number 12 and add up the probabilities for each event:

    $$0.5 + 0.23 + 0.25 = 0.98 = \textbf{98\%}$$

    METHOD 2 $\quad P(\text{gumball, sticker, bouncy ball}) = \dfrac{\text{gumball, sticker, bouncy ball}}{\text{total prizes}}$

    $$= \frac{50 + 25 + 23}{100} = 0.98 = \textbf{98\%}$$

    METHOD 3 $\quad P(\text{everything except the watches}) = 1 - 0.02 = 0.98 = \textbf{98\%}$

14. There are no key chain prizes in the gumball machine so the chances of getting a key chain is zero.

    $$P(\text{zero}) = \frac{\text{\# of key chains}}{\text{total prizes}} = \frac{0}{100} = 0 = \textbf{0\%}$$

15. **METHOD 1** $\quad 0.25 + 0.23 = 0.48 = \textbf{48\%}$

    METHOD 2

    $$P(\text{sticker or bouncy ball}) = \frac{\text{\# of stickers and bouncy balls}}{\text{total prizes}} = \frac{25 + 23}{100}$$

    $$= 0.48 = \textbf{48\%}$$

16. $P(\text{sticker}) = \dfrac{\text{\# of stickers}}{\text{total prizes}} = \dfrac{25}{100} = 0.25 = \textbf{25\%}$

17. 0—Include words like *impossible*, *no chance*, and *zero percent chance*. There is no chance I will wear a t-shirt to a wedding reception.

18. 0.1—Key words: *slim chance* or *possibility*, *tiny chance* or *possibility*, *very little chance* or *possibility*, and *unlikely*. Even though there are only ten people's names in the basket, it is unlikely my name will be drawn.

19. 0.25—Key words: *one in 4 chance*, *small chance*, and *unlikely*. During a game of four corners, the person in the middle needs to choose a corner to eliminate. There is a one in four chance the person will eliminate the corner I am in.

20. 0.4—There is a **40%** chance it will rain tomorrow.

21. 0.5—There is a **50%** chance I will flip a head on a fair two-sided coin.

22. 0.6—There are ten pints of ice cream left in the freezer. There are six chocolate and four vanilla. There is a **60%** chance I will get a chocolate if I do not get to choose the ice cream I want.

23. 0.75—It is likely I will need to travel for work next week.

24. 0.9—There is a **90%** chance we will have a test tomorrow since we just finished the chapter yesterday.

25. 0.99—I am **99%** certain my answers are correct since I double-checked all my answers and even worked backward.

26. 1—I am **100%** certain we will have a family reunion next year since we have had one every year for the last ten years.

Lesson 6.5: Probability Models

Practice, pages 191–194

1. A. Possible outcomes are heads and tails. There are two equally possible outcomes. The sample space has two outcomes.

   B. Yes, because the probability of each event is constant or the same. They have an equal chance of happening.

   C. Probability model for flipping a coin.

Result of a Coin Flip	Heads	Tails
Probability	$\frac{1}{2}$ = 0.5 = 50	$\frac{1}{2}$ = 0.5 = 50%

   D. Probability model for experimental probability.

Result of a Coin Flip	Heads	Tails	Total
Observed Frequency	23	27	50
Relative Frequency	$\frac{23}{50}$ = 0.46 = 46%	$\frac{27}{50}$ = 0.54 = 54%	$\frac{50}{50}$ = 1 = 100%

E. Heads = 0.46(200) = **92**

Tails = 0.54(200) = **108**

F. If we flipped the coin 100 times, 200 times, 500 times, and so on, we would observe that the proportion of flipping a coin and having it land on heads would eventually settle down to the true probability of **0.5**.

2. A. Probability model for selecting each colored marble.

Color	Probability
Red	$P(red) = \dfrac{red}{total} = \dfrac{3}{20} = 0.15 = 15\%$
Blue	$P(blue) = \dfrac{blue}{total} = \dfrac{7}{20} = 0.35 = 35\%$
Green	$P(green) = \dfrac{green}{total} = \dfrac{4}{20} = 0.2 = 20\%$
Yellow	$P(yellow) = \dfrac{yellow}{total} = \dfrac{6}{20} = 0.3 = 30\%$

B. No, because the probability for each event is not constant or the same.

C. Probability model for Jenna randomly selecting colored marbles.

Color	Approximate Frequency
Red	0.15(50) = 7.5
Blue	0.35(50) = 17.5
Green	0.2(50) = 10
Yellow	0.3(50) = 15

D. Long-term frequency in this situation means that the more times you draw, the closer to the theoretical probability the numbers become.

E. Jenna could continue to draw from one side and the bag of marbles could not be shaken up as well, which would make the same marble be drawn.

3. A. There are **36 total outcomes**.

    Sample space = {2, 3, 4, 5, 6, 7, 8, 9, 10, 11, 12}

    B. Probability model for each sum rolled.

Sum of the Dice	Number of Favorable Events	Probability of Each Event
2	1	$P(\text{rolling a sum of 2}) = \frac{1}{36} \approx 0.028 \approx 2.8\%$
3	2	$P(\text{rolling a sum of 3}) = \frac{2}{36} = \frac{1}{18} \approx 0.056 \approx 5.6\%$
4	3	$P(\text{rolling a sum of 4}) = \frac{3}{36} = \frac{1}{12} \approx 0.083 \approx 8.3\%$
5	4	$P(\text{rolling a sum of 5}) = \frac{4}{36} = \frac{1}{9} \approx 0.111 \approx 11.1\%$
6	5	$P(\text{rolling a sum of 6}) = \frac{5}{36} \approx 0.139 \approx 13.9\%$
7	6	$P(\text{rolling a sum of 7}) = \frac{6}{36} = \frac{1}{6} \approx 0.167 \approx 16.7\%$
8	5	$P(\text{rolling a sum of 8}) = \frac{5}{36} \approx 0.139 \approx 13.9\%$
9	4	$P(\text{rolling a sum of 9}) = \frac{4}{36} = \frac{1}{9} \approx 0.111 \approx 11.1\%$
10	3	$P(\text{rolling a sum of 10}) = \frac{3}{36} = \frac{1}{12} \approx 0.083 \approx 8.3\%$
11	2	$P(\text{rolling a sum of 11}) = \frac{2}{36} = \frac{1}{18} \approx 0.056 \approx 5.6\%$
12	1	$P(\text{rolling a sum of 12}) = \frac{1}{36} \approx 0.0278 \approx 2.78\%$
Total	36	$\frac{36}{36} = 1 = 100\%$

    C. No, because all the events do not have a constant probability.

D. Probability model for each sum rolled during the game.

Sum of Dice	Observed Frequency	Relative Frequency
2	1	P(rolling a sum of 2) = $\frac{1}{45}$ ≈ 0.022 ≈ 2.2%
3	2	P(rolling a sum of 3) = $\frac{2}{45}$ ≈ 0.044 ≈ 4.4%
4	3	P(rolling a sum of 4) = $\frac{3}{45}$ = $\frac{1}{15}$ ≈ 0.067 ≈ 6.7%
5	4	P(rolling a sum of 5) = $\frac{4}{45}$ ≈ 0.089 ≈ 8.9%
6	9	P(rolling a sum of 6) = $\frac{9}{45}$ = $\frac{1}{5}$ = 0.2 = 20%
7	8	P(rolling a sum of 7) = $\frac{8}{45}$ = $\frac{1}{5}$ = 0.178 = 17.8%
8	6	P(rolling a sum of 8) = $\frac{6}{45}$ = $\frac{2}{15}$ = 0.133 = 13.3%
9	5	P(rolling a sum of 9) = $\frac{5}{45}$ = $\frac{1}{9}$ = 0.111 = 11.1%
10	6	P(rolling a sum of 10) = $\frac{6}{45}$ = $\frac{2}{15}$ = 0.133 = 13.3%
11	1	P(rolling a sum of 11) = $\frac{1}{45}$ ≈ 0.022 ≈ 2.2%
12	0	P(rolling a sum of 12) = $\frac{0}{45}$ = 0 = 0%
Total	45	$\frac{45}{45}$ = 1 = 100%

E. As Amelia, Kelly, Ryan, and Angelia continue rolling the dice, the experimental probability should gradually reflect or get closer to the theoretical probability. For example, the theoretical probability of rolling a sum of 7 is 16.7%. In their game, the experimental probability of rolling a sum of 7 is 17.8%. If they rolled 100 more times, the experimental probability of rolling a 7 will be closer to **16.7%**.

F. The persons rolling the dice may not shake them as well as someone else. Plastic dice are less reliable since the weight of the plastic may not be as consistent as shaking the dice in a cup.

4. A. The sample space has **8 possible outcomes**: Zach, Sonia, Jason, Medha, Niel, Andrew, Hinako, and Evo.

   B. Probability model for each student's name being drawn.

Student	Probability
Zach	P(selecting Zach) = $\frac{1}{8}$ = 0.125 = 12.5%
Sonia	P(selecting Sonia) = $\frac{1}{8}$ = 0.125 = 12.5%
Jason	P(selecting Jason) = $\frac{1}{8}$ = 0.125 = 12.5%
Medha	P(selecting Medha) = $\frac{1}{8}$ = 0.125 = 12.5%
Niel	P(selecting Niel) = $\frac{1}{8}$ = 0.125 = 12.5%
Andrew	P(selecting Andrew) = $\frac{1}{8}$ = 0.125 = 12.5%
Hinako	P(selecting Hinako) = $\frac{1}{8}$ = 0.125 = 12.5%
Evo	P(selecting Evo) = $\frac{1}{8}$ = 0.125 = 12.5%
Total	$\frac{8}{8}$ = 1 = 100%

   C. Yes, because the probability of each event is constant or the same. They each have an equal chance of being chosen every day.

D. To find the relative frequency of each student, construct a probability model to represent the data as seen below.

Student	Observed Frequency	Relative Frequency
Zach	3	$P(\text{selecting Zach}) = \frac{3}{30} = \frac{1}{10} = 0.1 = 10\%$
Sonia	6	$P(\text{selecting Sonia}) = \frac{6}{30} = \frac{1}{5} = 0.2 = 20\%$
Jason	2	$P(\text{selecting Jason}) = \frac{2}{30} = \frac{1}{15} \approx 0.067 \approx 6.7\%$
Medha	3	$P(\text{selecting Medha}) = \frac{3}{30} = \frac{1}{10} = 0.1 = 10\%$
Niel	5	$P(\text{selecting Niel}) = \frac{5}{30} = \frac{1}{6} \approx 0.167 \approx 16.7\%$
Andrew	4	$P(\text{selecting Andrew}) = \frac{4}{30} = \frac{2}{15} \approx 0.133 \approx 13.3\%$
Hinako	5	$P(\text{selecting Hinako}) = \frac{5}{30} = \frac{1}{6} \approx 0.167 \approx 16.7\%$
Evo	2	$P(\text{selecting Evo}) = \frac{2}{30} = \frac{1}{15} \approx 0.067 \approx 6.7\%$
Total	30	$\frac{30}{30} = 1 = 100\%$

E. As Mrs. Massaro continues to draw names out of the bag randomly, the experimental probability should gradually reflect or get closer to the theoretical probability. For example, the probability of Evo's name being drawn is approximately 6.7%. If Mrs. Massaro draws 200 more names out of the bag, the probability of Evo's name being drawn will be closer to 12.5%.

F. External factors may be when the name is put back in the bag, the names may need to be shaken more evenly. Mrs. Massaro could also draw from a different part of the bag every time.

5. A. The table below shows how many students were there for each category.

Type of Transportation	Relative Frequency
Walk	0.25(340) = 85
Bike	0.3(340) = 102
Car—No Carpool	0.35(340) = 119
Car—Carpool	0.1(340) = 34
Total	1(340) = 340

B. 102 − 85 = 17. **17** more students biked than walked.

C. 119 − 34 = 85. **85** more students rode in a car but did not carpool compared to the ones that did carpool.

6. A.

Type of Drink	Approximating the Frequency
Original Milk Tea with Boba	0.42(900) = 378
Thai Ice Tea with Boba	0.26(900) = 234
Other	0.32(900) = 288
Total	1(900) = 900

144 more customers ordered the original milk tea compared to the Thai iced tea.

B. 378 − 234 = **144**.

Lesson 6.6: Probability of Compound Events

Practice, page 197

1. The probability of the puppy's name starting with a K or will have an A as a second letter is $\frac{6}{12} = \frac{1}{2}$.

Vowels			Letters		
		K	S	T	M
	A	KA	SA	TA	MA
	E	KE	SE	TE	ME
	U	KU	SU	TU	MU

2. The probability it will land on all heads or all tails is $\frac{2}{8} = \frac{1}{4}$.

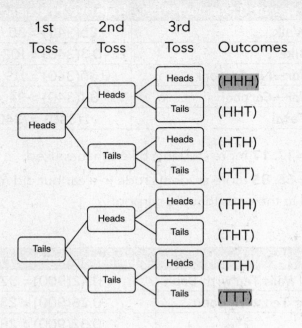

3. At least 2 heads means 2 or more heads. $\frac{11}{16}$

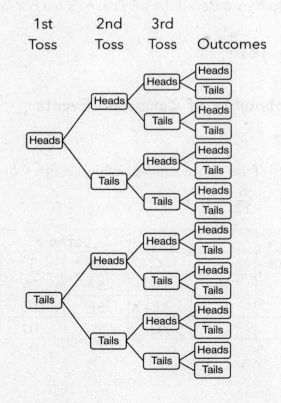

4. The probability it will land on a sum that is greater than 8 is $\frac{10}{36} = \frac{5}{18}$.

5. $\frac{18}{36} = \frac{1}{2}$

6. $\frac{4}{16} = \frac{1}{4}$

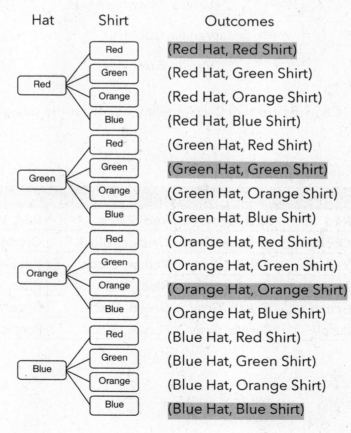

Hat	Shirt	Outcomes
	Red	(Red Hat, Red Shirt)
Red	Green	(Red Hat, Green Shirt)
	Orange	(Red Hat, Orange Shirt)
	Blue	(Red Hat, Blue Shirt)
	Red	(Green Hat, Red Shirt)
Green	Green	(Green Hat, Green Shirt)
	Orange	(Green Hat, Orange Shirt)
	Blue	(Green Hat, Blue Shirt)
	Red	(Orange Hat, Red Shirt)
Orange	Green	(Orange Hat, Green Shirt)
	Orange	(Orange Hat, Orange Shirt)
	Blue	(Orange Hat, Blue Shirt)
	Red	(Blue Hat, Red Shirt)
Blue	Green	(Blue Hat, Green Shirt)
	Orange	(Blue Hat, Orange Shirt)
	Blue	(Blue Hat, Blue Shirt)

7. $\frac{1}{12}$

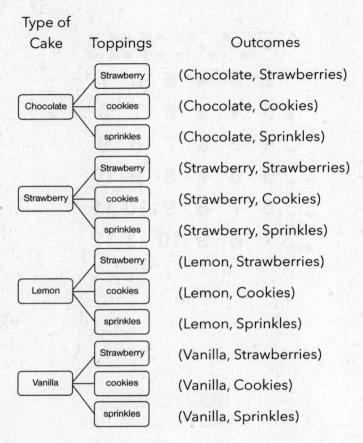

Type of Cake	Toppings	Outcomes

Type of Cake — Toppings — Outcomes

- Chocolate
  - Strawberry → (Chocolate, Strawberries)
  - cookies → (Chocolate, Cookies)
  - sprinkles → (Chocolate, Sprinkles)
- Strawberry
  - Strawberry → (Strawberry, Strawberries)
  - cookies → (Strawberry, Cookies)
  - sprinkles → (Strawberry, Sprinkles)
- Lemon
  - Strawberry → (Lemon, Strawberries)
  - cookies → (Lemon, Cookies)
  - sprinkles → (Lemon, Sprinkles)
- Vanilla
  - Strawberry → (Vanilla, Strawberries)
  - cookies → (Vanilla, Cookies)
  - sprinkles → (Vanilla, Sprinkles)

8. Odds are $\frac{1}{18}$. Chances are slim that Angelina will order the same combination as her sister.

Letters

Color of towel		Gray	Black	White
	Red	Red, Gray	Red, Black	Red, White
	Orange	Orange, Gray	Orange, Black	Orange, White
	Yellow	Yellow, Gray	Yellow, Black	Yellow, White
	Blue	Blue, Gray	Blue, Black	Blue, White
	Green	Green, Gray	Green, Black	Green, White
	Purple	Purple, Gray	Purple, Black	Purple, White

9. Answers may vary.

10. Answers may vary.

Chapter 7 Practice Test

Computer-Adaptive Test, pages 199–202

1. Honeybees need to secrete 21.84 pounds of honey to produce 2.6 pounds of wax in order to construct 100,000 cells.

   Let x = the amount of honey in pounds needed for 2.6 pounds of wax.

   $$\frac{8.4 \text{ pounds of honey}}{1 \text{ pound of wax}} = \frac{x \text{ pounds of honey}}{2.6 \text{ pounds of wax}}$$

   $$\frac{8.4 \text{ pounds of honey}}{1 \text{ pound of wax}} \cdot \frac{2.6}{2.6} = \frac{21.84 \text{ pounds of honey}}{2.6 \text{ pounds of wax}}$$

2. Bryan scored an **83%** on the exam.

   $30(3.5) + 7(5) - 9(1.25) - 3(0.375) = 70 + 35 - 11.25 - 2.25 = 91.5$

   Bryan's score in percents $= \dfrac{\text{score}}{\text{total}} = \dfrac{91.5}{110} = 0.831 = \textbf{83\%}$

3. $-4(3x - 2y) - 0.1(5y - 20x) - \dfrac{3}{4}(12x - y)$

   $-12x + 8y - 0.5y + 2x - 9x + 15y$

   $-12x + 2x - 9x + 8y - 0.5y + 15y$

   $-19x + 22.5y$

4. The five consecutive odd numbers are: **37**, **39**, **41**, **43**, and **45** and their sum is **205**.

   METHOD 1   Let s = the smallest number.

   1st odd number = s

   2nd odd number = $s + 2$

   3rd odd number = $s + 4$

   4th odd number = $s + 6$

   5th odd number = $s + 8$

   1st number + 2nd number + 3rd number + 4th number + 5th number = sum

   $$s + s + 2 + s + 4 + s + 6 + s + 8 = 205$$

   $$5s + 20 = 205$$

   $$5s + 20 - 20 = 205 - 20$$

   $$5s = 185$$

   $$\frac{5s}{5} = \frac{185}{5}$$

   $$s = \textbf{37}$$

1st odd number = s = 37

2nd odd number = s + 2 = 37 + 2 = 39

3rd odd number = s + 4 = 37 + 4 = 41

4th odd number = s + 6 = 37 + 6 = 43

5th odd number = s + 8 = 37 + 8 = 45

METHOD 2 Let L = the largest of the 5 odd consecutive numbers.

1st odd number = $L - 8$

2nd odd number = $L - 6$

3rd odd number = $L - 4$

4th odd number = $L - 2$

5th odd number = L

1st number + 2nd number + 3rd number + 4th number + 5th number = sum

$$L - 8 + L - 6 + L - 4 + L - 2 + L = 205$$

$$5L - 20 = 205$$

$$5L - 20 + 20 = 205 + 20$$

$$5L = 245$$

$$\frac{5L}{5} = \frac{245}{5}$$

$$L = \textbf{45}$$

1st odd number = $L - 8 = 45 - 8 = 37$

2nd odd number = $L - 6 = 45 - 6 = 39$

3rd odd number = $L - 4 = 45 - 4 = 41$

4th odd number = $L - 2 = 45 - 2 = 43$

5th odd number = $L = 45$

5.   The answer is **B**. The original cost of the printer is **$249.00**.

$$\text{Original cost}(100\% + 8.25\%) = 269.54$$

$$\text{Original cost}(108.25\%) = 269.54$$

$$\text{Original cost}(1.0825) = 269.54$$

$$\frac{\text{Original cost}(1.0825)}{1.0825} = \frac{269.54}{1.0825}$$

$$\text{Original cost} = \textbf{248.9976905}$$

6. The answer is **D**. Jane can send up to **eleven** articles of clothing without going over the weight limit. If she sends nine articles of clothing, she will be over the weight limit by 0.1875 pounds and be charged an additional fee.

$$\frac{1 \text{ pound}}{16 \text{ ounces}} = \frac{x \text{ pound}}{6.25 \text{ ounces}}$$

$$1(6.25) = 16x$$

$$\frac{6.25}{16} = \frac{16x}{16}$$

$$0.390625 = x$$

$$6.25 \text{ ounces} = 0.390625 \text{ pounds}$$

Let c = articles of clothing.

Weight of books + weight of clothing < weight limit

$$4.5 + 0.390625c < 9$$

$$4.5 + 0.390625c - 4.5 < 9 - 4.5$$

$$0.390625c < 4.5$$

$$\frac{0.390625c}{0.390625} < \frac{4.5}{0.390625}$$

$$c < 11.52$$

Article of Clothing	4.5 + 0.390625c < 9	True or False
11	4.5 + 0.390625(11) < 9 8.796875 < 9	True
12	4.5 + 0.390625(12) < 9 9.1875	False

7. The answer is **A**. Scale factor = **4**. Since triangle B is larger than triangle A, the scale factor must be greater than 1.

$$\text{Scale factor} = \frac{\text{scaled image}}{\text{original}} = \frac{20}{5} = \frac{16}{4} = \frac{12}{3} = \textbf{4}$$

8. The answer is **B**. One triangle is possible because $3^2 + 4^2 = 5^2$. This is a right triangle.

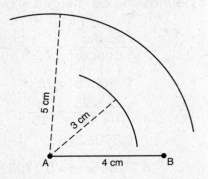

9. The answer is **C**. Kirill started off with **1,000 mL** of water.

   Let w = the original amount of water Kirill started off with.

$$w(100\% - 60\%) = 400$$

$$w(40\%) = 400$$

$$0.4w = 400$$

$$\frac{0.4w}{0.4} = \frac{400}{0.4}$$

$$w = \mathbf{1,000}$$

10. $-0.2 - (-0.02) - \frac{1}{2} \div -2(-0.2) + 20\%$

    $-0.2 + 0.02 + (0.25)(-0.2) + 0.2$

    $-0.2 + 0.02 - 0.05 + 0.2$

    −0.03

11. $-\dfrac{12}{28} \div \left(-\dfrac{6}{12}\right) \div \left(-\dfrac{5}{10}\right) = -\dfrac{\mathbf{12}}{\mathbf{28}}\left(-\dfrac{\mathbf{12}}{\mathbf{6}}\right)\left(-\dfrac{\mathbf{10}}{\mathbf{5}}\right) = -\dfrac{\mathbf{12}}{\mathbf{7}}$

12. $\dfrac{1}{6}(7) = \dfrac{\mathbf{7}}{\mathbf{6}}$ **hours each week Kate has lost.**

13. She is short $\mathbf{1\dfrac{5}{8}}$ cups of salt.

$$3\frac{1}{2} - 1\frac{7}{8} = 3\frac{4}{8} - 1\frac{7}{8} = 2\frac{12}{8} - 1\frac{7}{8} = \mathbf{1\frac{5}{8}}$$

14. 98 of $\dfrac{3}{10} = \dfrac{98}{1}\left(\dfrac{3}{10}\right) = \dfrac{\cancel{98}}{1}\left(\dfrac{3}{\cancel{10}}\right) = \dfrac{147}{5} = \mathbf{29.4\ calories\ of\ sugar}$

15. Ellen caught $5\frac{7}{24}$ **inches** of rain in her rain catcher.

$$3\frac{1}{2}-\frac{3}{8}+2\frac{5}{6}-\frac{2}{3}=3\frac{1}{2}-\frac{3}{8}+2\frac{5}{6}-\frac{2}{3}=3\frac{12}{24}+2\frac{20}{24}+\left(-\frac{9}{24}\right)+\left(-\frac{16}{24}\right)=5\frac{32}{24}+\left(-\frac{25}{24}\right)=\mathbf{5\frac{7}{24}}$$

16. $1{,}200\left(\frac{1}{480}\right)=\mathbf{2.5\ feet}$

17. Jeshua can make **14 trips**. Round down in this situation because if he made 15 trips, he would not have enough gas for the entirety of the trip.

$$13\div\frac{7}{8}=13\left(\frac{8}{7}\right)=\frac{104}{7}=\mathbf{14.86}$$

18. Kevin has **$151** left. 7(25) − 2(42) + 3(20)

175 − 84 + 60

$151

19. Chloe charges **$191.06** on her credit card each month.

$$\text{Average}=\frac{\text{total}}{\#}=\frac{\text{sum of each monthly charge}}{6}-\frac{1{,}146.36}{6}=\mathbf{-191.06}$$

20. Amount in piggy bank = 52(0.05) + 67(0.01) + 37(0.25) + 14(0.1)

= 2.6 + 0.67 + 9.25 + 1.4

= 13.92

Cost of two movie tickets = **2(7.5) = 15**

Amount Jake is short: 13.92 − 15 = **−$1.08**

21. Total points on Abby's math quiz:

12(2.5) + 3(−1.5) + 1(−2.25) = 30 + (−4.5) + (−2.25)

= **23.25**

22. Kaitlyn's snail crawled an average of **0.855 inches** per day.

$$\text{Average}=\frac{\text{total}}{\#}=\frac{0.25+0.8+1.32+1.05}{4}=\frac{3.42}{4}=\mathbf{0.855}$$

23. Isabella has only **4.25 cups**.

A. Number of cups of chocolate chips she needs:

3 batches (2.5 cups) = 7.5 cups

Number of cups she is short: 7.5 − 4.25 = 3.25 cups.

B. She needs one more bag of chocolate chips.

She will have half a cup of chocolate chips left over.

$$3.75 - 3.25 = 0.5 = \frac{1}{2}$$

24. $(5+4)3 - 2 = 9(3) - 2 = 27 - 2 = \mathbf{25}$

25. $2 - 3(4+5) = 2 - 3(9) = 2 - 27 = \mathbf{-25}$

26. Answers may vary. Here is one possible solution:

$$8\left(125\% + \frac{3}{4}\right) \div 0.16 - 99 = \mathbf{1}$$

27. $\frac{\mathbf{3}}{\mathbf{8}}$ is halfway between $\frac{1}{2}$ and $\frac{1}{4}$.

METHOD 1 Average $= \dfrac{\text{total}}{\#}$

$$\left(\frac{4}{8} + \frac{2}{8}\right)\frac{1}{2} = \frac{6}{8}\left(\frac{1}{2}\right) = \frac{\mathbf{3}}{\mathbf{8}}$$

METHOD 2 Half of the distance between the two.

Find the distance between the two points: $\dfrac{4}{8} - \dfrac{2}{8} = \dfrac{2}{8}$

Divide the distance in half: $\dfrac{2}{8}\left(\dfrac{1}{2}\right) = \dfrac{1}{8}$

Add it back to the point closest to 0: $\dfrac{2}{8} + \dfrac{1}{8} = \dfrac{3}{8}$

Check your answer by subtracting the halfway distance from the point farthest away from 0: $\dfrac{4}{8} - \dfrac{1}{8} = \dfrac{3}{8}$

Double check your answer by graphing all 3 points on the number line:

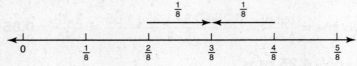

28. $-\dfrac{\mathbf{19}}{\mathbf{24}}$ is halfway between $-\dfrac{3}{4}$ and $-\dfrac{5}{6}$.

METHOD 1 Average $= \dfrac{\text{total}}{\#}$

$$-\frac{9}{12} + \left(-\frac{10}{12}\right)\frac{1}{2} = -\frac{19}{12}\left(\frac{1}{2}\right) = -\frac{\mathbf{19}}{\mathbf{24}}$$

METHOD 2 Half of the distance between the two.

Find the distance between the two points: $-\dfrac{10}{12}-\left(-\dfrac{9}{12}\right)=-\dfrac{1}{12}$

Divide the distance in half: $-\dfrac{1}{12}\left(\dfrac{1}{2}\right)=-\dfrac{1}{24}$

Add it back to the point closest to 0: $-\dfrac{9}{12}+\left(-\dfrac{1}{24}\right)=-\dfrac{18}{24}+\left(-\dfrac{1}{24}\right)=-\dfrac{19}{24}$

Check your answer by subtracting the halfway distance from the point farthest

away from 0: $-\dfrac{10}{12}-\left(-\dfrac{1}{24}\right)=-\dfrac{10}{12}+\dfrac{1}{24}=-\dfrac{20}{24}+\dfrac{1}{24}=-\dfrac{19}{24}$

Double check your answer by graphing all three points on the number line:

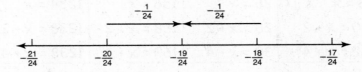

29. Think of the same expressions that work for each set of the four consecutive odd numbers.

$3 = x$	$11 = x$	$57 = x$	$121 = x$
$5 = x + 2$	$13 = x + 2$	$59 = x + 2$	$123 = x + 2$
$7 = x + 4$	$15 = x + 4$	$61 = x + 4$	$125 = x + 4$
$9 = x + 6$	$17 = x + 6$	$63 = x + 6$	$127 = x + 6$

Let x = the first number.

Write your equation in words: First # + second # + third # + fourth # = total

Use the expressions and plug in what you have: $x + x + 2 + x + 4 + x + 6 = 80$

Solve for x and find both numbers: $4x + 12 = 80$

$$4x + 12 - 12 = 80 - 12$$

$$4x = 68$$

$$\dfrac{4x}{4} = \dfrac{68}{4}$$

$$x = \mathbf{17}$$

Plug x into the original expressions to find the other three numbers.

First consecutive odd number $= x = 17$
Second consecutive odd number $= x + 2 = 17 + 2 = 19$
Third consecutive odd number $= x + 4 = 17 + 4 = 21$
Fourth consecutive odd number $= x + 6 = 17 + 6 = 23$

Articulate your solution in a sentence: The sum of these four consecutive odd numbers 17, 19, 21, and 23 is 80.

30. Think of the same expressions that work for each set of the three consecutive even numbers.

$8 = x$	$26 = x$	$156 = x$	$1234 = x$
$10 = x + 2$	$28 = x + 2$	$158 = x + 2$	$1236 = x + 2$
$12 = x + 4$	$30 = x + 4$	$160 = x + 4$	$1238 = x + 4$

Let $x =$ the first number.
Write your equation in words: First # + second # + third # = total
Use the expressions and plug in what you have: $x + x + 2 + x + 4 = 48$
Solve for x and find both numbers: $3x + 6 = 48$

$$3x + 6 - 6 = 48 - 6$$

$$3x = 42$$

$$\frac{3x}{3} = \frac{42}{3}$$

$$x = \mathbf{14}$$

Plug x into the original expressions to find the other two numbers

First consecutive even number $= x = 14$
Second consecutive even number $= x + 2 = 14 + 2 = 16$
Third consecutive even number $= x + 4 = 14 + 4 = 18$

Articulate your solution in a sentence: The sum of these three consecutive even numbers 14, 16, and 18 is 48.

31. The cost of the squeaky ball is **$1.65** and the cost of the frisbee is **$3.10**.

    Let b = the cost of the squeaky ball.

    Frisbee = $1.45 + b$

    Frisbee + squeaky ball = total cost

    $$1.45 + b + b = 4.75$$
    $$1.45 + 2b - 1.45 = 4.75 - 1.45$$
    $$2b = 3.3$$
    $$\frac{2b}{2} = \frac{3.3}{2}$$
    $$b = \mathbf{1.65}$$
    $$b + 1.45 = \mathbf{3.10}$$

32. Let w = the length of the width

    Width = w

    Length = $4w - 1$

    Perimeter = add up all sides

    $$36 = w + w + 4w - 1 + 4w - 1$$
    $$36 = 10w - 2$$
    $$36 + 2 = 10w - 2 + 2$$
    $$38 = 10w$$
    $$\frac{38}{10} = \frac{10w}{10}$$
    $$\mathbf{3.8} = w$$

    Length = $4w - 1 = 4(3.8) - 1 = 15.2 - 1 = \mathbf{14.2}$

    The length is 14.2 inches and the width is 3.8 inches.

    Check your answer: perimeter = 2(length) + 2(width)

    $$36 = 2(14.2) + 2(3.8)$$
    $$36 = 28.4 + 7.6$$
    $$\mathbf{36} = 36$$

Performance Task, pages 203-204

1. Kirsten spends approximately **$144.68** on soy milk every year for her soy lattes every morning.

   Let x = number of liters in one cup.

   $$\frac{4 \text{ cups}}{1 \text{ liter}} = \frac{1 \text{ cup}}{x \text{ liters}}$$

   $$\frac{4 \text{ cups}}{1 \text{ liter}} \div \frac{4}{4} = \frac{1 \text{ cup}}{0.25 \text{ liters}}$$

   Find the number of cups she can make from three half gallons of soy milk that would cost her $8.99 total.

   $$\frac{0.25 \text{ liters}}{1 \text{ cup of soy milk}} = \frac{3(1.89)}{c \text{ cups of soy milk}}$$

   $$\frac{0.25 \text{ liters}}{1 \text{ cup of soy milk}} = \frac{5.67}{c \text{ cups of soy milk}}$$

   $$\frac{0.25 \text{ liters}}{1 \text{ cup of soy milk}} \cdot \left(\frac{22.68}{22.68}\right) = \frac{5.67}{22.68 \text{ cups of soy milk}}$$

   Find the total amount she spends on soy milk in one year. Let t = total cost of soy milk for the year:

   $$\frac{22.68 \text{ cups of soy milk}}{\$8.99} = \frac{365 \text{ cups total}}{t}$$

   $$22.68t = 8.99(365)$$

   $$22.68t = 3281.35$$

   $$\frac{22.68t}{22.68} = \frac{3281.35}{22.68}$$

   $$t = \mathbf{144.68}$$

2. If Kassy used **24 tokens**, it would cost her **$6**.

Coordinates (x, y)	$\frac{y}{x} = k$
(3, 0.75)	$\frac{0.75}{3} = 0.25$
(5, 1.25)	$\frac{1.25}{5} = 0.25$

The constant of proportionality is 0.25. This means each token costs $0.25.

The equation: $0.25x = y$

$$0.25(24) = \mathbf{6}$$

3.

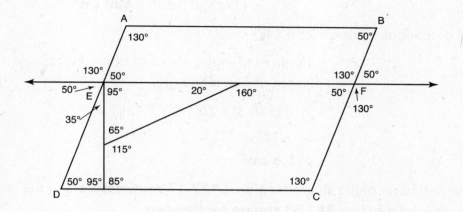

4.   Let $L = L$ of the rectangle

$W = 0.4L$

Perimeter = add up all sides

$$44.8 = L + L + 0.4L + 0.4L$$
$$44.8 = 2.8L$$
$$\frac{44.8}{2.8} = \frac{2.8L}{2.8}$$

$L = \mathbf{16}$

$W = 0.4(16) = \mathbf{6.4}$

Area = length(width) = $16(6.4) = \mathbf{102.4\ cm^2}$

5.   The dimensions of the base area are **12 cm by 12 cm**.

Volume of square pyramid $= \dfrac{Bh}{3} = \dfrac{(\text{area of square})\text{height}}{3}$

$$864 = \frac{18s^2}{3}$$
$$864 = 6s^2$$
$$\frac{864}{6} = \frac{6s^2}{3}$$
$$144 = s^2$$
$$\sqrt{144} = \sqrt{s^2}$$
$$\mathbf{12} = s$$

6. Kaia will need **425.6 square centimeters** of wrapping paper and **480 cubic centimeters** of candy to fill the triangular prism.

Volume of triangular prism = Bh = (area of triangle)(height of prism)

$$= (10)(8)(0.5)(12) = \textbf{480 cm}^3$$

SA of triangular prism = $2B + LA$

$$= 2(\text{area of triangle}) + \text{area of bottom rectangle} +$$
$$2(\text{area of side rectangle})$$

$$= 2(10)(8)(0.5) + 10(12) + 2(12)(9.4)$$

$$= 80 + 120 + 225.6$$

$$= \textbf{425.6 cm}^2$$

7. The perimeter of the shaded region is **127.17 centimeters**, and the area of the shaded region is **381.51 square centimeters**.

Area of the shaded region = area of big circle − 3(area of small circle)

$$= (3.14)(13.5)^2 - 3(3.14)(4.5)^2$$

$$= 3.14(182.25) - 3(3.14)(20.25)$$

$$= 572.265 - 190.755$$

$$= \textbf{381.51 cm}^2$$

Perimeter of shaded region = circumference of big circle + 3(circumference of small circle)

$$= 2(3.14)(13.5) + 3(3.14)(4.5)$$

$$= 84.78 + 42.39$$

$$= \textbf{127.17 cm}$$

8.

Item	Observed Frequency	Relative Frequency	Approximate Frequency
Pizza	47	$\frac{47}{145} \approx 0.324$	0.324(1,800) = 583.2
Hot Dogs	32	$\frac{32}{145} \approx 0.221$	0.221(1,800) = 397.8
Chicken Fingers	66	$\frac{66}{145} \approx 0.455$	0.455(1,800) = 819
Total	145	$\frac{145}{145} = 1$	(1)1,800 = 1,800

9.

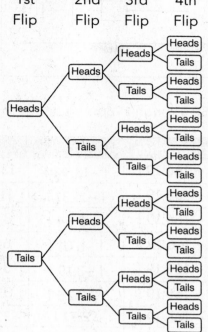

1st Flip	2nd Flip	3rd Flip	4th Flip

Outcomes

HHHH	THHH
HHHT	THHT
HHTH	THTH
HHTT	THTT
HTHH	TTHH
HTHT	TTHT
HTTH	TTTH
HTTT	TTTT

$$P(\text{flipping exactly 3 heads or 3 tails}) = \frac{\text{favorable events}}{\text{total events}} = \frac{8}{16} = \frac{1}{2} = 0.5 = \textbf{50\%}$$

10.

Population 1950 to 1960

Lower Half
- 152.27 —— LE = 152.27
- 154.88
- 157.55 —— Q1 = 157.55
- 160.18
- 163.03

Upper Half
- 165.93 —— Q2 = 165.93
- 168.90
- 171.98
- 174.88 —— Q3 = 174.88
- 177.83
- 180.67 —— UE = 180.67

Range = 180.67 − 152.27 = 28.4

IQR = 174.88 − 157.55 = 17.33

Population 2006 to 2016

Lower Half
- 298.38 —— LE = 298.38
- 301.23
- 304.09 —— Q1 = 304.09
- 306.77
- 308.11

Upper Half
- 310.45 —— Q2 = 310.45
- 312.76
- 314.96
- 317.34 —— Q3 = 317.34
- 319.70
- 321.93 —— UE = 321.93

Range = 321.93 − 298.38 = 23.55

IQR = 317.34 − 304.09 = 13.25

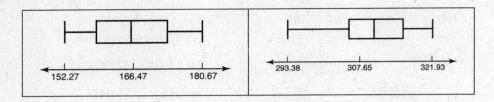

Population of the United States from 1950 through 1960:

Data	Data Value	Mean	Absolute Deviation		
1	152.27	166.19	| 152.27 − 166.19 |	| −13.92 |	13.92
2	154.88	166.19	| 154.88 − 166.19 |	| −11.31 |	11.31
3	157.55	166.19	| 157.55 − 166.19 |	| −8.64 |	8.64
4	160.18	166.19	| 160.18 − 166.19 |	| −6.01 |	6.01
5	163.03	166.19	| 163.03 − 166.19 |	| −3.19 |	3.19
6	165.93	166.19	| 165.93 − 166.19 |	| −0.26 |	0.26
7	168.90	166.19	| 168.90 − 166.19 |	| 2.71 |	2.71
8	171.98	166.19	| 171.98 − 166.19 |	| 5.79 |	5.79
9	174.88	166.19	| 174.88 − 166.19 |	| 8.69 |	8.69
10	177.83	166.19	| 177.83 − 166.19 |	| 11.64 |	11.64
11	180.67	166.19	| 180.67 − 166.19 |	| 14.48 |	14.48
Total	1,828.1				86.844
MAD	$\frac{total}{\#} = \frac{86.844}{11} = 7.88$				

Population of the United States from 2006 through 2016:

Data	Data Value	Mean	Absolute Deviation		
1	298.38	310.52	| 298.38 − 310.52 |	| −12.14 |	12.14
2	301.23	310.52	| 301.23 − 310.52 |	| −9.29 |	9.29
3	304.09	310.52	| 304.09 − 310.52 |	| −6.43 |	6.43
4	306.77	310.52	| 306.77 − 310.52 |	| −3.75 |	3.75
5	308.11	310.52	| 308.11 − 310.52 |	| −2.41 |	2.41
6	310.45	310.52	| 310.45 − 310.52 |	| −0.07 |	0.07
7	312.76	310.52	| 312.76 − 310.52 |	| 2.24 |	2.24
8	314.96	310.52	| 314.96 − 310.52 |	| 4.44 |	4.44
9	317.34	310.52	| 317.34 − 310.52 |	| 6.82 |	6.82
10	319.70	310.52	| 319.70 − 310.52 |	| 9.18 |	9.8
11	321.93	310.52	| 321.93 − 310.52 |	| 11.41 |	11.41
Total	3,415.72				68.8
MAD	$\dfrac{\text{total}}{\#} = \dfrac{68.8}{11} \approx 6.25$				

The MAD is higher from 1950 through 1960, which suggests that there was more variability then compared to the growth from 2006 through 2016.

Common Core Standards

Grade 7 Math Standards

Ratios and Proportional Relationships

Analyze proportional relationships and use them to solve real-world and mathematical problems

CCSS.Math.Content.7.RP.A.1 Compute unit rates associated with ratios of fractions, including ratios of lengths, areas, and other quantities measured in like or different units. *For example, if a person walks 1/2 mile in each 1/4 hour, compute the unit rate as the complex fraction $^{1/2}/_{1/4}$ miles per hour, equivalently 2 miles per hour.*

CCSS.Math.Content.7.RP.A.2 Recognize and represent proportional relationships between quantities.

CCSS.Math.Content.7.RP.A.2.a Decide whether two quantities are in a proportional relationship, e.g., by testing for equivalent ratios in a table or graphing on a coordinate plane and observing whether the graph is a straight line through the origin.

CCSS.Math.Content.7.RP.A.2.b Identify the constant of proportionality (unit rate) in tables, graphs, equations, diagrams, and verbal descriptions of proportional relationships.

CCSS.Math.Content.7.RP.A.2.c Represent proportional relationships by equations. *For example, if the total cost t is proportional to the number n of items purchased at a constant price p, the relationship between the total cost and the number of items can be expressed as t = pn.*

CCSS.Math.Content.7.RP.A.2.d Explain what a point (x, y) on the graph of a proportional relationship means in terms of the situation, with special attention to the points $(0, 0)$ and $(1, r)$ where r is the unit rate.

CCSS.Math.Content.7.RP.A.3 Use proportional relationships to solve multistep ratio and percent problems. Examples: simple interest, tax, markups and markdowns, gratuities and commissions, fees, percent increase and decrease, percent error.

Number Systems

Apply and extend previous understandings of operations with fractions

CCSS.Math.Content.7.NS.A.1 Apply and extend previous understandings of addition and subtraction to add and subtract rational numbers; represent addition and subtraction on a horizontal or vertical number line diagram.

CCSS.Math.Content.7.NS.A.1.a Describe situations in which opposite quantities combine to make 0. *For example, a hydrogen atom has 0 charge because its two constituents are oppositely charged.*

CCSS.Math.Content.7.NS.A.1.b Understand $p + q$ as the number located a distance $|q|$ from p, in the positive or negative direction depending on whether q is positive or negative. Show that a number and its opposite have a sum of 0 (are additive inverses). Interpret sums of rational numbers by describing real-world contexts.

CCSS.Math.Content.7.NS.A.1.c Understand subtraction of rational numbers as adding the additive inverse, $p - q = p + (-q)$. Show that the distance between two rational numbers on the number line is the absolute value of their difference, and apply this principle in real-world contexts.

CCSS.Math.Content.7.NS.A.1.d Apply properties of operations as strategies to add and subtract rational numbers.

CCSS.Math.Content.7.NS.A.2 Apply and extend previous understandings of multiplication and division and of fractions to multiply and divide rational numbers.

CCSS.Math.Content.7.NS.A.2.a Understand that multiplication is extended from fractions to rational numbers by requiring that operations continue to satisfy the properties of operations, particularly the distributive property, leading to products such as $(-1)(-1) = 1$ and the rules for multiplying signed numbers. Interpret products of rational numbers by describing real-world contexts.

CCSS.Math.Content.7.NS.A.2.b Understand that integers can be divided, provided that the divisor is not zero, and every quotient of integers (with a nonzero divisor) is a rational number. If p and q are integers, then $-(p/q) = (-p)/q = p/(-q)$. Interpret quotients of rational numbers by describing real-world contexts.

CCSS.Math.Content.7.NS.A.2.c Apply properties of operations as strategies to multiply and divide rational numbers.

CCSS.Math.Content.7.NS.A.2.d Convert a rational number to a decimal using long division; know that the decimal form of a rational number terminates in zeros or eventually repeats.

CCSS.Math.Content.7.NS.A.3 Solve real-world and mathematical problems involving the four operations with rational numbers.[1]

[1]Computations with rational numbers extend the rules for manipulating fractions to complex fractions.

Expressions and Equations

Use properties of operations to generate equivalent expressions

CCSS.Math.Content.7.EE.A.1 Apply properties of operations as strategies to add, subtract, factor, and expand linear expressions with rational coefficients.

CCSS.Math.Content.7.EE.A.2 Understand that rewriting an expression in different forms in a problem context can shed light on the problem and how the quantities in it are related. *For example, a + 0.05a = 1.05a means that "increase by 5%" is the same as "multiply by 1.05."*

Solve real-life and mathematical problems using numerical and algebraic expressions and equations

CCSS.Math.Content.7.EE.B.3 Solve multistep real-life and mathematical problems posed with positive and negative rational numbers in any form (whole numbers, fractions, and decimals), using tools strategically. Apply properties of operations to calculate with numbers in any form; convert between forms as appropriate; and assess the reasonableness of answers using mental computation and estimation strategies. *For example: if a woman making $25 an hour gets a 10% raise, she will make an additional 1/10 of her salary an hour, or $2.50, for a new salary of $27.50. If you want to place a towel bar 9 3/4 inches long in the center of a door that is 27 1/2 inches wide, you will need to place the bar about 9 inches from each edge; this estimate can be used as a check on the exact computation.*

CCSS.Math.Content.7.EE.B.4 Use variables to represent quantities in a real-world or mathematical problem, and construct simple equations and inequalities to solve problems by reasoning about the quantities.

CCSS.Math.Content.7.EE.B.4.a Solve word problems leading to equations of the form $px + q = r$ and $p(x + q) = r$, where p, q, and r are specific rational numbers. Solve equations of these forms fluently. Compare an algebraic solution to an arithmetic solution, identifying the sequence of the operations used in each approach. *For example, the perimeter of a rectangle is 54 cm. Its length is 6 cm. What is its width?*

CCSS.Math.Content.7.EE.B.4.b Solve word problems leading to inequalities of the form $px + q > r$ or $px + q < r$, where p, q, and r are specific rational numbers. Graph the solution set of the inequality and interpret it in the context of the problem. *For example, as a salesperson, you are paid $50 per week plus $3 per sale. This week you want your pay to be at least $100. Write an inequality for the number of sales you need to make, and describe the solutions.*

Geometry

Draw, construct, and describe geometrical figures and describe the relationships between them

CCSS.Math.Content.7.G.A.1 Solve problems involving scale drawings of geometric figures, including computing actual lengths and areas from a scale drawing and reproducing a scale drawing at a different scale.

CCSS.Math.Content.7.G.A.2 Draw (freehand, with ruler and protractor, and with technology) geometric shapes with given conditions. Focus on constructing triangles from three measures of angles or sides, noticing when the conditions determine a unique triangle, more than one triangle, or no triangle.

CCSS.Math.Content.7.G.A.3 Describe the two-dimensional figures that result from slicing three-dimensional figures, as in plane sections of right rectangular prisms and right rectangular pyramids.

Solve real-life and mathematical problems involving angle measure, area, surface area, and volume

CCSS.Math.Content.7.G.B.4 Know the formulas for the area and circumference of a circle and use them to solve problems; give an informal derivation of the relationship between the circumference and area of a circle.

CCSS.Math.Content.7.G.B.5 Use facts about supplementary, complementary, vertical, and adjacent angles in a multistep problem to write and solve simple equations for an unknown angle in a figure.

CCSS.Math.Content.7.G.B.6 Solve real-world and mathematical problems involving area, volume, and surface area of two- and three-dimensional objects composed of triangles, quadrilaterals, polygons, cubes, and right prisms.

Statistics and Probability

Use random sampling to draw inferences about a population

CCSS.Math.Content.7.SP.A.1 Understand that statistics can be used to gain information about a population by examining a sample of the population; generalizations about a population from a sample are valid only if the sample is representative of that population. Understand that random sampling tends to produce representative samples and support valid inferences.

CCSS.Math.Content.7.SP.A.2 Use data from a random sample to draw inferences about a population with an unknown characteristic of interest. Generate multiple samples (or simulated samples) of the same size to gauge the variation in estimates or predictions. *For example, estimate the mean word length in a book by randomly sampling words from the book; predict the winner of a school election based on randomly sampled survey data. Gauge how far off the estimate or prediction might be.*

Draw informal comparative inferences about two populations

CCSS.Math.Content.7.SP.B.3 Informally assess the degree of visual overlap of two numerical data distributions with similar variabilities, measuring the difference between the centers by expressing it as a multiple of a measure of variability. *For example, the mean height of players on the basketball team is 10 cm greater than the mean height of players on the soccer team, about twice the variability (mean absolute deviation) on either team; on a dot plot, the separation between the two distributions of heights is noticeable.*

CCSS.Math.Content.7.SP.B.4 Use measures of center and measures of variability for numerical data from random samples to draw informal comparative inferences about two populations. *For example, decide whether the words in a chapter of a seventh-grade science book are generally longer than the words in a chapter of a fourth-grade science book.*

Investigate chance processes and develop, use, and evaluate probability models

CCSS.Math.Content.7.SP.C.5 Understand that the probability of a chance event is a number between zero and one that expresses the likelihood of the event occurring. Larger numbers indicate greater likelihood. A probability near 0 indicates an unlikely event, a probability around 1/2 indicates an event that is neither unlikely nor likely, and a probability near 1 indicates a likely event.

CCSS.Math.Content.7.SP.C.6 Approximate the probability of a chance event by collecting data on the chance process that produces it and observing its long-run relative frequency, and predict the approximate relative frequency given the probability. *For example, when rolling a number cube 600 times, predict that a 3 or 6 would be rolled roughly 200 times, but probably not exactly 200 times.*

CCSS.Math.Content.7.SP.C.7 Develop a probability model and use it to find probabilities of events. Compare probabilities from a model to observed frequencies; if the agreement is not good, explain possible sources of the discrepancy.

CCSS.Math.Content.7.SP.C.7.a Develop a uniform probability model by assigning equal probability to all outcomes, and use the model to determine probabilities of events. *For example, if a student is selected at random from a class, find the probability that Jane will be selected and the probability that a girl will be selected.*

CCSS.Math.Content.7.SP.C.7.b Develop a probability model (which may not be uniform) by observing frequencies in data generated from a chance process. *For example, find the approximate probability that a spinning penny will land heads up or that a tossed paper cup will land open-end down. Do the outcomes for the spinning penny appear to be equally likely based on the observed frequencies?*

CCSS.Math.Content.7.SP.C.8 Find probabilities of compound events using organized lists, tables, tree diagrams, and simulation.

CCSS.Math.Content.7.SP.C.8.a Understand that, just as with simple events, the probability of a compound event is the fraction of outcomes in the sample space for which the compound event occurs.

CCSS.Math.Content.7.SP.C.8.b Represent sample spaces for compound events using methods such as organized lists, tables, and tree diagrams. For an event described in everyday language (e.g., "rolling double sixes"), identify the outcomes in the sample space that compose the event.

CCSS.Math.Content.7.SP.C.8.c Design and use a simulation to generate frequencies for compound events. *For example, use random digits as a simulation tool to approximate the answer to the question: If 40% of donors have type A blood, what is the probability that it will take at least four donors to find one with type A blood?*

Standards for Mathematical Practice

Note: All information in this Appendix is sourced from official Common Core website *http://www.corestandards.org/*.

The Standards for Mathematical Practice describe varieties of expertise that mathematics educators at all levels should seek to develop in their students. These practices rest on important "processes and proficiencies" with longstanding importance in mathematics education. The first of these are the NCTM process standards of problem solving, reasoning and proof, communication, representation, and connections. The second are the strands of mathematical proficiency specified in the National Research Council's report *Adding It Up*: adaptive reasoning, strategic competence, conceptual understanding (comprehension of mathematical concepts, operations, and relations), procedural fluency (skill in carrying out procedures flexibly, accurately, efficiently, and appropriately), and productive disposition (habitual inclination to see mathematics as sensible, useful, and worthwhile, coupled with a belief in diligence and one's own efficacy).

The Standards for Mathematical Practices

1. **CCSS.MATH.PRACTICE.MP1—Make sense of problems and persevere in solving them.**

   Mathematically proficient students start by explaining to themselves the meaning of a problem and looking for entry points to its solution. They analyze givens, constraints, relationships, and goals. They make conjectures about the form and meaning of the solution and plan a solution pathway rather than simply jumping into a solution attempt. They consider analogous problems, and try special cases and simpler forms of the original problem in order to gain insight into its solution. They monitor and evaluate their progress and change course if necessary. Older students might, depending on the context of the problem, transform algebraic expressions or change the viewing window on their graphing calculator to get the information they need. Mathematically proficient students can explain correspondences between equations, verbal descriptions, tables, and graphs or draw diagrams of important features and relationships, graph data, and search for regularity or trends. Younger students might rely on using concrete objects or pictures to help conceptualize and solve a problem. Mathematically proficient students check their answers to problems using a different method, and they continually ask themselves, "Does this make sense?" They can understand the approaches of others to solving complex problems and identify correspondences between different approaches.

2. **CCSS.MATH.PRACTICE.MP2—Reason abstractly and quantitatively.**

Mathematically proficient students make sense of quantities and their relationships in problem situations. They bring two complementary abilities to bear on problems involving quantitative relationships: the ability to *decontextualize*—to abstract a given situation and represent it symbolically and manipulate the representing symbols as if they have a life of their own, without necessarily attending to their referents—and the ability to *contextualize*, to pause as needed during the manipulation process in order to probe into the referents for the symbols involved. Quantitative reasoning entails habits of creating a coherent representation of the problem at hand; considering the units involved; attending to the meaning of quantities, not just how to compute them; and knowing and flexibly using different properties of operations and objects.

3. **CCSS.MATH.PRACTICE.MP3—Construct viable arguments and critique the reasoning of others.**

Mathematically proficient students understand and use stated assumptions, definitions, and previously established results in constructing arguments. They make conjectures and build a logical progression of statements to explore the truth of their conjectures. They are able to analyze situations by breaking them into cases, and can recognize and use counterexamples. They justify their conclusions, communicate them to others, and respond to the arguments of others. They reason inductively about data, making plausible arguments that take into account the context from which the data arose. Mathematically proficient students are also able to compare the effectiveness of two plausible arguments, distinguish correct logic or reasoning from that which is flawed, and—if there is a flaw in an argument—explain what it is. Elementary students can construct arguments using concrete referents such as objects, drawings, diagrams, and actions. Such arguments can make sense and be correct, even though they are not generalized or made formal until later grades. Later, students learn to determine domains to which an argument applies. Students at all grades can listen or read the arguments of others, decide whether they make sense, and ask useful questions to clarify or improve the arguments.

4.   **CCSS.MATH.PRACTICE.MP4—Model with mathematics.**

Mathematically proficient students can apply the mathematics they know to solve problems arising in everyday life, society, and the workplace. In early grades, this might be as simple as writing an addition equation to describe a situation. In middle grades, a student might apply proportional reasoning to plan a school event or analyze a problem in the community. By high school, a student might use geometry to solve a design problem or use a function to describe how one quantity of interest depends on another. Mathematically proficient students who can apply what they know are comfortable making assumptions and approximations to simplify a complicated situation, realizing that these may need revision later. They are able to identify important quantities in a practical situation and map their relationships using such tools as diagrams, two-way tables, graphs, flowcharts, and formulas. They can analyze those relationships mathematically to draw conclusions. They routinely interpret their mathematical results in the context of the situation and reflect on whether the results make sense, possibly improving the model if it has not served its purpose.

5.   **CCSS.MATH.PRACTICE.MP5—Use appropriate tools strategically.**

Mathematically proficient students consider the available tools when solving a mathematical problem. These tools might include pencil and paper, concrete models, a ruler, a protractor, a calculator, a spreadsheet, a computer algebra system, a statistical package, or dynamic geometry software. Proficient students are sufficiently familiar with tools appropriate for their grade or course to make sound decisions about when each of these tools might be helpful, recognizing both the insight to be gained and their limitations. For example, mathematically proficient high school students analyze graphs of functions and solutions generated using a graphing calculator. They detect possible errors by strategically using estimation and other mathematical knowledge. When making mathematical models, they know that technology can enable them to visualize the results of varying assumptions, explore consequences, and compare predictions with data. Mathematically proficient students at various grade levels are able to identify relevant external mathematical resources, such as digital content located on a website, and use them to pose or solve problems. They are able to use technological tools to explore and deepen their understanding of concepts.

6. **CCSS.MATH.PRACTICE.MP6—Attend to precision.**

   Mathematically proficient students try to communicate precisely to others. They try to use clear definitions in discussion with others and in their own reasoning. They state the meaning of the symbols they choose, including using the equal sign consistently and appropriately. They are careful about specifying units of measure, and labeling axes to clarify the correspondence with quantities in a problem. They calculate accurately and efficiently and express numerical answers with a degree of precision appropriate for the problem context. In the elementary grades, students give carefully formulated explanations to each other. By the time they reach high school they have learned to examine claims and make explicit use of definitions.

7. **CCSS.MATH.PRACTICE.MP7—Look for and make use of structure.**

   Mathematically proficient students look closely to discern a pattern or structure. Young students, for example, might notice that three and seven more is the same amount as seven and three more, or they may sort a collection of shapes according to how many sides the shapes have. Later, students will see 7×8 equals the well remembered $7 \times 5 + 7 \times 3$, in preparation for learning about the distributive property. In the expression $x^2 + 9x + 14$, older students can see the 14 as 2×7 and the 9 as $2 + 7$. They recognize the significance of an existing line in a geometric figure and can use the strategy of drawing an auxiliary line for solving problems. They also can step back for an overview and shift perspective. They can see complicated things, such as some algebraic expressions, as single objects or as being composed of several objects. For example, they can see $5 - 3(x - y)^2$ as 5 minus a positive number times a square and use that to realize that its value cannot be more than 5 for any real numbers x and y.

8. **CCSS.MATH.PRACTICE.MP8—Look for and express regularity in repeated reasoning.**

   Mathematically proficient students notice if calculations are repeated, and look both for general methods and for shortcuts. Upper elementary students might notice when dividing 25 by 11 that they are repeating the same calculations over and over again, and conclude they have a repeating decimal. By paying attention to the calculation of slope as they repeatedly check whether points are on the line through (1, 2) with slope 3, middle school students might abstract the equation $(y - 2)/(x - 1) = 3$. Noticing the regularity in the way terms cancel when expanding $(x - 1)(x + 1)$, $(x - 1)(x^2 + x + 1)$, and $(x - 1)(x^3 + x^2 + x + 1)$ might lead them to the general formula for the sum of a geometric series. As they work to solve a problem, mathematically proficient students maintain oversight of the process while attending to the details. They continually evaluate the reasonableness of their intermediate results.

Connecting the Standards for Mathematical Practice to the Standards for Mathematical Content

The Standards for Mathematical Practice describe ways in which developing student practitioners of the discipline of mathematics increasingly ought to engage with the subject matter as they grow in mathematical maturity and expertise throughout the elementary, middle, and high school years. Designers of curricula, assessments, and professional development should all attend to the need to connect the mathematical practices to mathematical content in mathematics instruction.

The Standards for Mathematical Content are a balanced combination of procedure and understanding. Expectations that begin with the word "understand" are often especially good opportunities to connect the practices to the content. Students who lack understanding of a topic may rely too heavily on procedures. Without a flexible base from which to work, they may be less likely to consider analogous problems, represent problems coherently, justify conclusions, apply the mathematics to practical situations, use technology mindfully to work with the mathematics, explain the mathematics accurately to other students, step back for an overview, or deviate from a known procedure to find a shortcut. In short, a lack of understanding effectively prevents a student from engaging in the mathematical practices.

In this respect, those content standards that set an expectation of understanding are potential "points of intersection" between the Standards for Mathematical Content and the Standards for Mathematical Practice. These points of intersection are intended to be weighted toward central and generative concepts in the school mathematics curriculum that most merit the time, resources, innovative energies, and focus necessary to qualitatively improve the curriculum, instruction, assessment, professional development, and student achievement in mathematics.

Index

373

PREPARE STUDENTS FOR SUCCESS

Let's Prepare for the PARCC . . . Tests

FULLY ALIGNED WITH NEW STATE STANDARDS

This series of books introduces students to the PARCC assessment administered across the country. It offers comprehensive subject reviews and practice tests designed to familiarize students with the PARCC grade level test and prepares them to do their best on test day.

Students will find everything they need in order to prepare—and succeed—on the PARCC tests.

Let's Prepare for the PARCC Grade 6 ELA/Literacy Test
ISBN 978-1-4380-0817-2

Let's Prepare for the PARCC Grade 6 Math Test
ISBN 978-1-4380-0818-9

Each book: Paperback, 7 13/16" x 10", $12.99, *Can$15.50*

SBAC Books

This series of books introduces students to the Smarter Balanced Assessment Consortium (SBAC), a series of next-generation assessment tests based on the Common Core Standards. These fair and reliable standards prepare students for 21st century learning, including the use of computers on test day. Each Grade 6 book features one practice test; an overview of the tests, including the computerized format of the exams; all questions thoroughly answered and explained; practice exercises that cover the different types of SBAC questions; test-taking tips and strategies; and more. It's the perfect way to help students reach their highest potential on the grade-specific SBAC tests.

SBAC Grade 6 ELA
ISBN 978-1-4380-1057-1

SBAC Grade 6 Math
ISBN 978-1-4380-1029-8

Each book: Paperback, 7 13/16" x 10", $14.99, *Can$18.50*

Available at your local bookstore
or visit **www.barronseduc.com**

Barron's Educational Series, Inc.
250 Wireless Blvd.
Hauppauge, NY 11788
Order toll-free: 1-800-645-3476

In Canada: Georgetown Book Warehouse
34 Armstrong Ave.
Georgetown, Ontario L7G 4R9
Canadian orders: 1-800-247-7160

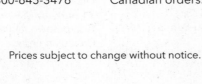

Prices subject to change without notice.

(#311c) R10/17

Really. This isn't going to hurt at all . . .

Learning won't hurt when middle school and high school students open any *Painless* title. These books transform subjects into fun—emphasizing a touch of humor and entertaining brain-tickler puzzles that are fun to solve.

Bonus Online Component—each title followed by (*) includes additional online games to challenge students, including Beat the Clock, a line match game, and a word scramble.

Each book: Paperback

Painless Algebra, 4th Ed.*
Lynette Long, Ph.D.
ISBN 978-1-4380-0775-5, $9.99, Can$11.99

Painless American Government
Jeffrey Strausser
ISBN 978-0-7641-2601-7, $9.99, Can$11.99

Painless American History, 2nd Ed.
Curt Lader
ISBN 978-0-7641-4231-4, $9.99, Can$11.99

Painless Chemistry, 2nd Ed.*
Loris Chen
ISBN 978-1-4380-0771-7, $9.99, Can$11.99

Painless Earth Science
Edward J. Denecke, Jr.
ISBN 978-0-7641-4601-5, $11.99, Can$14.99

Painless English for Speakers of Other Languages, 2nd Ed.
Jeffrey Strausser and José Paniza
ISBN 978-1-4380-0002-2, $9.99, Can$11.50

Painless Fractions, 3rd Ed.
Alyece Cummings, M.A.
ISBN 978-1-4380-0000-8, $10.99, Can$13.99

Painless French, 3rd Ed.*
Carol Chaitkin, M.S., and Lynn Gore, M.A.
ISBN 978-1-4380-0770-0, $9.99, Can$11.99

Painless Geometry, 2nd Ed.
Lynette Long, Ph.D.
ISBN 978-0-7641-4230-7, $9.99, Can$11.99

Painless Grammar, 4th Ed.*
Rebecca Elliott, Ph.D.
ISBN 978-1-4380-0774-8, $9.99, Can$11.99

Painless Italian, 2nd Ed.
Marcel Danesi, Ph.D.
ISBN 978-0-7641-4761-6, $9.99, Can$11.50

Painless Math Word Problems, 2nd Ed.
Marcie Abramson, B.S., Ed.M.
ISBN 978-0-7641-4335-9, $11.99, Can$14.99

Painless Poetry, 2nd Ed.
Mary Elizabeth
ISBN 978-0-7641-4591-9, $9.99, Can$11.99

Painless Pre-Algebra, 2nd Ed.*
Amy Stahl
ISBN 978-1-4380-0773-1, $9.99, Can$11.99

Painless Reading Comprehension, 3rd Ed.*
Darolyn "Lyn" Jones, Ed.D.
ISBN 978-1-4380-0769-4, $9.99, Can$11.99

Painless Spanish, 3rd Ed.*
Carlos B. Vega and Dasha Davis
ISBN 978-1-4380-0772-4, $9.99, Can$11.99

Painless Spelling, 3rd Ed.
Mary Elizabeth
ISBN 978-0-7641-4713-5, $9.99, Can$11.99

Painless Study Techniques
Michael Greenberg
ISBN 978-0-7641-4059-4, $9.99, Can$11.99

Painless Vocabulary, 3rd Ed.*
Michael Greenberg
ISBN 978-1-4380-0778-6, $9.99, Can$11.99

Painless Writing, 3rd Ed.*
Jeffrey Strausser
ISBN 978-1-4380-0784-7, $9.99, Can$11.99

Prices subject to change without notice.

SUPPORTS STATE STANDARDS

Available at your local bookstore or visit **www.barronseduc.com**

Barron's Educational Series, Inc.
250 Wireless Blvd.
Hauppauge, N.Y. 11788
Order toll-free:
1-800-645-3476